The Greensboro Symphony Guild
Greensboro, N.C.

Cover and Divider Page Art
designed by
Lauren Worth

The Greensboro Symphony Guild is a 670 member non-profit organization whose goal is to promote and foster musical culture and education by aiding the Greensboro Symphony Society in the promotion of an orchestra for the community.

All the proceeds from the sale of BRAVO benefit the educational projects of the Greensboro Symphony Guild. The recipes in this book have been collected from various sources by members of the Greensboro Symphony Guild and neither the Guild nor any contributor, publisher, printer, distributor or seller of this book is responsible for errors or omissions. Brand names have been used only when necessary.

For additional copies,
see order blanks in back of book or write:
BRAVO
Greensboro Symphony Guild
P.O. Box 29224
Greensboro, N.C. 27408

Printed in USA by
S.C. Toof & Co.
Memphis, TN

Contents

COOKBOOK COMMITTEE

Chairman: Sally Millikin
Editor: Sallie Nolan
Testing: Irene Mnick, Delores Wellmaker
Typing: Jan Meadows, Earle's Secretarial

Assistant Chairman	Pat Austin
Advisor	Jane Armfield
Secretary-Treasurer	Jean Ware
Recipe Editor	Nancy Beard
Recipe Editing	Margaret Albright, Peggy Brame, Helen Davidson, Glenda Johnson, Juanita Linton, Sylvia Smith
Tasting	Nancy Balderacchi, Helene Belfi, Alice Gaines, Sally Sherrill, Beverly Stocks, Evelyn Sturm
Copy Editing	Peggy Wyatt, Mary Hoffler, Ann Rives, Janelle Snider, Betty Willhauck
Personalities	Karen Johnston, Caroline Lee
Marketing	Pam Allen, Jane Gibson
"Bravo Bash" Kickoff	Caroline Lee
Gourmet Dinner Prize	Pat Haley
Cookbook Orders	Anne Callicott, Nan Price
At Large	Martha Best, Allison Callicott, Bonnie Cordes, Gail Huggins, Rachel Hull, Donna Hunt, Peggy Johnson, Judy Jolly, Barbara Kretzer, Susan Lowe, Judy Murray, Donna Moore, Sally Morgan, Pat Neill, Iris O'Donnell, Alice Pearce, Emily Pernice, Peggy Ritchie, Marilyn Robinson, Joyce Somers, Irene Snowberger, Lorraine Vallituto, Happy Waller, Darlene Young

Cookbook name submitted by: Donna Thornton

The cookbook committee gratefully acknowledges all who submitted recipes and participated in testing luncheons. Because of duplication and limited space, we were unable to include all of the 1,200 recipes offered to our committee. A sincere thanks to all of you.

Introduction

If we, as members of the Greensboro Symphony Guild and residents of Greensboro, North Carolina, had to describe in one word the idea behind BRAVO, it would be "celebration." We proudly present this book to you in celebration of the officially designated "Number 1" city in America and its most treasured resource — the Greensboro Symphony Orchestra. This publication will aid in the development of numerous musical projects for our children, and the continued success of the Greensboro Symphony under the direction of Maestro Peter Paul Fuchs. The recipes published in this cookbook will provide you with a true "taste of Greensboro," her citizens, and their dedication to music. To you who use this book, please join us in a resounding "BRAVO"!

William Sidney Porter, known to the world as O. Henry —
the master of the short story, was born in Southern Guilford
County in 1862. In 1865 his father moved back to his home
town of Greensboro and young Will began his life and his
world of fantasies in the town. A man who enjoyed and
wrote about his fellow man, William Sidney Porter intro-
duces our appetizer recipes — delicious accompaniments
for any social gathering or as a special introduction to a
memorable meal.

Appetizers

O. HENRY

APRICOT CHUTNEY

Preparation: 15 minutes
Cooking: 1 hour and 30 minutes

Yield: 6 cups

1 can (29-ounce) apricot halves
2 cups packed brown sugar
2 cups distilled white vinegar
1 cup chopped onion
½ cup diced crystalized ginger
1 teaspoon chili powder

1 teaspoon ground cloves
1 teaspoon salt
1 clove garlic, minced
1 cup golden raisins
2 tablespoons mustard seeds

Drain and dice apricots. Reserve syrup. Heat syrup and remaining ingredients (except apricots) to boiling and reduce heat. Simmer uncovered 45 minutes. Stir in apricots and simmer 45 minutes longer. Serve with cream cheese and crackers.

Louise Glover

APPLE WALNUT PÂTÉ

Preparation: 45 minutes

Serves: 20

1 cup shelled walnuts (broken up)
3 large shallots (2 to 3 ounces)
2 garlic cloves, minced
1 medium onion (4 ounces)
1 stick unsalted butter
2 apples (peeled, cored, quartered, chopped)
1 pound chicken livers

8 ounces hot sausage
¼ cup apple brandy
8 ounces cream cheese
½ teaspoon salt
½ teaspoon tarragon
⅛ teaspoon thyme
⅛ teaspoon allspice

Lightly butter mold. Chop walnuts and set aside. Mince shallots and garlic. Chop onions. Melt 3 tablespoons butter in saucepan. Sauté onions, shallots, and garlic. Add chopped apples and cook until soft. Remove from pan. Melt remaining butter in skillet and sauté liver and sausage until cooked. Slowly warm brandy. Ignite and pour over meat. Allow to burn down and cool. Combine onion/apple mixture with meat mixture. Puree. Add cream cheese and seasonings and mix completely. Add walnuts. Transfer to a mold or to many smaller containers.

Anne Adams

SIX LAYER AVOCADO DIP

Preparation: 15 minutes   Serves: **12 to 16**

2 large avocados
⅛ teaspoon garlic powder
⅛ teaspoon garlic salt
1 tablespoon lemon juice
2 tablespoons mayonnaise
1 (8-ounce) carton sour cream
2 (8-ounce) jars Picante sauce
  (mild)

¾ cup chopped ripe olives
3 medium tomatoes, peeled and
  diced
1½ cups grated sharp cheese
Tostados (plain, not Nachos
  flavored, for dipping)

1st layer: Mash avocadoes, and blend in garlic salt, garlic powder, lemon juice and mayonnaise. Spread in bottom of 12 × 8 × 2 inch Pyrex dish.
2nd layer: Cover with sour cream.
3rd layer: Drain mild Picante sauce and spread over sour cream.
4th layer: Sprinkle on chopped ripe olives.
5th layer: Add on chopped tomatoes.
6th layer: Sprinkle on grated cheddar cheese.
Can be made in the morning, then refrigerated. Allow dip to sit at room temperature about an hour before serving.

Vivien Bauman

TARAMOSALATA IN RAGOUT SHELLS

Preparation: 30 minutes   Serves: **18**

4 slices French bread, 1 inch thick
½ cup cold water
1 large russet potato (10 ounces),
  cooked, cooled to room
  temperature, peeled and
  shredded
1 cup tarama (Greek carp roe)
1 small onion, quartered
1 clove garlic, minced
3 tablespoons fresh lemon juice

1½ cups olive oil (or Safflower oil)
½ grapefruit crown
Fresh strawberries marinated with
  Kirsch (optional)
Ragout shells (or substitute any
  appetizer toasts available like
  English Water Biscuits, Sesame
  or Cracked Wheat Cracker, or
  Wasa Wheat Bread.)

Soak bread thoroughly in water. Squeeze dry. Combine bread with potato, tarama, onion, garlic, and lemon juice in processor or batches in blender. Mix well. With machine running, drizzle in oil until mixture is thickened to mayonnaise consistency. If too thick, blend in ¼ cup water to thin to spreading consistency. Spoon mixture in ragout shells. Place filled shells on serving platter centered with a grapefruit crown and garnished with fresh strawberries.

Recipe shared by Harry Gianaris, local advertising executive, who received it from his "little old Greek mother"!

CHEESE SPREAD FOR FRENCH BREAD

Preparation: 10 minutes · Yield: 1¾ pounds

1 pound margarine
½ pound grated sharp cheddar
cheese
¼ pound grated Parmesan cheese

1 teaspoon Worchestershire sauce
1 teaspoon garlic powder
½ teaspoon paprika

Whip ingredients together until light and fluffy. Spread on slices of French or sour dough bread and broil until hot, melted and slightly browned. Can be stored in the refrigerator in a closed container.

Marilyn Robinson

GREEN CHILIES AND CHEESE DIP

Preparation: 10 minutes · Serves: 10 to 12

1 (4-ounce) can green chilies
12 ounces cheddar cheese

12 ounces Monterey Jack cheese
1 egg, beaten

Wash and seed green chilies. Drain and chop. Grate cheeses. In a 1½ quart baking dish alternate layers of green chilies, Monterey Jack, green chilies, cheddar cheese. Repeat layering until dish is filled. Pour egg over top layer using a fork to penetrate all layers. Bake at 375 degrees for 25 minutes. Serve hot with party rye bread.

Marian Ferrel

INDIA DIP

Preparation: 10 minutes · Serves: 8

8 ounces cream cheese
½ cup blue cheese, crumbled
¼ cup chutney

¼ cup chopped dates (optional)
1 tablespoon lemon juice
¾ cup chopped pecans

Mix all ingredients, except the pecans, until smooth. Refrigerate. Just before serving, sprinkle with pecans. Serve with Triscuits or wheat crackers.

Beverly Rogers

BROCCOLI DIP

Preparation: 20 minutes   Serves: 10 to 12

2 onions, chopped
1 stick butter
2 cups celery, chopped
1 package frozen chopped broccoli

1 roll garlic cheese
1 can cream of mushroom soup
8 ounces cream cheese, softened
1 package slivered almonds

Sauté onions in butter. Add celery, simmer until tender. Add remaining ingredients and heat thoroughly. Serve hot in chafing dish with crackers or chips.

Marian Ferrel

AVOCADO DIP

Preparation: 30 minutes   Serves: 10

2 very ripe avocados
Lemon juice to taste (1 to 2
   lemons)
2 medium tomatoes, peeled and
   chopped

1 medium onion, chopped fine
1 green pepper, chopped fine
1 slice bacon fried crisp, and
   crumbled
Salt

Mash avocados with fork. Add lemon juice to keep from discoloring. Add remaining ingredients. Serve with nachos.

Better than guacamole!

Donna Moore

HOT PEPPER JELLY

Preparation: 30 minutes   Yield: 9 to 11 cups

½ cup green bell pepper, chopped
½ cup hot green chili pepper,
   chopped
6½ cups sugar
1½ cups vinegar
1 cup water

¼ cup red bell pepper, chopped,
   optional
Green food coloring as desired.
1 bottle Certo

Combine all ingredients except Certo. Bring to full boil and cook for 10 minutes. Add Certo and boil 1 minute. Bottle immediately. Seal with paraffin.

A tasty topper for cream cheese!

Marilyn Robinson

11

MEXICAN SURPRISE

Preparation: 15 minutes   Serves: 16

*1 can Bean Dip
1 (8-ounce) carton sour cream
*1 can Picante Sauce
1 ripe avocado, chopped

1 ripe tomato, chopped
1½ cups shredded cheddar cheese
Tostitos

*These can be found on the Frito-Lay display rack

Spread the bean dip in a circular shape on a flat platter. About 7 inches across is a nice size. Spread the sour cream on top of the bean dip, but stopping about ½ inch from the circle edges. Sprinkle ¼ can of the Picanté Sauce over the sour cream. Scatter the avocado and the tomato on top. Sprinkle enough Picanté Sauce to suit your taste. The more you use the more "surprised" you will be. Three-fourths can works well for the entire "Surprise." Lightly press the cheese over the entire shape. Refrigerate for one hour. Remove from refrigerator and let stand for at least 20 minutes. It is much tastier at room temperature.

For lovers of hot, spicy foods!

Jackie Peoples

BAKED NACHO DIP

Preparation: 30 minutes   Serves: 20 to 25
Cooking: 15 to 20 minutes

1 (8-ounce) cream cheese
   (softened)
1 (8-ounce) carton sour cream
1 (10½-ounce) can jalapeno bean
   dip
1 (1¼-ounce) package chili
   seasoning mix

5 drops hot sauce
2 teaspoons chopped fresh parsley
¼ cup taco sauce
1¼ cup (5 ounces) shredded
    Monterey Jack, divided
¾ cup cheddar cheese, grated

Combine cream cheese and sour cream. Beat until smooth. Stir in bean dip, chili seasoning mix, hot sauce, parsley, taco sauce, ¾ cup Monterey Jack cheese, and ¾ cup cheddar cheese. Heat until soft and hot in oven in 12 x 8 x 2 inch baking dish topped with the rest of cheese. Bake at 325 degrees for 15 to 20 minutes. Serve hot with tortilla chips, yields about 3½ cups.

Bobbie Hill

EASY TACO DIP

Preparation: 20 minutes   Serves: 20

1 (16-ounce) can refried beans
1 envelope taco seasoning mix
1 (16-ounce) carton sour cream
1 small onion, chopped
1 (6-ounce) can ripe pitted olives,
   sliced

¼ head lettuce, shredded
1 tomato, chopped
8 ounces sharp cheddar cheese,
   grated

Mix beans and taco seasoning mix. Spread in large glass or silver tray. Spread sour cream over bean layer. Sprinkle onions, olives, lettuce, tomato, and cheese in layers on top of sour cream. Refrigerate until ready to serve. Best served with plain or nacho cheese tostitos.

Sally Millikin

TOASTED PECANS

Preparation: 10 minutes   Serves: 12 to 18
Cooking: 30 minutes

4 cups pecans
¼ pound butter
½ teaspoon tabasco

1 tablespoon garlic salt
4 teaspoons Worcestershire

Melt butter in large flat baking sheet in oven. Stir in next three ingredients. Add pecans. Stir to coat well. Bake in 300 degree oven for 30 minutes.

Juanita Linton

PRAIRIE FIRE

Preparation: 5 minutes   Serves: 12
Cooking: 30 minutes

1 (4-ounce) can whole hot green
   chili peppers
1½ cup onions
1 (1-pound) can chili without
   beans

1 pound grated sharp cheddar
   cheese
Salt to taste
Large tortilla chips

In blender, combine peppers and onions. Blend in chili. Add cheese. Pour into greased 8 x 8 inch dish and bake 30 minutes at 350 degrees. Serve with large tortilla chips.

Mary Adams

EASY NACHO SNACK

Preparation: 20 minutes   Yield: 3 dozen

1 (12-ounce) package tortilla chips
1 (16-ounce) can refried beans
½ cup chopped green onions

1 cup shredded Cheddar cheese
1 (11½-ounce) jar pickled hot
   jalapeno pepper slices

Place about 3 dozen tortilla chips on ungreased baking sheet. Spread 2 teaspoons refried beans on each chip. Sprinkle with green onions and cheese. Top each with slice of jalapeno pepper. Bake at 350 degrees for 5 minutes.

Omit jalapeno pepper for a milder taste.

Judy Pajak

CHUTNEY GLAZED CHEESE PÂTÉ

Preparation: ½ hour   Serves: 12

6 ounces cream cheese
4 ounces (1 cup) sharp cheddar
   cheese, shredded
3 tablespoons dry sherry
¾ tablespoons curry powder
¼ teaspoon salt

Topping:
½ cup chopped mango chutney (or
   more if desired)
2 medium scallions (including the
   greens), finely chopped

Thoroughly beat the cream cheese, cheddar cheese, sherry, curry powder, and salt. Spread this mixture ½ inch thick on a serving platter and chill until firm. At serving time, spread the top with a generous ½ cup chopped mango chutney and sprinkle with very finely sliced scallions.

Mary Jane Sevier, Jean Ware

BRIE WITH BROWN SUGAR AND ALMONDS

Preparation: 10 minutes   Serves: 16

1 (2-pound) wheel Brie
¼ cup light brown sugar

½ stick butter
½ cup almonds, sliced

Place Brie in lightly buttered 9-inch quiche dish. Heat in 300 degree oven for 15 minutes (or microwave on high for 3 minutes). Melt butter. Stir in brown sugar and almonds. Pour over Brie. Broil until lightly toasted. Serve with French bread.

Recipe shared by Greensboro caterer, Dotte McMasters.

BRIE EN CROUTE

Preparation: 10 minutes
Cooking: 15 to 20 minutes

Serves: 20 to 25

1 egg yolk
1 (8-inch) wheel of Brie cheese

1 Pepperidge Farm Frozen Puff
   Pastry sheet

Beat egg yolk with 1 tablespoon water. Thaw 1 sheet of puff pastry 20 minutes, then unfold. Roll out large enough to cover the top and sides of the wheel of Brie. Put pastry sheet cover over Brie and place in quiche dish. Brush top of pastry with egg mixture. If desired, decorate with cut-outs made from pastry scraps and apply with egg mixture. Brush the cut-outs with egg. Place in the middle of a preheated 375 degree oven. Bake for 15 to 20 minutes or until golden brown. Serve with crackers.

An elegant Brie!

Irene Mnick
Beverly Stocks

TIROPETES
(Cheese Puffs)

Preparation: 2½ hours
Cooking: 20 minutes

Yield: 60

4 eggs, well-beaten
1 (8-ounce) package cream
   cheese, softened
1 pound Feta cheese, crumbled

1 pound phyllo dough, comes
   frozen
1 pound clarified butter (See
   Baklava in Index for
   instructions)

Beat eggs until fluffy. Add cream cheese and continue beating until well blended. Remove from mixer. Crumble feta cheese with fork. Combine with egg mixture. Stir in 3 tablespoons of the melted butter. Cut phyllo dough into 6 x 12 inch pieces. For each triangle, lightly brush ½ of the dough with butter and fold over other half to make a strip 3 inches wide. Brush lightly with butter. Place 1 teaspoon cheese mixture at one end of each strip. Fold strip diagonally until traingles are formed (like folding a flag). Brush tops with melted butter and place on greased baking sheet. Bake at 350 degrees for 20 minutes or until golden brown. Serve warm. May be frozen (before baking) for at least 2 months.

Titsa Dermatis

SUE'S SWEET AND SOUR MUSTARD SAUCE

Preparation: 10 minutes   Yield: One quart

3 tablespoons flour
1 cup sugar
¼ pound melted butter
½ cup vinegar

6-ounce jar prepared mustard
2 well-beaten eggs with 1 teaspoon
  salt
1 can Campbell's boullion soup

Mix flour and sugar. Add melted butter, vinegar, prepared mustard, and eggs. Stir in boullion soup. Cook over medium heat until thick as a custard. Serve hot or cold. Keeps indefinitely in refrigerator. Also may be frozen.

A wonderful compliment for cold meats!

Sandra Burns

CHEESIE BLACK OLIVE SPREAD

Preparation: 15 minutes   Serves: 25
Cooking: 5 minutes

1 cup pitted black olives
½ cup green onions
2 cups sharp cheese (cut into
  small cubes)

½ teaspoon salt
½ cup mayonnaise
½ teaspoon curry powder
party rye bread

Place all ingredients except rye bread in food processor. Blend until of spreading consistency. Remove and store in refrigerator until ready to spread on bread slices. Heat in hot oven (400 degrees to 450 degrees) for about 5 minutes, until cheese becomes bubbly.

Anne Rendleman

SPINACH STUFFED MUSHROOMS

Preparation: 10 minutes   Serves: 6
Cooking: 20 to 25 minutes

1 pound mushrooms, stemmed
1 (12-ounce) package frozen
  spinach soufflé, thawed

1 teaspoon grated onion
Salt and pepper to taste
Parmesan cheese

Remove stems from mushrooms and chop. Mix thawed soufflé, chopped mushroom stems, onion, salt, and pepper. Fill washed caps with spinach mixture and place on cookie sheet. Sprinkle with Parmesan cheese. Bake in 350 degree oven 20 to 25 minutes.

Carolyn Maddux

SIMPLE SNOW CAPPED PÂTÉ

Preparation: 20 minutes   Serves: 6 to 8

Pâté:
1 small clove garlic, peeled
1 package (8-ounce) liverwurst, cut up
½ teaspoon each: basil, instant minced onion

Topping:
1 small clove garlic
1 (3-ounce) package cream cheese, chilled and cut into 3 pieces
1 teaspoon mayonnaise
Dash hot pepper sauce

For Pâté: Position knife blade in food processor. Drop garlic through food chute with processor running, and mince. Turn off and add liverwurst, basil and onion. Process 10 seconds. Stop and scrape sides of bowl. Process 10 more seconds. Press mixture into a 2-cup mold or small dish. Chill several hours or overnight. Unmold by running small metal spatula around edge and invert on serving plate.

Topping: Position knife blade in food processor. Drop garlic through chute with processor running and mince. Turn off. Add cream cheese, mayonnaise, and hot pepper sauce. Process 5 seconds. Scrape sides and process 5 more seconds. Frost sides and top of pâté. Chill until serving time. Serve with crackers.

June Rutherford

HERB CRUNCH

Preparation: 5 minutes   Serves: 10 to 12

1 box regular or small size oyster crackers
½ cup corn oil
1 tablespoon dill seed or dill weed

1 package Hidden Valley Buttermilk salad mix
½ teaspoon lemon pepper

Warm oil in a cup in hot water. Do not put oil directly into water. After oil is warm, mix oil, dill seed, lemon pepper and package of Hidden Valley Buttermilk salad mix. Stir together until well blended. Place crackers on cookie sheet or broiler pan and pour mixture over the crackers. Toss lightly until thoroughly coated. Let set a few minutes. Serve like any other "party mix" with drinks.

Good for the bridge table!

Janelle Snider

SPINACH PINWHEEL

Preparation: 1 hour
Cooking: 45 minutes

Serves: 16 to 20

Pastry:
2 sticks margarine, softened
2 cups plain four
1 cup cottage cheese
½ teaspoon salt

Filling:
8 slices bacon
2 (10-ounce) packages chopped
   spinach
2 teaspoons garlic salt
3 small onions, chopped
2 cups sharp cheddar cheese,
   grated

Pastry: Cut margarine into flour and salt. Add cottage cheese. Mix and form into 3 balls. Wrap each in plastic wrap and chill 6 hours or longer.
Filling: Fry bacon until crisp. Set aside. Pour off all but ¼ cup of drippings. Sauté the chopped frozen spinach, cook 10 minutes, then drain spinach well. Stir garlic salt, chopped onions and grated cheese into spinach mixture. Crumble bacon and add to mixture.
Roll out dough on floured board about 6 x 10 inches. Spread on ⅓ of spinach mixture. Roll up jelly roll fashion. Complete other 2 rolls. Bake on cookie sheets 45 minutes at 350 degrees. Let cool about 8 minutes. Slice into pieces and serve.

Vivien Bauman

DELECTABLE CHEESE STRAWS

Preparation: 45 minutes
Cooking: 10 to 15 minutes

Serves: 18

2 cups extra sharp grated cheese
1 stick butter or margarine
1½ cups all purpose flour
1 teaspoon baking powder

½ teaspoon cayenne pepper
1 teaspoon Tabasco
1 (16-ounce) box confectioners
   sugar

Cream together cheese and margarine. Add flour, baking powder, cayenne pepper. Mix by hand, adding Tabasco last. Place dough in cookie press and squeeze onto counter-top. Cut in one inch pieces and place on greased cookie sheet. (Or roll out dough and cut in short length strips.) Bake at 300° for 10 or 15 minutes. Remove from oven and place straws on waxed paper. Sprinkle while hot with powdered sugar. When straws have cooled, store in a tin container.

Mary Hoffler

MUSHROOM PUFFS

Preparation: 30 minutes
Cooking: 10 to 15 minutes

Serves: 16

1 pound mushrooms, chopped
½ stick butter
1 (8-ounce) package cream cheese
1 tablespoon Jane's Krazy Mixed
   Up Salt or your favorite
   Seasoned Salt

2 packages Pillsbury Crescent
   Dinner Rolls
1 egg, slightly beaten

Sauté the chopped mushrooms in ½ stick butter. Do not drain. Mix with cream cheese and salt. Set aside. Divide rolls into 8 rectangles (4 from each package). Enlarge rectangle with a rolling pin after closing seams. Spread ⅛ mushroom mixture on each rectangle and roll up jelly roll fashion. Pinch sides to seal. Partially freeze and then cut each roll into 1 inch slices. May freeze at this point. Brush each puff with beaten egg just before baking. Bake at 400 degrees 10 to 15 minutes or until lightly browned.

Janelle Snider

SPANAKOPETES
(Greek Spinach Pies)

Preparation: 1 hour
Cooking: 15 to 20 minutes.

Yields: 130 pieces

1 medium onion
2 tablespoons butter
1 pound spinach either fresh or
   frozen, chopped
6 ounces pot or small curd cottage
   cheese
3 eggs, lightly beaten

¼ cup bread crumbs
Salt and pepper
½ pound feta cheese
½ teaspoon dill (optional)
½ pound Phyllo dough
1 cup butter, melted (for brushing
   dough)

Preheat oven to 425 degrees. Sauté onion in 2 tablespoons butter. Add drained spinach until most moisture has evaporated. Stir in cheeses, eggs, salt, pepper, crumbs and dill. Cut phyllo into strips 2 inches wide. Brush one strip at a time with melted butter. Cover rest of phyllo with wax paper and lightly dampened dish towel. Put one teaspoon filling at one end of each strip then fold as if folding a flag over and over into a small triangle. Arrange on a baking sheet and brush with melted butter. Bake 15 to 20 minutes, at 325 degrees or until golden brown. Freeze, unbaked, then bake before thawing.

You can never have too many of these in your freezer!

Iris O'Donnell

CHERRY TOMATOES AND SESAME SEEDS

Preparation: 20 minutes

Serves: 15

Cherry tomatoes
Toasted sesame seeds
1 cup mayonnaise

½ cup mustard
3 tablespoons horseradish
6 drops Tabasco sauce

Wash tomatoes but leave stems in place. Toast sesame seeds in a warm oven (250 degree) until golden brown. Be careful to shake the pan so that they brown evenly. Make a sauce of mayonnaise, mustard, horseradish and Tabasco sauce. (Add more horseradish and tabasco if desired.) Pile the tomatoes in a serving bowl. Put the mayonnaise sauce in another bowl and the toasted sesame seeds in another. Dip the tomatoes in the sauce and seeds, and enjoy!

Alice Gaines

ARTICHOKE SQUARES

Preparation: 25 minutes
Cooking: 30 minutes

Yields: 20 squares

2 (6-ounce) jars marinated
   artichokes
1 small onion, chopped fine
1 clove garlic, minced
¼ cup fine bread crumbs
⅛ teaspoon salt
⅛ teaspoon pepper

Tabasco to taste
¼ teaspoon oregano
½ pound sharp Cheddar cheese,
   grated
2 eggs
2 tablespoons parsley

Drain marinade from 1 jar of artichokes into frying pan. Chop artichokes. To liquid add onion, garlic and sauté. Beat eggs in bowl. Add bread crumbs and seasonings. Stir in cheese, parsley, artichokes and sautéed mixture. Turn into greased 7 x 11 inch baking dish and bake at 325 degrees for 30 minutes. Let stand 5 minutes after baking and cut into small squares. May be wrapped in foil and frozen at this point for later use. To serve when frozen, thaw and reheat in foil 15 minutes at 325 degrees.

This appetizer is served often at the Governor's mansion!

Carolyn Hunt

Carolyn Hunt

CHEESE BALL

Preparation: 15 minutes   Serves: 8-10

½ pound sharp cheddar cheese
3 packages cream cheese
¼ pound Roquefort (or Blue)
   cheese
1 medium onion

1 cup chopped parsley
1 cup chopped pecans
1 tablespoon Worcestershire

Grind cheddar, Roquefort and onion in food chopper. Add cream cheese and one-half parsley and nuts. Form in ball. Roll in parsley and pecans.

This is a tasty, make-ahead appetizer for the Dole's busy lifestyle.

Elizabeth H. Dole

Elizabeth Dole

BLACK CAVIAR PIE

Preparation: 30 minutes   Serves: 25 to 30

6 hard-boiled eggs, chopped
3 tablespoons mayonnaise
1 large purple onion, finely
   chopped (about 1½ cups)
1 (8-ounce) package cream
   cheese, softened

⅔ cup sour cream
1 (3½-ounce) jar black caviar
lemon wedges and parsley

Grease bottom and sides of an 8-inch springform pan. In a mixing bowl, combine eggs and mayonnaise until well blended. Spread mixture in bottom of pan to make an even layer. Sprinkle with onion. Combine cream cheese and sour cream. Beat until smooth. By spoonfuls, drop onto onion. With wet table knife, spread gently to smooth. Cover and chill at least 3 hours or overnight. At serving time, top with a layer of drained caviar, distributing it to the edges of the pan. Run a knife around sides of pan. Loosen and lift off sides. Arrange lemon wedges in middle of pie in an open pinwheel. Fill to center with parsley. Serve with fresh bakery pumpernickel bread, cut in triangles. (Cocktail pumpernickel is too dry.)

Irene Mnick

STUFFED SNOW PEAS

Preparation: 30 minutes   Serves: 10 to 12

½ pound snow peas
1 (2½-ounce) package thinly sliced
   smoked beef
1 teaspoon prepared horseradish

1 cup sour cream
½ teaspoon prepared mustard
⅛ teaspoon pepper

Blanch snow peas in boiling water for one minute. Immerse in cold water, drain and refrigerate for 30 minutes before filling. Chop smoked beef very fine and mix with remaining ingredients. Carefully slit one side of pea pod with a sharp knife and fill with mixture, using a small spoon. Arrange on baking sheet with raised sides. Pea pods need to touch to stay upright. Refrigerate one hour.

Sally Millikin

SPINACH DIP

Preparation: 20 minutes   Serves: 15 to 20

2 (10-ounce) packages frozen
   spinach (thaw and squeeze all
   of water out)
1 package Knorr Swiss vegetable
   soup mix
1 (8-ounce) package cream cheese

1 pint sour cream
1 can water chestnuts, chopped
1 cup green onions, chopped

Mix all of the above and serve in a large (2-pound), round loaf of hollowed out rye bread. Cube bread removed from center and arrange around outside of large loaf to use for dip.

Betty Baxter, Sonja Andrew

PEANUT BUTTER STRIPS

Preparation: 15 minutes   Yield: 45 pieces
Cooking: 15 minutes

⅔ cup oil
⅔ cup peanut butter

½ cup sugar
9 slices bread

Mix peanut butter, oil, and sugar. Trim crusts from bread. Cut 8 slices into 5 strips per slice. Toast strips, extra piece of bread, and crusts for 15 minutes at 400 degrees. Place crusts and slice of bread in blender and make fine crumbs. Dip strips into peanut butter mixture and then roll in crumbs. Store in covered container.

Liz McGarr

ZUCCHINE SUISSE

Preparation: 15 minutes
Cooking: 25 minutes

Yield: 4 dozen squares

3 cups pared zucchini, shredded
1 cup Bisquick
½ cup chopped onion
½ cup Parmesan cheese
2 teaspoons snipped parsley
½ teaspoon salt

½ teaspoon seasoned salt
½ teaspoon dried marjoram
Dash pepper
1 clove garlic, finely chopped
½ cup vegetable oil
4 eggs, slightly beaten

All of the ingredients may be mixed into one large mixing bowl. Stir well to blend and pour into greased oblong pyrex 13 x 9 x 2 inch dish. Bake in oven for 25 minutes at 350 degrees.

Muriel Wilson

BACON SNAPS

Preparation: 5 minutes
Cooking: 10 minutes

Oscar Mayer Bacon (retains its
    shape best)

brown sugar

Cut bacon strips into 3 pieces. Dip each piece in brown sugar, coating on both sides. Set strips on cookie sheet with raised sides. Bake in 400 degree oven until sugar is melted and bacon looks cooked, about 10 minutes. Remove and place on wax paper to cool. (Should be crunchy.)

Judy Wein

CHEESE FESTIVE APPETIZER

Preparation: 10 minutes

Serves: 10

2 (8-ounce) packages cream
    cheese
1 (8-ounce) package sharp
    cheddar cheese
1 tablespoon chopped pimentos
1 tablespoon chopped green
    pepper

1 teaspoon chopped onion
1 teaspoon lemon juice
2 teaspoons Worcestershire sauce
Dash cayenne pepper
Dash pepper
Dash salt
Chopped pecans or paprika

Grate cheddar cheese. Add all ingredients in mixer except pecans. Mix thoroughly. Roll into ball. Roll in pecans or sprinkle with paprika. Better made 24 hours before serving. May be frozen. Serve with crackers.

Juanita Linton

CRABBIES

Preparation: 15 minutes   Serves: 25

1 stick butter or margarine
1 jar Olde English Cheese Spread
   (or cheddar cheese spread)
1½ teaspoons mayonnaise

½ teaspoon garlic salt
½ teaspoon seasoned salt
1 can (7-ounce) crab meat
6 English muffins

Allow butter and cheese to soften to room temperature. Cream together. Mix mayonnaise with salts. Add crab meat and butter/cheese mixture. Spread on split English muffins. Freeze 20 minutes, then cut into eighths and broil until bubbly crisp. Otherwise store in freezer and bring out when you're in a hurry.

An easy, delicious make-ahead appetizer!

Joy Smith
Nancy Brown

PARTY SHRIMP DIP

Preparation: 5 minutes   Serves: 12

8 ounces cream cheese, softened
4 tablespoons lemon juice
1 cup mayonnaise

1 cup chopped green onion tops
2 small cans party shrimp —
   crushed

Blend lemon juice and cream cheese together. Add mayonnaise. Blend. Stir in green onion and shrimp. Refrigerate at least 2 hours.

Several drops of red food color may be added to give a pale pink color.

Sue Gillison

SHRIMP AND CRABMEAT APPETIZER

Preparation: 30 minutes   Serves: 8 to 10
Cooking: 30 to 40 minutes

1 cup cooked shrimp, chopped
1 can crab meat (6 ounces)
1 cup chopped celery
1 cup herb stuffing mix
   (Pepperidge)

1 cup mayonnaise
1 can sliced water chestnuts (6
   ounce or small can)

Mix and bake 350 degrees for 30 to 40 minutes.

Janelle Snider

MARINATED SHRIMP

Preparation: 2 hours   Serves: 25

5 pounds cooked, deveined shrimp
3 or 4 medium onions, sliced thin
1 cup tarragon vinegar
2 cups salad oil (Wesson)

1 (10-ounce) bottle Durkee's Sauce
   (no substitute please)
1 tablespoon sugar
1 teaspoon salt
Bay leaves

Layer shrimp, onions, bay leaves in a large glass or ceramic jar. Mix tarragon vinegar, oil, Durkee's Sauce, sugar and salt. Pour over shrimp, gently stirring and turning jar to coat the shrimp. Chill for 24 hours. To serve, drain off some of marinade and arrange in pretty glass bowl or shell server.

Betty Baxter

HOT OR COLD CRAB DIP

10 ounces king crab, crabmeat
   supreme, or backfin crab meat
16 ounces cream cheese

3 or 4 ounces horseradish
1 cup mayonnaise

Beat cream cheese, mayonnaise, and horseradish until smooth. Stir in crab meat. Sprinkle cracked black pepper on top. Serve cold or hot with crackers.

Recipe shared by Greensboro caterers Jean Brandenburg and Margie Haines.

SCAMPI à la PETITE MARMITE

Preparation: 20 minutes   Serves: 8
Cooking: 5 minutes

Enough shrimp for 8 people
2 shallots
½ clove garlic
½ ounce Worcestershire sauce
salt

½ cup fresh lemon juice
½ cup sherry
½ pound butter
2½ to 5 ounces American
   mustard, yellow
Seasoned bread crumbs

Shrimp: Peel and butterfly shrimp, leaving tails on. Arrange on oven preheated platter or platters. Brush with oil and sprinkle with seasoned bread crumbs. Broil for 5 minutes or until done, depending on size shrimp. Remove from oven and pour hot Scampi sauce over shrimp and serve immediately.
Scampi Sauce: Grind the shallots and garlic, add Worcestershire, lemon juice and sherry. Mix mustard with butter until smooth and add this to the first mixture. Boil for 5 minutes, stirring constantly.

Sharon Masters

STUFFED CLAMS

Preparation: 15 minutes
Cooking: 20 minutes

Serves: 4

4 tablespoons margarine
½ cup finely chopped onion
½ teaspoon or so minced green
   pepper
2 tablespoons flour
¼ teaspoon salt

1 tablespoon Parmesan cheese
1 small can clams
Dash Worcestershire sauce
Dash Tabasco sauce
Tiny bit of breadcrumbs to thicken

Melt margarine in sauce pan and add onion and green pepper. Sauté until golden and soft. Add flour, salt and Parmesan cheese and mix well. Add clams and allow mixture to bubble. Add Worcestershire and Tabasco sauce, mixing well. Use a little breadcrumbs to thicken mixture. Put into 4 clam shells and bake at 400 degrees about 20 minutes, until brown and bubbly.

Clam shells can be purchased at gourmet or gift shops.

Debbie Bielski

BAKED CLAMS KAI

Preparation: 15 minutes

Serves: 12

1½ sticks butter or margarine
4 large garlic cloves, minced
1 can (10 ounces) water chestnuts,
   drained, rinsed, and chopped
   fine
1 can (10 ounces) minced clams

½ cup coarse breadcrumbs
Salt and pepper to taste
Paprika
Clam shells 12 to 15

Melt butter in skillet and sauté garlic until golden. Place clams in large bowl and remove half the juice (reserve). Add all but 2 tablespoons garlic butter to clams. Add water chestnuts, breadcrumbs, salt and pepper. Mix well. Set aside 5 minutes to thicken. Mixture should be soft and pliable. Spoon into clam shells and sprinkle with paprika. Combine reserved clam juice with remaining garlic butter and drizzle over clam mixture. Broil until hot, bubbly and brown. Serve with lemon wedges.

Nancy Smith

SMOKED OYSTER SPREAD

Preparation: ½ hour   Serves: 12 to 15

2 (8-ounce) packages cream
  cheese, softened
2 (3¾-ounce) cans smoked oysters
¼ cup milk or cream (or 2 to 4
  tablespoons of milk if firmer
  loaf desired)
2 to 3 tablespoons mayonnaise

1 tablespoon lemon juice
1 tablespoon Worcestershire sauce
Dash Tabasco
Salt and garlic powder to taste
Chopped parsley (fresh), paprika,
  chopped pecans

Cream the cheese and chop the oysters. Mix all the above ingredients
except parsley and paprika. Cover and refrigerate for several hours. Form
one loaf or spread in attractive shallow crystal bowl. Cover with parsley,
pecans, and paprika. Serve with buttery sesame seed crackers.

May also be used as a stuffing for cherry tomatoes.

Betty Baxter

YUMMY HAM/CHEESE FINGER ROLLS

Preparation: 30 minutes   Serves: 20
Cooking: 15 minutes

3 sticks margarine
2 grated onions
2 tablespoons mustard
2 tablespoons poppy seed

1 pound sliced boiled ham
1 pound sliced Swiss cheese
5 packages of party rolls
  (Pepperidge Farm or other
  brand)

Cook first four ingredients together until margarine is melted and mixture is
bubbly. Keep warm and set aside. Slice party rolls in half, preparing one
package at a time. Slice ham and Swiss cheese in pieces to fit size of party
rolls. Spread melted mixture on both sides of cut rolls. Add a slice of ham
and a slice of cheese to each roll. Return rolls to aluminum pan and heat
until cheese is melted, approximately 15 minutes at 350 degrees. Be sure
rolls are covered with foil. If you plan to freeze the rolls, let them thaw
slightly before heating.

*In a hurry? Slice the whole package of party rolls in half, spread melted
mixture on each whole half, layer ham and cheese on bottom half, cover
with top half of rolls THEN slice each individual roll apart!*

Merle Frazier

LAYERED CRAB MEAT SUPREME

Preparation: 15 minutes   Serves: 8 to 10

12 ounces softened cream cheese
2 tablespoons Worcestershire
   sauce
1 tablespoon fresh lemon juice
2 tablespoons mayonnaise
1 small onion, grated

Dash garlic salt
½ bottle chili sauce
12 ounces fresh backfin lump crab
   meat

Combine first 6 ingredients and blend until smooth. Spread in a large, shallow serving dish (a silver tray may be used). Spread ½ bottle chili sauce over this. Arrange fresh crab on top of sauce and cream cheese mixture. Sprinkle with fresh parsley. Serve immediately or chill overnight. Serve with assorted crackers.

This party favorite is equally good topped with shrimp!

Debby Legare
Pat Neill

OYSTERS ROCKEFELLER

Preparation: 30 minutes   Serves: 8
Cooking: 5 minutes

1 package frozen chopped spinach
2 tablespoons butter
2 tablespoons flour
1 cup milk

¼ teaspoon salt
Sprinkle of fresh pepper
Select oysters and oyster shells
Bacon, cooked and crumbled

Cook spinach and drain well. Make white sauce by combining butter, flour, milk and salt. Mix with spinach. Put a small amount in oyster shells. Place an oyster on each shell. Make hollandaise sauce (see recipe below). Pour hollandaise sauce over oysters and sprinkle with bacon. Bake 4 to 5 minutes in preheated 450 degree oven. Do not overcook.

Pat Haley

HOLLANDAISE SAUCE

2 egg yolks
½ stick butter

Juice of ½ lemon
Salt and pepper to taste

Place egg yolks, butter, lemon, salt and pepper in a saucepan and allow to get to room temperature. When ready to use, place over boiling water and stir until thick.

Pat Haley

BEST-EVER CRAB SPREAD

Preparation: 15 minutes   Serves: 10
Cooking: 20 minutes

1 (6-ounce) Wakefield frozen snow
   crab meat
1½ cups white American cheese,
   grated

¾ cup mayonnaise
1½ tablespoons grated onion
Dash Tabasco

Thaw crabmeat overnight in refrigerator. When ready to assemble ingredients, squeeze liquid from crab meat. Mix with rest of ingredients. Place in ovenproof dish. Bake 20 minutes in 350 degree oven. Serve surrounded by crackers.

Emily Pernice

ROAST BEEF FOR A LARGE GROUP

Preparation: 5 minutes   Serves: 30

10 to 30 pound round of beef
Oil
Salt

Cover beef with cooking oil. Coat with salt. Cook on 500 degrees for 45 minutes for small roast and 1 hour for larger one. Turn oven to 200 degrees and cook 15 minutes per pound or use meat thermometer for desired doneness.

Pat Carter

MAKE-AHEAD HAM SPREAD

Preparation: 1 hour   Serves: 24

3 pound canned ham (Hostess
   ham or deli ham)
1 cup mayonnaise
½ cup mustard, brown
½ cup Pommery mustard

2 tablespoons brown sugar
1 tablespoon wine vinegar
1 cup pickles, sweet and/or dill
   cubes with juice
1½ tablespoons liquid smoke

Chop ham in grinder or food processor. Mix remaining ingredients in separate bowl. Add to chopped ham. Store in refrigerator.

Ginny White

CHINESE BARBEQUED PORK (Char Siew)

Preparation: 5 minutes
Cooking: 20 minutes

Serves: 8

½ cup soy sauce
½ cup sugar
½ teaspoon garlic powder
2 tablespoons ketchup

½ teaspoon MSG
¼ teaspoon salt
1 pound pork tenderloin (in 2 strips)
Toasted sesame seed

Combine first 6 ingredients in mixing bowl. Add pork strips and marinate at least 3 hours, turning often. Drain pork and broil at 425 degrees for 20 minutes or until well done. Turn the strips each 10 minutes while broiling. Slice into ¼ inch pieces. Arrange over-lapping on a platter and sprinkle with toasted sesame seed.

An excellent appetizer but also good for sandwiches!

Darlene Young

MEATBALLS CHARCUTERIE

Preparation: 30 to 45 minutes
Cooking: 1 hour

Serves: 6 to 8

Butter
1 pound ground pork
1 cup dry bread crumbs
1 egg
Salt and pepper
⅓ cup chopped onion
1 tablespoon crushed black peppercorns
½ cup red wine vinegar
⅔ cup peeled, diced, chopped tomato

2 tablespoons tomato puree
1 (10½-ounce) can brown gravy
1 tablespoon chopped parsley
½ teaspoon dried thyme (or to taste)
½ teaspoon dried tarragon (or to taste)
Cold water as needed
1 to 2 tablespoons Dijon mustard

Combine pork, bread crumbs, egg, and salt and pepper to taste. Form into small meatballs and brown in butter. Cook gently until done and set aside. Sauté onion in butter remaining in pan. Pour off excess fat. Add remaining ingredients except mustard and water. Simmer for 10 minutes. Thin with cold water if you find the sauce too thick. Add mustard to taste. Add meatballs. Cool. Refrigerate for several days. Reheat and serve.

B. J. Pearce

MUSHROOM FARCI

Preparation: 35 minutes
Cooking: 25 minutes

Serves: 8

40 mushrooms, 1 to 2" in diameter
½ cup grated Parmesan cheese
½ cup dry bread crumbs
¼ cup grated onions
2 small cloves garlic minced
   (optional)

2 tablespoons chopped parsley
½ teaspoon salt
¼ teaspoon pepper
½ teaspoon oregano (optional)
1 stick butter, melted

Wash and dry mushrooms. Trim ends of stalks and carefully remove them from caps. Chop stalks and mix with cheese, bread crumbs, onions, garlic, parsley, salt, pepper and oregano. Fill mushroom caps with this mixture. (Do not overstuff.) Place caps in a shallow baking dish. Spoon butter over mushrooms, being sure to wet each cap. Bake in preheated oven (350 degrees) for 25 minutes. Excellent served with before dinner drinks.

Sylvia Smith

SIEW MAI

Preparation: 15 minutes
Cooking: 8 to 10 minutes

Yield: 3 dozen

Filling:
½ pound pork (more lean than fat)
4 dried Chinese mushrooms (soak
   in cold water until soft) and
   remove stems
1 piece canned bamboo shoot
½ carrot
30 pieces wonton skin
2 stalks spring onion, thinly sliced

Seasoning:
1 egg, beaten
¼ teaspoon salt
½ teaspoon MSG
1 teaspoon sugar
¼ teaspoon pepper
½ teaspoon sesame oil
½ teaspoon rice wine or dry sherry
1½ tablespoons cornflour

Mince pork, mushrooms, bamboo shoot and carrot finely (in blender or food processor). Add seasoning ingredients to minced ingredients and mix well. Divide into 30 portions. Trim wonton skins into rounds. Place a portion of filling on each piece of wonton skin. Gather the edges of the skin together to enclose filling cuplike. Press down the filling so it is compact. Arrange the dumplings on a steamer tray. Each dumpling should be 1 to 2 inches apart. Steam over medium heat for 8 to 10 minutes. Arrange on a serving plate. Garnish with thinly sliced spring onions. Serve hot.

Delicious with hot chili sauce purchased from Oriental section of grocery store.

Irene Snowberger

FRESH HAM BAR-BE-QUE

Preparation: 1 hour   Serves: 24
Cooking: 5 to 6 hours

2 pork shoulder arms picnic ham,
    5 to 6 pounds each (fresh)

Bake hams fat side up in 325 degree oven until fork tender. Takes 5 to 6 hours or more. Be sure to bake in deep roasting pan. Remove fat and chop up ham. This will be very tender and easy to chop. (But a greasy job!)

Sauce:
1 cup butter	2 tablespoons sugar
1 cup vinegar	2 onions (chopped)
2 cups water	Salt and pepper
4 tablespoons mustard	2 cups ketchup
	½ cup Worcestershire

Sauce: Simmer all ingredients for 10 minutes, then add ketchup and Worcestershire. Mix well with meat. Refrigerate or freeze.

Jackie Adams

PEPPERY SAUSAGE APPETIZER

Preparation: 30 minutes   Yields: 40 pieces
Cooking: 12 minutes

1 pound hot bulk sausage	½ teaspoon salt
1 pound lean ground sirloin	½ teaspoon pepper
1 pound Velveeta Cheese	1 teaspoon garlic powder
1 teaspoon Worcestershire	1 (1-pound) loaf small cocktail rye
1 teaspoon oregano (leaf)	(preferably Hickory Farms)

Sauté sausage in skillet, draining fat off as it accumulates. Place in separate bowl. In same skillet, sauté sirloin until red color is gone. Cut Velveeta into chunks and add to meat mixture. Add rest of ingredients and stir over low heat until mixture is well blended and cheese completely melted. Spread on cocktail rye slices and place on cookie sheet and freeze. When frozen, pop into freezer bags. To serve, remove number of slices desired and bake on cookie sheet for 12 minutes at 350 degrees.

Emily Pernice

CARIBBEAN GOULASH

Preparation: 15 minutes   Serves: 20

1½ pounds cooked shrimp
1 (6-ounce) can pitted ripe olives,
   drained
1 (6-ounce) can water chestnut,
   drained
1 basket cherry tomatoes
½ medium head cauliflower, cut in
   florets

Sauce:
2 cups mayonnaise
½ teaspoon MSG
½ teaspoon salt
½ cup prepared creamed
   horseradish
2 teaspoons dry mustard
2 teaspoons lemon juice

Mix with sauce being careful not to break tomatoes. Marinate for at least 8 hours. Serve in large glass bowl with toothpicks. Very colorful.

Lucy Hilder

PARTY BEEF ROLLS

Preparation: 20 minutes   Serves: 20
Cooking: 20 minutes

1 package Pepperidge Farm Party
   Rolls (20 to a package)
½ pound of thinly slice rare roast
   beef (from Delicatessen)

Softened butter
Lawry's seasoned salt

Slice rolls in half. Butter both sides, lightly. Trim fat from roast beef and cut into pieces to fit rolls. Layer beef on rolls and sprinkle liberally with Lawry's seasoned salt. Bake at 350 degrees for 20 minutes, covered with foil. (Punch small holes in foil so they don't get too soft.)

Delores Wellmaker

CREAM CHEESE WITH JEZEBEL SAUCE

Preparation: 10 minutes   Yield: 4 cups

14 ounces apple jelly
14 ounces pineapple preserves
5 ounces horseradish

2 tablespoons freshly ground
   pepper
Cream cheese

Mix all ingredients except cream cheese. Pour in covered containers and store in refrigerator until needed. Serve with cream cheese and crackers.

Dianne Shope

SHREDDED BARBEQUE BEEF

Preparation: 45 minutes
Cooking: 5 hours

Serves: 12 to 15

3 pound chuck roast
1 large onion, chopped
1 stalk celery, cut into pieces
1 large green pepper
1½ quarts water
2 cloves garlic
1 teaspoon salt
1 small bottle catsup
2 tablespoons brown sugar

2 tablespoons vinegar
1 teaspoon allspice and dry
  mustard
½ teaspoon chili powder
2 to 3 drops hot sauce
1 teaspoon Worcestershire
1 bay leaf
¼ teaspoon garlic salt
¼ teaspoon paprika

Place roast and vegetables in a large pot and add water. Cook covered for 4 hours. Remove meat. Cool and shred. Return meat to top of stove with 1½ cups of broth from cooking pot. Add remaining ingredients. Slowly boil uncovered for 1 hour. Add additional broth if needed. Serve on party rolls from a chafing dish.

Makes terrific leftovers!

Anne Rendleman

CHICKEN WINGS SHANGHAI STYLE

Preparation: 35 minutes
Cooking: 35 minutes

Serves: 12 to 16

2–3 pounds chicken wings
⅓ cup water
⅓ cup soy sauce
2 tablespoons brown sugar

1 tablespoon dry sherry
1 teaspoon powdered ginger
3 or 4 cloves of star anise
  (optional)

Combine everything in a large saucepan or teflon skillet. Bring to a boil, reduce heat, cover and simmer for 20 minutes only. Stir occasionally to give all the wings an equal turn in the liquid. After 20 minutes remove the cover, increase the heat slightly and continue cooking for 15 minutes. Because of the sugar in the liquid, it will begin to thicken into a rich brown glaze. Toss and stir to coat each wing with the sauce as it thickens.

Incredibly Easy!

Nancy Durham

ITALIAN SAUSAGE LOAF

Preparation: 10 minutes   Serves: 8 to 10
Cooking: 25 to 30 minutes

1 pound mild Italian sausage   Olive oil
2 (10-ounce) packages chopped   salt and pepper
   frozen spinach   Oregano
2 sheets of puff pastry

Slit casing and remove sausage. Brown in sauce pan, chopping with spoon to crumble. Cook spinach (see package directions). Squeeze water from spinach. Mix with drained sausage. Flour board. Roll each sheet of puff pastry to smooth out creases. Dress each piece of pastry lightly with olive oil. Spread with spinach and sausage and add seasonings as desired. Roll each loosely into a loaf similar to jelly roll (do not roll tightly or the inside pastry won't get done). Pinch ends of loaves together. Brush top and sides with a beaten egg. Sprinkle with paprika. Bake at 350 degrees for 25 to 30 minutes or until medium golden brown. Slice in 1 inch pieces.

Irene Mnick

ZESTY MEATBALLS

Preparation: 1 hour   Serves: 15 to 20
Cooking: 20 minutes

1½ cups catsup   2½ teaspoons Worcestershire
3 tablespoons mustard   sauce
3 tablespoons India relish   3 tablespoons lemon juice
6 tablespoons brown sugar

Using your favorite meatball recipe, prepare 1½ to 2 pounds ground beef and roll into balls. Bake at 375 degrees for 10 minutes. Combine above ingredients in large bowl and pour over meatballs. Bake covered an additional 10 minutes. Meatballs may be kept warm in crockpot or chafing dish.

Sherry Bailey

GRANOLA

Preparation: 30 minutes
Cooking: 1 to 1½ hours

2 or 3 pounds rolled oats   1½ cups safflower oil
2 cups coconut   1½ cups honey
2 cups nuts and seeds (cashews,   ⅔ cup water
   almonds, hulled sunflower   3 tablespoons vanilla
   seeds)   1 cup white raisins or dried fruits
2 cups wheat germ   after cooking
1 tablespoon salt

Mix first 4 ingredients and add remaining except raisins and dried fruits. Mix well. Heat in oven for 1 to 1½ hours at 250 degrees in shallow pans. Turn frequently. Remove from oven. Add fruits and raisins.

Nancy Bray

In 1925, the Greensboro Historical Museum opened its doors. An exhibit of 186 items had been collected and arranged by a society of volunteers formed in 1924. Over the years the permanent collection has developed into an increasingly important exhibition of Greensboro and surrounding area memorabilia. Museum membership as well as various civic and arts organizations have enjoyed the ambiance of the historical setting for both business and social meetings. The soups featured on the following pages are a tasty accompaniment or a hearty main dish for any group gathered for business or pleasure.

Soups

GREENSBORO HISTORICAL MUSEUM

CREAM OF CAULIFLOWER SOUP

Preparation time: 1 hour   Serves: 6

1 medium cauliflower
1 medium potato
1 large tomato
5 cups milk
5 minced green onions
1 tablespoon minced parsley

½ teaspoon savory seasoning
2 teaspoons salt
¼ teaspoon white pepper
½ pint whipping cream
Chopped chives

Separate cauliflower into florets. Peel and dice potato. Peel and chop tomato. Combine milk, cauliflower, potato, tomato, green onions, parsley and seasonings in Dutch oven. Simmer until vegetables are tender. Pour mixture through colander, reserving liquid. Place the vegetables, ⅓ at a time, into blender container with enough liquid to process easily until pureed. Return puree and remaining liquid to Dutch oven. Slowly stir in whipping cream. (Soup can be made ahead to this point.) Place over low heat and heat through, stirring frequently, until hot. Do not boil. Pour into bowls and sprinkle with chopped chives. May be served chilled or hot.

A tantalizing soup for both simple and grand occasions!

Lucy Major

CARROT SOUP

Preparation: 20 minutes   Serves: 6 to 8
Cooking: 20 minutes

¼ cup finely chopped onion
4 cups pared and sliced carrots
2 cans clear chicken broth
   (13¾-ounce cans)
¾ cup water

¼ teaspoon ground nutmeg
1½ tablespoon peanut butter
   (creamy style)
¼ cup heavy cream
Parsley to garnish

In 3 quart saucepan, bring onion, carrots, chicken broth, water and nutmeg to boil until carrots are tender, about 20 minutes. Cool. In the blender take ½ the carrot mixture and blend until smooth. Put into a saucepan. Whirl the other ½ of carrot mixture in blender and add peanut butter. Blend until smooth. Add to the first batch of soup. Stir in the cream. Reheat soup (do not boil, just simmer). Stir often and serve. Can be refrigerated in a tight container and reheated at serving time. Garnish with parsley.

An adaptation of a Trader Vic's recipe!

Nancy Balderacchi

CRAB SOUP WONDERFUL

Preparation: 5 minutes
Cooking: 5 minutes

Serves: 6 to 8

1 (10¾-ounce) can tomato soup
1 (10¾-ounce) can beef consommé
1 (10¾-ounce) can pea soup

1 cup sherry
1 cup heavy cream
1 (6¾-ounce) can crab meat

Heat all ingredients except crab meat. When mixture is hot, add crab meat and serve.

Mary Elam

MIDNIGHT SOUP

Preparation: 15 minutes
Cooking: 2½ hours

Serves: 4 to 6

1 pound hot bulk sausage
2 (16-ounce) cans tomatoes
2 (16-ounce) cans kidney beans, drained

1 large bell pepper, chopped
1 onion, chopped

Lightly brown and crumble sausage. Drain. Set aside. Combine remaining ingredients in saucepan. Simmer 30 minutes. Add sausage and simmer 2 hours. Season as desired.

Nancy Jones

FRITO CHILI SOUP

Preparation: 10 minutes
Cooking: 10 minutes

Serves: 8

2 regular size cans Ranch style pinto beans
1 (19-ounce) can Wolf Brand chili
1 regular size can Rotell tomatoes

1 regular size can tomatoes — stewed or sliced
½ pound grated American cheese
½ pint sour cream
1 large bag regular size Fritos

Mix in large pot first five ingredients. Heat thoroughly. Just before serving, add the sour cream. Put small amount of Fritos into each soup bowl and pour soup over them. Serve while still hot.

Katy Blanton

HEARTY POTATO SOUP

Preparation: 45 minutes
Cooking: 1½ hours

Serves: 6 to 8

8 to 10 medium potatoes, peeled and diced
1 to 2 mild onions, chopped
1 to 2 carrots, scraped and grated
1 stalk celery, halved and sliced
1 teaspoon bacon drippings
2 chicken bouillon cubes
1 (13-ounce) can evaporated milk
1 (10¾-ounce) can Campbell's Potato Soup
½ teaspoon garlic powder

2 tablespoons dillweed
1 tablespoon Worcestershire
¼ teaspoon poultry seasoning
¼ cup chopped fresh parsley or 2 tablespoons dried parsley
Salt and pepper to taste
¼ cup Parmesan cheese
6 to 8 slices bacon, fried and crumbled
Milk to thin to desired consistency

In a large pot, combine potatoes, onions, carrots, celery. Add water just to cover and bring to a boil. Stir in bacon drippings and bouillon cubes. Cover and cook until vegetables are just tender. With a large spoon, stir cooked vegetables vigorously until mixture thickens. Add evaporated milk and canned soup. Blend in garlic powder, dill, Worcestershire, poultry seasoning, parsley, salt, pepper, cheese, and bacon. Stir well and thin to desired consistency with whole milk. Cover and simmer on low heat for 1 hour, stirring frequently. Serve topped with additional Parmesan cheese and seasoned croutons.

Flavor improves when refrigerated 12 to 24 hours before serving!

Jane Gibson

QUICK & EASY BEAN SOUP

Preparation: 15 minutes
Cooking: 20 minutes

Serves: 8

5 cups water
2 cups milk (homogenized)
¼ cup finely chopped onion
2 teaspoons salt
¼ teaspoon pepper

1 envelope instant mashed potatoes (French's)
1 to 2 cups finely diced ham
1 (1-pound) can pork and beans
1 tablespoon parsley

Combine water, milk, onion, salt and pepper in a large saucepan. Bring to a boil. Remove from heat. Gradually stir in contents of potato envelope. Add ham, beans and parsley. Heat 10 minutes or longer.

Betty Baxter

ONION WINE SOUP

Preparation: 30 minutes   Serves: 6 to 8
Cooking: 35 to 40 minutes

¼ cup butter
5 large onions, chopped
5 cups beef broth
½ cup celery leaves
1 large potato, sliced
1 cup dry white wine

1 tablespoon vinegar
2 teaspoons sugar
1 cup light cream
1 tablespoon minced parsley
Salt and pepper

Melt butter in large saucepan. Add chopped onion and mix well. Add beef broth, celery leaves and potato. Bring to boil. Cover and simmer for 30 minutes. Puree mixture in a blender. Return to saucepan and blend in wine, vinegar and sugar. Bring to boil and simmer 5 minutes. Stir in cream, parsley and salt and pepper to taste. Heat thoroughly but do not boil.

*The addition of cream gives a unique flavor to this
White House specialty!*

Nancy Reagan

Nancy Reagan

CHILLED, DILLED ZUCCHINI SOUP

Preparation: 20 minutes   Serves: 6
Cooking: 25 minutes

4 medium zucchini, cut in ½-inch
  slices
2 cans chicken broth
1 bunch scallions, chopped
Salt and pepper to taste

2 (8-ounce) packages cream
  cheese, softened
1 cup sour cream
1½ tablespoons fresh dill (or 1½
  teaspoons dry dill)
1 tablespoon freshly chopped
  chives

In a large saucepan, bring to a boil zucchini, chicken broth, scallions, salt and pepper. Cover, reduce heat and simmer for 20 to 25 minutes or until zucchini is soft. Allow to cool 10 to 15 minutes. In food processor or blender, combine cream cheese, sour cream, dill and chives. Process until smooth. Add the cooled zucchini mixture (liquid and all) and process until smooth. May need to divide into several batches if capacity of processor is too small. Chill 6 hours or overnight. Add salt and pepper to taste. Do not freeze.

Garnish with a lemon slice and fresh snipped dill or sour cream.

Karen Johnston

GERMAN VEGETABLE SOUP

Preparation: 30 minutes   Serves: 10
Cooking: 20 to 25 minutes

¼ to ½ cup finely diced bacon
3 tablespoons butter, melted
½ cup chopped cabbage
½ cup chopped leeks or green
   onions
½ cup regular onion, chopped
½ cup diced celery

½ cup diced carrots
½ cup diced parsnips
3 to 4 tablespoons flour
3 cups chicken broth
1 cup heavy cream
Salt and pepper to taste

Lightly sauté finely diced bacon in melted butter. Sauté vegetables about 5 minutes over medium heat. Add flour and mix well. Slowly add chicken broth, stirring to prevent lumping. Cook for 20 to 25 minutes. Remove from heat and stir in heavy cream. Add salt and pepper to taste. Return to heat and continue cooking to just before boiling. (When reheating, do not allow soup to boil.)

A very rich soup that's nice for company.

Gale East

OLD KENTUCKY CREAM OF BROCCOLI SOUP

Preparation: 30 minutes   Serves: 8 to 10
Cooking: 15 minutes

1½ quarts water or 6 cups
1 (10-ounce) package frozen
   chopped broccoli
¾ cup finely chopped onion
2 teaspoons salt
2 teaspoons MSG
2 teaspoons white pepper
1 teaspoon garlic powder

8 ounces (2 cups) shredded
   American cheese (like Velveeta
   Cheese)
1 cup milk, not skim
1 cup whipping cream
¼ cup butter
⅓ cup all-purpose flour
½ cup cold water

In a 3-quart saucepan, bring 1½ quarts of water to boil. Add broccoli and onion and boil 10 to 12 minues. Add seasonings and shredded cheese. Stir until cheese melts. Add milk, cream, and butter. Stir and heat to boiling. Slowly add water to flour, stirring constantly until texture is smooth. Slowly add to hot mixture, stirring rapidly. Cook and stir until soup is consistency of heavy cream.

Best if made a day ahead!

Beverly Gwynn

CALIFORNIA'S BEST GAZPACHO

Preparation: 30 minutes   Serves: 6 to 8

2 large tomatoes, peeled
1 large cucumber, pared
1 medium onion
1 medium green pepper
1 pimento, drained
2 (12-ounce) cans tomato juice
⅓ cup olive oil
⅓ cup red wine vinegar

¼ teaspoon Tabasco
½ teaspoon salt
⅛ teaspoon black pepper
½ cup croutons
¼ cup chopped chives
1 clove garlic (optional)

In blender, combine tomato, cucumber, green pepper, onion, pimento and ½ cup tomato juice. Blend at high speed 30 seconds to puree the vegetables. In a large bowl, mix pureed vegetables with remaining tomato juice, olive oil, vinegar, Tabasco, salt and pepper and crushed garlic. Refrigerate covered at least 2 hours before serving. (Keeps well for several days.) Serve in chilled bowls and top with chopped chives and croutons. (Cucumber, green pepper and onion also make an attractive garnish.)

Makes a satisfying low-calorie summer lunch or appetizer.

Wanda Poole

FRESH BROCCOLI CHOWDER

Preparation: 30 minutes   Serves: 8
Cooking: 10 minutes

2 pounds fresh broccoli
3 cups chicken stock
3 cups milk
1 cup ham cooked and diced
2 teaspoons salt

¼ teaspoon freshly ground pepper
1 cup half and half cream
2 cups grated Swiss cheese
¼ cup butter

Wash broccoli and remove any leaves and coarse stem ends. Place the broccoli in a large pot adding ½ the stock. Bring to a boil, then reduce the heat and cover. Simmer for 7 minutes. Remove broccoli from stock and chop coarsely. Add remaining stock, milk, ham, salt and pepper to the stock in the pot and stir well. Bring to a boil over medium heat, stirring occasionally. Stir in cream, cheese, butter, and broccoli and heat until the cheese is melted. Do not boil.

Jimmie Johnson

THE COUNTESS SPINACH-CREAM SOUP

Preparation: 30 minutes
Cooking: 15 minutes

Serves: 4

1½ pounds spinach
2½ tablespoons butter
2 chopped pearl onions
2½ tablespoons flour
2 cups beef bouillon

Salt, pepper, nutmeg
1 cup milk
4 tablespoons whipped cream
4 lemon slices
Croutons (optional)

Wash spinach well and remove stems. Cook 3 minutes in salted water. Remove from water and drain. Melt butter in pot. Add the thinly chopped pearl onions and sauté 2 to 3 minutes. Add flour and stir until mixture is "straw yellow." Add bouillon, water and spinach. Bring to boil. Cover pot and cook on low heat for 15 minutes. Put in blender to form a puree. Return mixture to pot and add milk, salt, pepper and a pinch of nutmeg. Serve in small soup bowl with a tablespoon of whipped cream on top and a lemon slice. Serve croutons with soup.

An old favorite that was served in the Esterhazy Palace in Austria, where Joseph Haydn started his musical career.

Jill Froehlich

EASY ONION SOUP

Preparation: 20 minutes
Cooking: 4 to 5 hours

Serves: 6 to 8

2 pounds onions
¼ pound butter or margarine
3 (10¾-ounce) cans consomme
  soup
1 soup can water (optional)
Worcestershire sauce to taste
Salt and pepper to taste

½ to ¾ cup dry red wine
Toasted French bread slices (for
  each bowl of soup)
Melted butter
Sharp cheddar cheese, grated

Peel onions and slice. In large saucepan, melt butter or margarine. Add onion slices, a few at a time, and cook to a golden brown. Add consomme. To each 3 cans of consomme, add 1 soup can of water if needed. Stir and heat slowly. Add Worcestershire sauce, salt and pepper to taste. Then add dry red wine. Simmer, covered (do not boil), for 4 to 5 hours, stirring occasionally. If soup is too thick, add more wine. When ready to serve, put soup in onion bowls. Top with a slice of toasted French bread and drizzle with melted butter. Generously top with grated sharp cheddar cheese.

Joan Calvert

FRESH MUSHROOM SOUP

Preparation: 30 minutes   Serves: 8 to 10
Cooking: 20 minutes

1 pound fresh mushrooms, chopped or sliced	Pepper to taste
½ cup butter	⅓ cup flour
1 medium onion, chopped	½ teaspoon Worcestershire sauce
1 small clove garlic, minced	1 cup chopped celery
½ teaspoon salt (optional)	2 carrots, sliced
½ teaspoon dry mustard	6 cups beef broth
	1 cup white wine

Sauté mushrooms in ¼ cup butter and set aside. Sauté onion and garlic in remaining butter. Blend in salt, pepper, mustard and flour. Add Worcestershire sauce, celery, carrots and beef broth. Cook, stirring constantly until slightly thickened. Lower heat. Cook covered for 20 minutes. Strain. Add wine and mushrooms to strained broth. Heat thoroughly or until mushrooms are tender.

Madelyn Phillips

ACORN SQUASH SOUP

Preparation: 20 minutes   Serves: 6
Cooking: 1½ hours

3 medium acorn squash	2 stalks celery, cut in 6 pieces
Salt and pepper	1½ cups grated cheddar cheese
6 tablespoons butter	2 cups half and half cream
1 onion, diced	

Prepare squash by leveling each end, cutting squash in half, (using a zig-zag pattern, if desired) and scooping out seeds and membranes from centers. Place squash "bowls" on a foil lined baking sheet. Sprinkle insides with salt and pepper and dot with 3 tablespoons butter. Into each "bowl" place a portion of the onion, 1 piece of celery, a portion of the cheese (reserving ½ cup for final broiling) and a portion of half and half. Dot tops of squash with remaining 3 tablespoons butter. Cover loosely with foil. Place in 350 degree oven and bake 1½ hours, or until tender when pierced with a fork. (More half and half may be added for a thinner soup.) Remove foil and finish cooking by topping with remaining cheese and broiling 1 minute until cheese has melted and is browned on top.

A memorable first course!

Trish Green

45

OYSTER/GREEN PEA SOUP

Preparation: 25 minutes   Serves: 8 to 10
Cooking: 20 minutes

6 tablespoons butter
½ cup finely chopped onion
2 packages (10 ounces each)
    frozen green peas
2 cups milk
1 quart shucked fresh oysters with
    their liquor

2 cups clam juice
½ cup dry white wine
Salt and pepper to taste
2 cups heavy cream

Melt 2 tablespoons butter in a saucepan and cook onions until they are wilted but not brown. Add peas and milk and simmer just until peas are tender. Add oysters and clam juice and simmer over very low heat 5 minutes or until oysters curl. Add wine, remaining butter, salt and pepper. When butter melts, puree half the mixture in an electric blender. Pour both mixtures (pureed and non-pureed) into saucepan. When ready to serve, preheat broiler and whip cream seasoned with a little salt. Heat soup almost to boiling and spoon it into hot, heatproof serving dishes. Top each serving with a generous spoonful of whipped cream and slide under broiler until cream is toasted dark brown. Serve immediately.

The heavy cream may be eliminated. It is delicious "as is."

Louise Glover

CHEESE SOUP

Preparation: 15 minutes   Serves: 6 to 8
Cooking: 30 minutes

1 small onion, minced
2 tablespoons butter
1 pint chicken broth
1 pint half and half
1 small jar cheese whiz (8-ounce),
    or 1 pound sharp cheddar
    cheese

1 cup milk and 1 teaspoon flour
    for thickening
Garnish with prepared seasoned
    croutons

Sauté onion in 2 tablespoons butter. Do not brown. Add chicken broth and let onions cook until done. Add half and half and small jar cheese whiz or 1 pound cheddar cheese, grated. Mix milk and flour. Pour into soup mixture. Cook on medium heat until desired thickness is reached and set aside. (Do not boil.)

Perfect with a green salad for lunch!

Joan Shumate

SEAFOOD BISQUE

Preparation: 30 minutes   Serves: 10 to 12
Cooking: 20 minutes

½ pound bay scallops   ½ cup flour
½ pound peeled shrimp   1 teaspoon Spanish paprika
½ pound crab meat   1 bay leaf
1 teaspoon lemon juice   1 ½ quart hot milk
4 ounces butter   Salt, pepper, sherry wine to taste

Cook scallops and shrimp until just done in 1 pint water seasoned with salt, lemon juice and bay leaf. Drain and save liquid. Sauté ¼ cup finely chopped onion in 4 ounces of butter. DO NOT BROWN. Sprinkle 1 teaspoon Spanish paprika and ½ cup flour. Stir and add liquid and 1½ quart of heated milk. Cook on low heat until simmering. Stir to keep from scorching. DO NOT BOIL. Chop shrimp and scallops. Add to milk. Add ½ pound crabmeat and season to taste with salt, white pepper and sherry wine. Makes approximately 12 servings.

This recipe shared by Chef Franklin Beal of Greensboro Country Club.

NEW ENGLAND CLAM CHOWDER

Preparation: 30 minutes   Serves: 8 to 10
Cooking: 30 minutes

1 pint clams, chopped   1 cup water
2 tablespoons bacon fat   3 cups Half-and-Half
3 tablespoons all-purpose flour   ½ teaspoon salt
½ cup celery, chopped   ½ teaspoon pepper
½ cup onion, chopped   Dash of Texas Pete
1 teaspoon thyme leaves   2 tablespoons butter or margarine
2 cups diced potatoes   1 chicken or clam bouillon cube
1 bay leaf

In sauce pan put bacon fat and butter or margarine over medium heat. Cook onion and celery until tender. Add flour and clam water into mixture blended. Mix and cook. Sitr until slightly thickened. Stir in potatoes and all spices above. Add chicken or clam bouillon cube. Cook until potatoes are tender. Add Half-and-Half. Stir. Cook about 8 minutes. Makes 10 cups.

This recipe was shared by Chef McConnell
of Greensboro Country Club at Carlson Farms.

CHELSEA CREAM OF CUCUMBER

Preparation: 1 hour   Serves: 4

2 large cucumbers
2 tablespoons butter
Pinch of sugar
Salt to taste
White pepper to taste
1 cup half and half

½ medium onion, chopped
1 bay leaf
1 tablespoon butter
1 tablespoon flour
1 cup chicken broth
4 tablespoons heavy cream

Peel cucumbers. Slice in half lengthwise and seed. Slice thinly, blanch in boiling water for 2 minutes, and drain well. Melt 2 tablespoons butter in saucepan and add the cucumber, sugar, and seasonings. Cover and cook gently for 15 minutes or until cucumber is soft. Combine half and half, onion, and bay leaf in saucepan. Bring to a boil and remove from heat. Add to cucumbers. Let mixture stand to infuse for 10 minutes, and strain. Meanwhile, prepare white sauce as follows to use for thickening soup. Melt 1 tablespoon butter and blend in 1 tablespoon flour. Stir in chicken stock and heavy cream. Bring just to boiling, stirring constantly. Stir in the strained milk. Bring to a low boil, stirring constantly, and cook gently 2 to 3 minutes. Serve immediately. Recipe may be doubled.

An elegant soup for a spring luncheon!

Jean Anne Finley

CREAM OF BROCCOLI SOUP

Preparation: 20 minutes   Serves: 4
Cooking: 20 minutes

1 head broccoli, minced
1 small potato, minced
1 small onion, minced
3 tablespoons fresh parsley,
    minced
6 cups chicken broth

3 cups milk
6 tablespoons butter
5 tablespoons flour
Salt and pepper

Melt butter, add flour and stir over low heat 3 minutes. Add heated milk. Beat with whisk until smooth. Boil broccoli, potato, onion and parsley in chicken broth 10 minutes. Add to milk mixture and simmer 5 to 10 minutes. Season with salt and pepper.

Joanne White

EASY BRUNSWICK STEW

Preparation: 20 minutes   Serves: 6
Cooking: 2 hours

3 to 4 chicken breasts
1 onion, chopped
1 (16-ounce) can corn
1 (8-ounce) can tomato sauce
1 teaspoon Worcestershire sauce
1 teaspoon catsup
Dash of Tabasco

½ teaspoon salt
⅛ teaspoon pepper
1 (16-ounce) can butterbeans
2 potatoes, diced
1 teaspoon lemon juice
¼ cup butter

In Dutch oven, cook chicken in boiling, salted water until done, 30 to 45 minutes. Cool and remove chicken from bones. Cut into bite size chunks. Strain broth and return to Dutch oven. Add all other ingredients and cook, simmering, about 1 hour, or longer if desired. Stir occasionally. May be thickened with small amount of cornstarch mixed with ½ cup water. Can be frozen.

Peggy Wyatt

HOT CUCUMBER SOUP OXFORD

Preparation: 45 minutes   Serves: 4 to 6
Cooking: 15 minutes

3 ounces butter
1 onion, chopped
4 to 5 cucumbers (peeled & seedless), chopped
1 leek chopped (use white and light green)
1 can (13¾ ounce) chicken broth
2 tablespoons fresh dill or 2 teaspoon dried

½ cup whipping cream
1 teaspoon cornstarch
1 teaspoon lemon juice
1 teaspoon lemon pepper
½ teaspoon salt
½ teaspoon sugar

Melt butter in pan. Add onion and cook until soft. Add cucumber and leek and cook 5 minutes. Add can of chicken broth and 1 tablespoon fresh dill or 1 teaspoon dried dill. Simmer until tender, 10 to 15 minutes. Puree in blender or food processor. In a separate small bowl, mix whipping cream and cornstarch. Add to cucumber puree. Add lemon juice, lemon pepper, salt, sugar and the remaining dill. Taste and add more salt if needed. Can serve in bowls with a garnish of sour cream and dill on top. For a main course add small pieces of shrimp. Serve with hot garlic bread.

Lynn Beauchamp

DELICIOUS CHICKEN RICE SOUP

Preparation: 45 minutes
Cooking: 2½ hours

Serves: 6 to 8

1 (3½ to 4 pound) fryer-broiler
10 cups water
¼ teaspoon dried whole basil
¼ teaspoon celery salt
⅛ teaspoon garlic salt
1 tablespoon chopped fresh
    parsley

1 bay leaf
2 teaspoons salt
¼ teaspoon pepper
4 medium carrots, chopped
1 small onion, chopped
½ cup Uncle Ben's rice

Combine first 9 ingredients in a large Dutch oven. Cook 1½ hours, or until chicken is tender. Remove chicken and discard bay leaf. Let chicken cool. Remove meat from bones and dice meat. Set aside. Bring chicken broth to a boil. Add carrots, onions and rice. Simmer 30 minutes. Add meat and rice. Cook 15 minutes.

Lorraine Dodds

SAVORY MINESTRONE

Preparation: 20 minutes
Cooking: 40 minutes

Serves: 6 to 8

3 slices bacon, finely chopped
1 cup chopped onion
2 large cloves garlic, minced
1 teaspoon crushed basil leaves
1 can beef broth
1 can bean and bacon soup
2 soup cans of water

1 (16-ounce) can tomatoes,
    undrained
½ cup elbow macaroni
½ cup cabbage, cut into small
    pieces
2 to 3 small zucchini squash,
    cubed

In large saucepan, brown bacon and cook onion with garlic and basil until tender. Stir in soups, water, tomatoes, and macaroni. Bring to boil, cover, reduce heat. Simmer 15 minutes. Add cabbage and squash. Cook 15 minutes more or until squash is done. Stir occasionally and add more water if needed. Makes about 8 cups.

Delicious served with Italian bread, fruit and cheese.

Cookie McAdoo

SQUASH SOUP

Preparation: 30 minutes
Cooking: 40 minutes

Serves: 8 to 10

6 leeks
½ stick butter
2 pounds yellow squash
4 cups chicken broth

1 cup heavy cream
Salt and pepper to taste
Nutmeg (optional)

In large saucepan, sauté the white parts of 6 leeks (washed and minced) in ½ stick butter, until soft. Wash 2 pounds yellow squash. Dice. Add to saucepan with 4 cups chicken broth. Bring to a boil and simmer, covered, about 30 minutes. In a blender or food processor, puree mixture in batches and return to saucepan. Stir in 1 cup heavy cream with salt and pepper to taste. Adding a pinch or two of nutmeg makes a delicious flavor.

Jeanne Sutherland

CREAM OF MUSHROOM SOUP

Preparation: 25 minutes
Cooking: 15 minutes

Serves: 4

3 cups sliced mushrooms
2 tablespoons minced onions
3 tablespoons butter
3 tablespoons flour
½ teaspoon salt
⅛ teaspoon pepper

1 quart milk
2 chicken boullion cubes
1 tablespoon catsup
½ teaspoon Worcestershire sauce
2 tablespoons chopped chives

Sauté mushrooms and onions in butter. Blend flour with salt and pepper and add to the mushrooms and onions, stirring constantly for 2 to 3 minutes. Gradually add milk, then bouillon cubes, catsup and Worcestershire sauce. Cook on low heat, stirring constantly, until thickened (about 15 minutes). Sprinkle chives on soup when ready to serve.

Emily Pernice

One of the centers of social activity in the mid 1800's was Blandwood, home of North Carolina governor, John Motley Morehead. Today the mansion is open to the public, continuing its tradition as an elegant backdrop for many Greensboro social events. Like Blandwood, our bread recipes reflect the old and the new with options for the most simple to the most sophisticated meal.

Breads

THE BLANDWOOD MANSION

BLENDER YEAST ROLLS

Preparation: 2½ hours   Yield: 24 rolls
Cooking: 10 minutes

½ cup nonfat dry milk   1 package active dry yeast
2 eggs   ¼ cup oil
⅓ cup sugar   1 cup hot water
1 teaspoon salt   4 cups flour

Blend all ingredients except flour for 1 minute in an electric blender. Place flour into separate bowl, and make a "well" in center of flour. Pour in the blended mixture. Mix well, and let rise until doubled (about 2 hours). Mixture can then be refrigerated for 3 to 4 days and used as needed. It may also be kneaded, rolled and made into rolls. To prepare rolls, let dough rise again for 2 hours and bake at 350 degrees for approximately 10 minutes, or until golden brown. Cool 10 minutes before removing from pan. (If desired, this mixture also can be used to make 2 loaves of bread. Cook 30 minutes if using that variation.)

May use food processor instead of blender to prepare dough.

Connie Carter

HEART SHAPED BISCUITS

Preparation: 15 minutes   Yield: 12
Cooking: 8 to 10 minutes

2 cups biscuit mix   ⅔ cup milk

Preheat oven to 400 degrees. Mix biscuit mix and milk until soft dough forms. Beat for 30 seconds. (If dough is too sticky, gradually add enough biscuit mix to make dough easy to handle.) Put on cloth covered board, well dusted with biscuit mix. Gently coat dough with baking mix. Shape into a ball, and knead 10 times. Roll ½ inch thick. Cut with heart shaped cookie cutter dipped in baking mix. Bake on ungreased cookie sheet until golden brown, 8 to 10 minutes.

Heart shaped beaten biscuits were tradionally served at wedding receptions at Blandwood in the late 1800's. In its original form, this recipe calls for beaten biscuits; however, they are such a production that they are seldom made now.

Mary Lewis Edmunds

CRUMB COFFEE CAKE

Preparation: 35 minutes   Serves: 16 to 20
Cooking: 1 hour

Cake mixture:
1 stick margarine (Parkay)
¼ cup Crisco oil (only)
2 eggs
1 teaspoon baking powder
¼ teaspoon baking soda

¾ cup milk
1 cup sugar
2¼ cups cake flour, sifted
2 teaspoons vanilla flavoring

Topping mixture:
1 can cherry pie filling (or whatever you prefer)

Crumb mixture:
½ stick margarine
3 cups Bisquick

1 cup sugar
2 teaspoons cinnamon

Mix margarine, oil and one cup sugar thoroughly. Then add 2 eggs and beat well. Combine flour, baking powder, and baking soda. Add the flour mixture, a little at a time, alternating with the ¾ cup milk. Add vanilla and mix well. Pour into 10 x 14 or 16 inch pan, (don't use a 13 x 9 inch pan). Spread cherry pie filling evenly on batter. Mix the crumb mixture ingredients by hand. Sprinkle over cake batter. Bake in oven at 375 degrees for 35 to 45 minutes. If using pyrex pan, 350 degrees 45 to 50 minutes. Cool. Sprinkle with confectioners sugar. Cut in squares. Freezes well.

Lorraine Valitutto

APPLE BREAD

Preparation: 35 minutes   Yield: 1 loaf
Cooking: 1 hour

½ pound margarine or butter
1 cup sugar
2 eggs, beaten
2 cups flour
1 teaspoon baking soda, dissolved
   in 2 tablespoons buttermilk
1 teaspoon vanilla
2 cups diced tart apples

Topping:
4 tablespoons melted butter
4 tablespoons flour
1½ teaspoons cinnamon
4 tablespoons sugar

Cream sugar and margarine. Add beaten eggs. Add flour and buttermilk/baking soda mixture. Add vanilla. Stir in diced apples. Combine topping ingredients. Pour batter into greased 9 x 5 inch bread pan and top with topping. Bake 1 hour at 350 degrees.

Ellen Taft

CINNAMON FLUFF COFFEE CAKE

Preparation: 20 minutes
Cooking: 40 minutes

Serves: 10 to 12

Cake:
1 cup sugar
½ cup butter
1 egg, beaten
1 cup milk
2 cups flour
2½ teaspoons baking powder

Filling:
½ cup brown sugar
1½ teaspoons cinnamon
2 tablespoons flour
2 tablespoons melted butter
½ cup chopped pecans

Topping:
⅓ cup sugar
⅓ cup flour

1 tablespoon butter
½ teaspoon cinnamon

Cake:
Cream together sugar, butter, and egg. Add milk, flour, and baking powder. Spread half of cake batter in a 9 x 12 inch glass baking dish. Combine filling ingredients and sprinkle all but 2 tablespoons (reserve for topping) over batter. Pour rest of batter over filling.

Topping:
Sift flour and sugar together. Mix in softened butter until crumbly. Add the 2 tablespoons of filling and ½ teaspoon cinnamon. Sprinkle over top of batter. Bake 40 minutes at 350 degrees.

Bonnie Cordes

GERMAN PANCAKE

Preparation: 20 minutes
Cooking: 20 minutes

Serves: 10

1 cup sifted all-purpose flour
½ teaspoon baking powder
½ teaspoon salt
1 cup skim milk

5 eggs
1 tablespoon vegetable oil
1 (16-ounce) can diet-packed fruit,
    drained or any fresh fruit

Sift flour, baking powder and salt into mixing bowl. Using rotary beater, beat in milk, then eggs, one at a time. Heat oil in a large (9-inch) skillet with oven-proof handle. Pour in batter, all at once. Cook one minute over medium heat. Bake in hot oven (425 degrees) 20 minutes or until pancake is browned and puffy. Top with drained, sliced fruit. Serve at once.

When in season, try topping pancake with fresh strawberries or peaches sprinkled with confectioner's sugar for brunch!

Joan Calvert

CUBAN BREAD

Preparation: 3 hours   Serves: 8 to 10
Cooking: 30 to 40 minutes

1 package yeast   1 tablespoon sugar
2 cups lukewarm water   6 to 7 cups flour
1¼ tablespoons salt   Corn meal

Dissolve yeast in water in large bowl. Add salt and sugar. Stir. Add flour, 1 cup at a time. With wooden spoon, stir to make stiff dough. (May have to knead in last cup of flour.) Shape into ball and grease top. Cover with towel and let stand in warm place until doubled (about 1½ hours). With floured hands, shape into two long, thin loaves. Arrange on baking sheet heavily sprinkled with cornmeal. Allow to rest 5 minutes. Slash tops with sharp knife and brush with water for crisp crust. Place a pan of boiling water on bottom rack of oven. Bake at 400 degrees for 30 to 40 minutes. Do not preheat.

Lynda Middlemas

BASIC CREPE

Preparation: 1 hour   Yield: 30

6 eggs   ½ teaspoon salt
1 cup plus 2 tablespoons flour   3 cups milk
1½ tablespoons sugar   ¼ pound butter (or less)

Beat eggs. Add flour, sugar, and salt. Beat until smooth. Gradually add milk, beating constantly. Melt 1 teaspoon butter in 7-inch skillet. Pour 2 tablespoons batter to cover bottom of skillet. Cook until golden brown on bottom. Turn with spatula and cook other side until light brown. Transfer cooked crepe to wax paper. Repeat for each crepe. To freeze, separate each crepe with wax paper and store in airtight container.

Marian Ferrel

ICE CREAM SWEET ROLLS

Preparation: 5 minutes   Yield: 6 to 12
Cooking: 10 to 15 minutes

1 cup self-rising flour   1 cup softened ice cream, any flavor

Mix flour and ice cream and spoon into greased muffin tins. Fill ⅔ full. Bake 400 degrees for 10 to 15 minutes. Makes 12 small or 6 large muffins.

Jeanne Rives

QUICK CROISSANTS

Preparation: 20 minutes
Cooking: 30 to 40 minutes

Serves: 12

1 package yeast
1 cup lukewarm water
¾ cup evaporated milk
1½ teaspoon salt
⅓ cup sugar
1 egg

5 cups plain four, unsifted
¼ cup butter, melted and cooled
1 cup firm butter, refrigerator
 temperature
1 egg beaten with 1 tablespoon
 water

Soften yeast in water. Add milk, salt, sugar, egg, and 1 cup of flour. Beat until smooth, and add melted butter. Set aside. In large bowl, cut 1 cup firm butter into remaining 4 cups flour until butter pieces are about the size of dried kidney beans. Pour yeast batter over, and blend until moistened. Cover with plastic wrap and refrigerate at least 4 hours (or up to 4 days). Remove dough from refrigerator and knead 6 times. Divide dough into 4 balls (refrigerate unused portion). Roll each ball into circle, and cut each circle into 8 wedges. Roll each wedge into crescent form. Cover rolls, and let rise 4 to 6 hours in warm place. Brush with egg/water mixture, and bake 30 to 40 minutes at 325 degrees. Can mix dough as much as four days before baking. Baked rolls may be frozen and reheated at 350 degrees for 10 minutes.

Ann Rives
Rosli Clark

STRAWBERRY BREAD

Preparation: 30 minutes
Cooking: 1 hour

Serves: 20

3 cups flour
1 teaspoon soda
½ teaspoon salt
1 tablespoon cinnamon
2 cups sugar

3 eggs, beaten
1 cup oil
2 (10-ounce) packages frozen
 strawberries (thawed)

Preheat oven to 350 degrees. Grease and flour two loaf pans. Combine first 5 ingredients and mix well. Combine eggs, oil and strawberies. Add strawberry mixture to dry ingredients. Mix well. Bake in greased and floured loaf pans at 350 degrees for 1 hour. Let stand in pan until cool.

Spread with cream cheese for a delectable treat!

Sylvia Smith

APPLESAUCE PUFFS

Preparation: 10 to 15 minutes   Yield: 24
Cooking: 12 minutes

2 cups packaged biscuit mix
¼ cup sugar
1 teaspoon cinnamon
½ cup applesauce
¼ cup milk
1 egg, slightly beaten
2 tablespoons salad oil

Topping:
1 teaspoon cinnamon
½ cup sugar
2 tablespoons melted margarine

Combine biscuit mix, ¼ cup sugar and 1 teaspoon cinnamon. Add applesauce, milk, egg and oil. Beat vigorously for 30 seconds. Grease 2 small
muffin tins and fill ⅔ full (yields 24) or 1 regular muffin tin (yields 12). Bake
in 400 degree oven for 12 minutes. Dip tops in melted butter and then into
sugar mixed with cinnamon. Can be frozen.

Best when served warm with coffee.

Juanita Linton
Janet Sheffield

JAM AND CHEESE LOAF

Preparation: 1 hour   Yield: 1 loaf
Cooking: 25 minutes

½ cup warm water (110 to 115
    degrees)
1 package active dry yeast
2½ cups biscuit mix
1 egg

½ cup plus 1 tablespoon sugar
1 (8-ounce) cream cheese, softened
1 tablespoon lemon juice
¼ cup jam or preserves

In mixing bowl, dissolve yeast in water. Stir in biscuit mix, egg and 1
tablespoon sugar. Mix well. Turn onto floured surface and knead for 20
strokes. Place dough in center of greased 15½ x 12 inch baking sheet. Roll
to 14 x 9 inches. In a mixing bowl, combine cream cheese, ½ cup sugar and
juice. Spread mixture lengthwise down center third of the rectangle. Make
3-inch-long cuts at 1 inch intervals on both long sides. Fold strips at an
angle over filling. Cover, chill overnight. Bake in 350 degree oven for 20
minutes. Spoon jam down center of loaf. Bake 5 minutes more. Cool 10
minutes.

Mary Adams

SWEDISH KRINGLE

Preparation: 15 to 20 minutes
Cooking: 55 to 60 minutes

Serves: 16

First layer:
1 cup flour
1 or 2 tablespoons cold water
½ cup butter

Second layer:
1 cup water
½ cup butter
1 cup flour
3 eggs
1 teaspoon almond extract

Frosting:
¾ cup confectioner's sugar
1 teaspoon almond extract
3 tablespoons water
Toasted almond slivers

First layer:
Blend flour, water, and butter with pastry blender or two knives until consistency of corn meal. Pat in two strips on a cookie sheet (3 × 8 inches long) with space in between.
Second layer:
Put water in pan with butter and heat to boiling point. Remove from heat, add flour and stir until smooth. Stir in eggs, one at a time, beating well after each addition. Add 1 teaspoon almond extract and spread on dough strips. Bake at 350 degrees for 55 to 60 minutes. Cool and frost with the following glaze:
Frosting:
Combine confectioner's sugar, extract, and water. Spread on warm kringle. Top with toasted almond slivers. Cut into squares or diamond shapes.

Rosli Clark

SCONES

Preparation: 10 minutes

Serves: 18

2 cups self-rising flour
½ teaspoon salt
¾ stick butter
½ tablespoon superfine sugar

1 egg
2 tablespoons milk

Mix salt into flour and rub in the butter to a crumb like consistency. Whisk sugar, egg and milk together. Stir into flour mixture to make soft dough. Roll out about ¾ inch thick. Cut in rounds (2 inch cutter) or triangles. Bake in center of oven 400 degrees to 425 degrees for 10 minutes. Serve with butter, jam, whipped cream.

Janie Hunt

TRUE BLUEBERRY MUFFINS

Preparation: 25 minutes   Serves: 12
Cooking: 10 minutes

½ cup shortening   2½ cups flour
2 eggs   2½ teaspoons baking powder
1⅓ cups sugar   ½ teaspoon salt
1 (16½-ounce) can blueberries,   1 teaspoon vanilla
   including juice   ½ teaspoon almond flavoring

Combine shortening and sugar in mixing bowl and beat until fluffy. Add eggs one at a time. Stir in blueberries and juice. Add flavorings. Stir in flour by hand (do not beat). Place in refrigerator. Will keep up to 3 days. When ready to bake, fill greased muffin tins ⅓ full and bake at 375 degrees for 30 minutes or until lightly browned on top.

The use of canned blueberries makes this an easy recipe that is delicious at any time of the year!

Jo Smith

ORANGE MUFFINS

Preparation: 30 minutes   Yields: 6 dozen
Cooking: 15 to 20 minutes

4 eggs   1 teaspoon lemon extract
2 cups sugar   2 teaspoons baking powder
2 cups flour
1 cup milk   Icing:
¼ pound butter   1½ cups granulated sugar
Pinch salt   juice and rind of 1 orange and
1 teaspoon vanilla   1 lemon

Beat eggs well. Stir in sugar, flour and mix well. All beating *must* be done by hand. Heat milk, butter, salt. Add to milk mixture vanilla and lemon extract. Pour milk mixture into egg mixture, beating constantly. Stir in baking powder before baking. Fill well-greased pans not quite half full. Bake at 375 degrees for 15 to 20 minutes. Dip warm muffins in icing and drain. Makes 75 small or 50 larger muffins.

Wonderful for a morning coffee!

Bonnie Cordes

SIX WEEKS MUFFINS

Preparation: 15 minutes
Cooking: 20 minutes

Yield: 4 to 5 dozen

1 (15-ounce) box Raisin Bran
1 quart buttermilk
3 cups sugar
5 teaspoons soda
2 teaspoons salt

1 cup oil
4 eggs
5 cups flour (all purpose, sifted
   after measured)

Mix Raisin Bran and milk in large bowl. Let stand a few minutes until bran is soft. Add all other ingredients and mix with spoon or hands. Use muffin papers or grease muffin tins. Fill muffin cups ⅔ full. Bake at 400 degrees for 20 minutes. Freeze well.

Mix may be kept in refrigerator up to 6 weeks. Use for hot breakfast muffins or any occasion.

Sylvia Smith
Julie Blalock

PUMPKIN MUFFINS

Preparation: 10 minutes
Cooking: 25 minutes

Yield: 24

2 eggs
1 cup milk
1 stick butter, melted
1¼ cups granulated sugar
1½ cups bread flour
1¼ cups canned or fresh pumpkin
   (mashed)

2 teaspoons baking powder
1 teaspoon cinnamon
¼ teaspoon nutmeg
¼ teaspoon salt
¼ cup chopped pecans or walnuts
½ cup raisins

Bring all ingredients to room temperature. Cream butter, sugar and pumpkin until smooth. Add eggs. Blend all four ingredients well. Sift flour, baking powder and spices and add alternately with milk to egg batter. Do not overmix. Fold in nuts and raisins. Sprinkle little cinnamon/sugar on top before baking. Bake in greased muffin tins at 400 degrees. for approximately 25 minutes or until done. Muffins can be frozen and reheated.

Recipe may be used for sweet potato muffins, substituting 1¼ cups mashed sweet potato for pumpkin.

Elizabeth West

BRAN MUFFINS

Preparation: 15 minutes   Yield: 24
Cooking: 15 minutes

1 cup Bran Buds
1 cup boiling water
¾ cup margarine
1½ cups sugar
2 eggs
2½ cups flour

2½ teaspoons baking soda
Dash salt
2 cups buttermilk
2 cups All-Bran
1½ cups raisins (optional)

Soak Bran Buds in boiling water. Set aside to cool. Cream margarine, sugar and eggs and add to soaked Bran Buds. Add flour, baking soda and salt. Fold in buttermilk and All-Bran. Spoon batter into lightly greased muffin tins. Bake in 400-degree oven for 15 minutes. Will keep 4 weeks in refrigerator and longer in freezer.

Light texture, and you'll agree they are the best you've ever eaten!

Rachel Hull

CREAM CHEESE DANISH

Preparation: 15 minutes   Yield: 12
Cooking: 30 minutes

2 (8-ounce) packages cream cheese
2 (8-ounce) packages crescent rolls
2 eggs
½ cup sugar

2 teaspoons vanilla
½ cup raisins or glazed red
    cherries, chopped in small
    pieces, optional.

Beat cream cheese, eggs and sugar until smooth. Add vanilla and mix at medium speed for 5 minutes. Add fruit and stir. Line a pan (9 x 13") with aluminum foil (overlap on sides of pan). Spread 1 package of crescent rolls in pan, (flatten out by hand). Pour cream cheese mixture over crescent dough. Take the other package of crescent rolls and spread on top of the cream cheese mixture (seal perforated pieces). Beat 1 egg yolk and brush the top of cake. Bake in 350 degree oven for 30 minutes. Cool. Remove cake from pan with aluminum foil. Cut into squares (according to the size you prefer). Wrap in aluminum foil and refrigerate. Can be frozen.

Terrific and easy!

Lorraine Valitutto

SESAME LEMON MUFFINS

Preparation: 10 minutes   Yield: 12
Cooking: 25 minutes

1 cup flour   ¼ cup butter
¼ cup sugar   1 cup yogurt
2 teaspoons baking powder   1 teaspoon grated lemon rind
½ teaspoon salt   1 egg
2 tablespoons sesame seeds

Combine dry ingredients, reserving a few sesame seeds for topping. Beat in egg and yogurt and butter. Place remaining sesame seeds on top of the muffin to brown. Bake at 400 degrees for 25 minutes.

Jimmie Johnson

SOUR CREAM MUFFINS

Preparation: 10 minutes   Yield: 24 muffins
Cooking: 20 to 30 minutes

2 cups self-rising flour   ½ pint sour cream
1½ sticks butter, melted

Combine all ingredients and spoon into small ungreased muffin tins. Bake at 350 degrees for 20 to 30 minutes. May be frozen.

Nancy Beard

GRANDMA'S NUT BREAD

Preparation: 20 minutes   Yield: 2 loaves
Cooking: 1 hour

1 egg   ½ teaspoon salt
1½ cups sugar   4 large teaspoons baking powder
2 cups milk   2 cups walnuts, chopped
4 cups flour   1 cup seedless raisins

Mix egg, sugar, milk and 3 cups of flour. Add salt. Combine remaining cup of flour with baking powder. Mix together all ingredients. Pour into two greased loaf pans and bake at 350 degrees for 1 hour. (Check after 45 minutes to make sure tops are not getting too brown.) Tops will crack. Cover pans with towel and let sit for one hour.

Donna Tibbles

THE VERY BEST ZUCCHINI BREAD

Preparation: 30 minutes
Cooking: 55 minutes

Serves: 8 to 10

3 eggs, beaten
1 cup oil
2 cups sugar
2 cups shredded zucchini
2 teaspoons vanilla
3 cups flour

1 teaspoon baking soda
¼ teaspoon baking powder
3 teaspoons cinnamon
1 teaspoon salt
1 cup raisins
Chopped nuts or coconut, optional

Preheat oven to 350 degrees. Beat eggs well. Add oil, sugar, zucchini and vanilla. Mix well. In separate bowl, sift together dry ingredients. Add to zucchini mixture. Add raisins, and nuts or coconut if desired. Pour into 2 greased loaf pans (9 × 5½ × 2½ inch). Bake 55 minutes at 350 degrees. Do not overcook.

Serve at a meeting or present as a hostess gift.

Caroline Lee

BANANA BREAD

Preparation: 1 hour
Cooking: 50 to 60 minutes

Yield: 1 large or 3 small loaves

1 cup brown sugar, firmly packed
½ cup margarine
2 eggs, beaten
4 tablespoons sour milk
1½ cups ripe bananas, mashed
   (about 3)

2 cups plain flour
1 teaspoon baking soda
1 cup chopped pecans

Preheat oven to 350 degrees. Grease 1 large loaf pan (9 x 5 x 3 inches) or 3 small loaf pans (5 x 2 x 2 inches), and cover bottoms with wax paper. Cream brown sugar and margarine. Add remaining ingredients, mixing well after each addition. Pour into pan(s). Bake large loaf for 60 minutes. Small loaves for 50 minutes. Test for doneness by sticking toothpick in center.

NOTE: Sour milk may be made by adding ¼ teaspoon vinegar to 4 tablespoons milk.

Joy Morrison

SANDY'S HOMEMADE PANCAKE MIX

Preparation: 10 minutes   Yield: 5¼ cups

2½ cups unbleached white flour
2 cups whole wheat or buckwheat
  flour

¼ cup baking powder
½ cup sugar
2 teaspoons salt

Mix ingredients together and store in covered container in refrigerator. When ready to use, stir dry pancake mix and measure.

Pancakes:
1 egg, slightly beaten
1 cup milk

1½ tablespoons oil
1 cup pancake mix

Combine egg, milk and oil. Stir in pancake mix until moistened. Pour by scant ¼ cupfuls, well apart, onto a lightly oiled hot griddle.

Makes a great gift!

Dianne Shope

POTATO ROLLS

Preparation: 1 hour
Cooking: 15 to 20 minutes

Yield: 3 to 4 dozen

1 package dry yeast
2 teaspoons salt
¼ cup sugar
½ cup lukewarm water
2 eggs

1 cup milk, scalded
⅔ cup shortening, melted
1 cup warm mashed potatoes
4½ to 5 cups flour (all purpose)
½ stick butter, melted

Place yeast, salt and sugar into mixing bowl. Add water. Mix 3 minutes until yeast is bubbly. Add eggs. Mix 3 minutes. Scald milk, melt shortening, and cool to lukewarm. Combine with warm mashed potatoes. Add potato mixture to the yeast mixture and continue mixing. Add flour one cup at a time, stirring until dough is smooth and firm. When the mixture becomes too heavy for the mixer, stir by hand. Transfer to a larger bowl if necessary. Place dough on a floured board. Knead well. Place in a large bowl, brush with melted butter, cover, and let rise until doubled in bulk (1 hour approximately). Roll out ½" thick on floured board. Brush with melted butter. Cut with a biscuit cutter (floured 2½" size). Grease a large roll pan. Fold each roll over and place on pan. Brush with melted butter and let rise until doubled. Bake at 400 degrees for 15 to 20 minutes. Brush with melted butter.

Judy Jolly

CORN PUDDING BREAD

Preparation: **10 minutes**   Serves: **10 to 12**
Cooking: **45 minutes**

1 (12-ounce) package Flako muffin   ½ pint sour cream
   mix   3 eggs, room temperature
1 (16-ounce) can Del Monte cream   ½ teaspoon salt
   corn   ½ cup oil

Mix all ingredients together. Pour into 9 x 13 inch buttered casserole and bake 45 minutes at 375 degrees.

Jackie Adams

CORN ON THE NARROW

Preparation: **10 minutes**   Serves: **15**
Cooking: **10 minutes**

1 (8¾-ounce) can creamed yellow   2 cups packaged biscuit mix
   corn   1 stick butter

Mix corn and biscuit mix. Roll and cut into biscuits. The thinner they are, the crisper. Melt 1 stick butter and coat each side of biscuit. Bake at 450 degrees 10 minutes.

Virginia Ann Fowlkes

SKILLET CORN BREAD

Preparation: **15 minutes**   Serves: **6 to 8**
Cooking: **25 minutes**

3 tablespoons oil or margarine   2 cups cornmeal
1 cup buttermilk   ½ teaspoon soda
1 egg, beaten

Melt margarine (or heat oil) in skillet in oven. In a mixing bowl, combine cornmeal with buttermilk. Add soda. Add beaten egg. Pour most of hot melted shortening in bread batter. Pour mixture into hot skillet. Bake at 350 degrees about 25 minutes. Bread is done when nice and brown and toothpick comes out clean. Cut into wedges to serve.

Serve hot with lots of butter!

Jeanette Meadows

BAKED BANANAS

Preparation: 5 minutes
Cooking: approximately 10 minutes

Serves: 4

1 package cresent rolls
2 bananas

Butter and cinnamon sugar for basting

Take 2 triangular rolls and press together to form a rectangle of pastry. In the middle of the pastry place ½ of a banana and wrap pastry around the banana tucking ends underneath. Melt margarine and brush on top of each pastry. Sprinkle with cinnamon sugar. Bake at 350 degrees until golden brown.

Hope Hull

EASY CHEESE BISCUITS

Preparation: 10 minutes
Cooking: 9 minutes

Yield: 10

1 can (10-ounce) Pillsbury
   Buttermilk Refrigerated Biscuits
   (not flaky)

½ stick butter or margarine
½ cup sharp cheddar cheese

With floured scissors, cut each biscuit into fourths. Pack close together in 9 inch pie plate or cake pan. Melt butter or margarine with cheese. Pour over biscuits, covering completely. Bake for 9 minutes at oven temperature listed on biscuit can (or until done).

Jean Payne

REAL SOUTHERN BISCUITS

Preparation: 10 minutes
Cooking: 8 to 10 minutes

Serves: 12

2 cups self-rising flour
½ cup Crisco (regular)

1 teaspoon baking powder
1 cup buttermilk

Measure flour and baking powder. Cut in Crisco with pastry blender. Add buttermilk. Knead 12 to 14 times on a floured surface. Roll out to desired thickness and cut with small biscuit cutter. Bake at 450 degrees on ungreased cookie sheet for 8 to 10 minutes or until golden brown.

These biscuits are easy to prepare, and deliciously moist!

Carolin Powell

ONION SHORTCAKE

Preparation: 25 minutes   Serves: 9
Cooking: 25 to 30 minutes

1 large sweet Spanish onion
¼ cup butter
1 (12-ounce) package corn muffin
  mix
1 egg, beaten
⅓ cup milk

1 cup cream-style corn
2 drops hot pepper sauce
1 cup sour cream
¼ teaspoon salt
¼ teaspoon dill weed
1 cup grated sharp cheddar cheese

Preheat oven to 425 degrees. Peel and slice onion and sauté in butter. Set aside. Combine muffin mix, egg, milk, corn and hot pepper sauce. Pour into buttered 8 inch square pan. Add sour cream, salt, dill weed and ½ cup cheese to onions. Spread over batter. Sprinkle with remaining cheese. Bake at 425 degrees for 25 to 30 minutes.

Delicious served warm and topped with additional sautéed onions.

Louise Glover

COMPANY ROLLS

Preparation: 30 minutes   Yield: 3 dozen rolls
Cooking: 12 to 15 minutes

1 cup shortening
½ cup sugar
2 teaspoons salt
1 cup boiling water

2 eggs
2 packages dry yeast
1 cup lukewarm water
6 cups flour

Pour 1 cup boiling water over first 3 ingredients. Stir until dissolved. Cool. Beat 2 eggs and add. Dissolve 2 packges dry yeast in 1 cup lukewarm water and stir into mixture. Stir in 6 cups flour (add more flour if needed). Knead until elastic but not sticky. Put in greased bowl and grease top of mixture. Put in freezer and chill. Remove and put lid over bowl. Refrigerate again. When ready to use, shape into pocket rolls. Dip each side in melted butter. Let rise about 1½ hours. Bake at 400 degrees for 12 to 15 minutes.

Light texture, and can be prepared in a mixer the night before serving!

Pat Carter

SOUR DOUGH BREAD

Preparation: 2 hours
Cooking: 30 minutes

Serves: 16

1½ cups warm water (not hot)
1 package yeast
1 cup Sour Dough Starter (listed below)
4 cups unsifted flour
2 teaspoons sugar
2 teaspoons salt
½ teaspoon baking soda

2 cups unsifted flour, approximately
½ stick melted butter

Sour Dough Starter:
4 cups plain flour
4 cups milk

To make starter: Mix equal parts of flour and milk. Leave uncovered at room temperature until bubbly (about 5 or 6 days). Cover and refrigerate. Replenish at least every three weeks by discarding half of starter and adding fresh flour and milk. If crust forms, stir and add a little milk.

To make bread: Dissolve yeast in warm water. Add starter, 4 cups flour, salt and sugar. Stir about 4 minutes. Turn into large greased bowl. Cover with a towel and let rise in a warm place until doubled in bulk (1 to 1½ hours). Mix soda with 1 cup of flour and stir. (Dough will be stiff.) Turn onto a floured board and knead 5 to 8 minutes. Using remaining cup of flour to control stickiness, shape into loaves. Place on a lightly greased cookie sheet. Cover and let rise until doubled in bulk (1 to 1½ hours). Place shallow pan of water on bottom shelf of oven. Bake at 375 degrees for 30 minutes or until medium brown. Brush top with melted butter. Serve hot.

Nan Price

SOUR DOUGH PANCAKES

Preparation: 10 minutes
Cooking: several minutes

Yield: 18 to 24

¼ cup Sour Dough Starter (see Index)
½ cup undiluted evaporated milk
½ cup warm water
1 cup unsifted flour

1 egg
1 tablespoon sugar
¼ teaspoon salt
½ teaspoon soda

Combine starter, milk, water and flour in a large bowl. Mix to blend and leave uncovered at room temperature overnight. Before adding remaining ingredients, remove some of mixture back to starter bowl to replenish starter. Then add egg, sugar, salt and soda. Mix well but do not beat. Cook on greased griddle.

For buckwheat cakes, substitute ¾ cup buckwheat flour and ¼ cup white flour for the 1 cup of flour.

Nan Price

UP AND DOWN BISCUITS

Preparation: 1½ hours
Cooking: 12 minutes

Yield: 1 dozen

2 cups flour
½ teaspoon salt
4 teaspoons baking powder
½ teaspoon cream of tartar
3 tablespoons sugar

½ cup shortening
⅔ cup milk
¼ cup melted margarine or butter
¼ cup sugar
1 tablespoon cinnamon

Sift first 5 ingredients into mixing bowl. Cut in shortening until mixture resembles coarse crumbs. Add milk all at once and stir until dough "follows" fork around bowl. Turn onto floured board and knead gently ½ minute. Roll dough to ¼ inch thickness. Brush with melted butter. Sprinkle with ¼ cup sugar and cinnamon. Cut into 2 inch strips. Stack strips 5 high. Cut off 2 inch pieces and place, cut side down, in greased muffin tins. Bake at 425 degrees for 12 minutes.

Great for breakfast or brunch!

Alice Pearce

BEST PUMPKIN BREAD

Preparation: 10 minutes
Cooking: 50 minutes

Serves: 12

2⅔ cups sugar
⅔ cup butter or margarine
4 eggs, beaten
2 cups canned pumpkin
3⅓ cups plain flour
½ teaspoon baking powder
2 teaspoons soda

1 teaspoon salt
1 teaspoon cinnamon
½ teaspoon ground cloves
⅔ cup water
⅔ cup chopped pecans
⅔ cup raisins

Preheat oven to 350 degrees. Cream sugar and butter. Add eggs and pumpkin. Combine dry ingredients and add alternately with water. Mix well. Stir in nuts and raisins. Bake 50 minutes in two 9 x 5 x 3 inch loaf pans or 50 minutes in 6 small (5 x 2 x 2 inch) loaf pans. (Grease pans with butter and pat wax paper on bottom. When cool, loaves are easy to remove intact by running knife around edge and inverting pan.)

Joy Morrison

The Greensboro, High Point, Winston-Salem Airport is a beautiful contemporary facility that provides quick, efficient transportation for an active, fast-growing metropolitan area. The busy lives of Greensboro residents often require a streamlined but nutritious approach to food preparation. Our pasta, cheese and egg section is healthy, tasty and easy cooking for those people on the go.

Pasta, Cheese and Eggs

GREENSBORO-HIGH POINT-WINSTON SALEM
REGIONAL AIRPORT

PASTA PRIMAVERA

Preparation: 20 minutes   Serves: 4

3 small zucchini
12 small whole green beans
2 carrots
2 scallions (including green part)
1/2 cup peas

2/3 cup olive oil
2 tablespoons lemon juice
1 clove garlic, minced
Salt and freshly ground pepper
1 pound thin spaghetti or linguine

Clean vegetables. Slice zucchini thin, cut green beans into 1/4 inch slices. Cut carrots into thin slices, then quarter the slices. Slice scallions 1/8 inch thick. Steam zucchini, beans, carrots and peas over boiling water just until the peas are tender, about 4 or 5 minutes. Combine oil, lemon juice and garlic and mix well. Mix with steamed vegetables and scallions. Toss so that vegetables are well coated. Meanwhile, cook 1 pound pasta according to package instructions until it is al dente. Drain thoroughly. Place in a warmed, buttered serving dish and pour on warm vegetable-oil dressing. Toss to mix well and serve at once. Pass the pepper grinder and grated Parmesan cheese.

Irene Mnick

TORTELLINI LIBERTY OAK

Preparation: 45 minutes   Serves: 6

1/2 pound egg tortellini
1/2 pound spinach tortellini
1/2 pound smoked ham, julienne
1 (8-ounce) can artichoke hearts,
   cut in quarters
1/4 pound cherry tomatoes, cut in
   quarters
2 green peppers julienne
Fresh parsley, chopped fine
1 purple onion, diced
Salt and freshly ground pepper

Dressing:
2 cloves garlic
1 tablespoon lemon juice
3 tablespoons balsamico vinegar
1/2 cup virgin olive oil
1/2 cup vegetable oil
2 teaspoons Dijon mustard
1 teaspoon basil
1 teaspoon oregano
1/2 teaspoon thyme

Cook both tortellini for 8 minutes in boiling water. Strain. Cool off with cold water. Add remaining ingredients. Mix well. Dressing: Mix together all ingredients in food processor or blender. Add to tortellini. Mix again and serve.

Recipe shared by Liberty Oak Restaurant.

PESTO

Preparation: 10 minutes   Serves: 8

1½ cups fresh basil
2 cloves garlic
¼ cup pine nuts or walnuts

¾ cup Parmesan cheese, grated
¾ cup olive oil

Combine basil, garlic, and nuts in processor or blender. Add Parmesan. Process until thick. Slowly add olive oil and continue to process until mixture has a butter-like consistency. Serve tossed with pasta. Refrigerate.

Sally Millikin

COLD PASTA SALAD, EL GRECO

Preparation: 1 hour   Serves: 8 to 10

1 (3 pound) chicken
Carrot, onion, bay leaf,
    peppercorns and celery to boil
    with chicken
1 pound Orzo*
Salt, to taste
1 cup Moutard-Mayo Sauce (see
    recipe)
1 jar marinated mushrooms
1 jar artichoke hearts
1 jar spiced whole baby beets
Cherry tomatoes
Fresh parsley

Moutard-Mayo Sauce:
2 cups mayonnaise
1 cup Dijon mustard
Garlic, to taste
Fresh minced parsley, to taste
Onions or shallots (minced), to
    taste
Seasoned bread crumbs, to taste
Tabasco, to taste
1 teaspoon anchovy paste
Salt and fresh ground pepper
1 ounce Pernod, Sambuca, or
    Anisette
Lemon juice, to taste (must be
    fresh)

*Orzo is Greek, middle-Eastern, pasta shaped like rice, and is available at specialty food shops.

Boil chicken in salted water with carrot, onion, bay leaf, peppercorns, and celery until tender. Cool in liquid. Drain. Remove chicken from bones and cut into bite-size pieces. Cook pasta in boiling salted water until tender. (Orzo takes longer than spaghetti!) Drain and add moutard-mayo sauce while still warm. Add chicken pieces. Let season in refrigerator several hours. Before serving, garnish with mushrooms, artichoke hearts, beets and tomatoes. Sprinkle with fresh parsley.

Recipe shared by Harry Gianaris, local advertising executive and gourmet cook.

SPAGHETTI CARBONARA

Preparation: 30 minutes

Serves: 6 to 8

1 pound spaghetti
1/4 pound bacon
3/4 cup grated Parmesan or
   Romano cheese

4 eggs, lightly beaten
1/4 cup white wine
1 teaspoon pepper
2 tablespoons hot bacon fat

Sauté bacon until crisp. Cook spaghetti according to package directions. While spaghetti is cooking, add cheese and wine to beaten eggs. Drain spaghetti and return to pot. Pour egg mixture over hot noodles. Add pepper and hot bacon fat. Stir until egg mixture is cooked. Garnish with crumbled bacon and serve immediately. For variety, 1/2 bell pepper (diced) may be sautéed with bacon and additional bell pepper used as a garnish.

Sallie Nolan

PASTA WITH CHICKEN AND SUNDRIED TOMATOES

Preparation: 20 minutes

Serves: 4 to 6

1 pound boneless chicken breasts
Flour
2 tablespoons good quality olive
   oil
3 tablespoons dry white wine
1 cup heavy cream
1 tablespoon Dijon mustard

8 to 10 sundried tomatoes packed
   in olive oil, drained and coarsely
   chopped
Salt and pepper to taste
1 pound fresh pasta
Fresh snow peas or broccoli as
   garnish

Slice chicken against the grain of the meat with the knife held on the diagonal as though slicing flank steak for London broil. Toss lightly with flour. Heat olive oil in sauté pan. Add chicken, sauté 3 to 4 minutes. Do not overcook. Remove chicken from pan. Deglaze pan with wine. Add cream and mustard. Reduce 3 to 4 minutes. Add tomatoes and continue to reduce until slightly thickened. Return chicken to pan just to heat through. Pour over hot pasta. Serve in large decorative pasta bowl and garnish with fresh snowpeas or fresh broccoli.

A California Chardonnay or Gewurztraminer is suggested as the wine by the owners of Cook's Corner, Ltd. who shared this recipe.

Mary James Lawrence
Linda Lee
Harrison Turner, M.D.

ASPARAGUS FETTUCINE ALFREDO

Preparation: 25 minutes   Serves: 6

12 ounces Fettucine noodles
1/2 pound fresh asparagus, using
   top 2 inches cut into 1 inch
   pieces
1/4 pound mushrooms, sliced
2 small zucchini, sliced
2 cloves garlic, crushed

1/2 cup butter
1 cup whipping cream
1/2 cup grated Parmesan cheese
1 teaspoon salt
1/4 teaspoon white pepper
Parmesan cheese (topping)

Cook noodles according to package instructions. Meanwhile, sauté vegetables and garlic in butter until crisp, but tender. Add remaining ingredients and cook until hot. Do not boil. Pour over hot pasta, tossing to coat noodles. Sprinkle with additional Parmesan cheese. Serve at once.

Patsy Hoffman

FETTUCINE PARMESAN

Preparation: 20 minutes   Serves: 8

10 ounces medium noodles
3 ounces butter (3/4 stick)
1/2 pint sour cream
1/2 pint heavy cream
4 ounces Parmesan cheese, freshly
   grated

2 tablespoons finely chopped
   chives
1/4 teaspoon grated nutmeg
Salt
Pepper

Cook noodles according to package directions. Drain and set aside. (The fresher the noodles, the greater the taste!) Melt butter and add noodles. Add sour cream and stir one minute over low heat. Add cream and cook slowly for 5 minutes. Add the cheese, a sprinkling of nutmeg and 1 tablespoon chives. Continue stirring until cheese is melted. Sprinkle remaining chives on top. Serve immediately.

Hazel Blackwelder

LESLIE SILKWORTH'S PASTA SALAD

Preparation: 45 minutes   Serves: 10

2 (6-ounce) packages frozen
   Alaska crabmeat (or one 2½ to
   3 pound chicken, cooked and
   boned)
1 pound spiral macaroni, cooked
½ pound snow peas, cleaned and
   blanched
2 to 3 cups broccoli florets,
   blanched
1 pint cherry tomatoes, cleaned
   and halved
1 cup canned water chestnuts,
   sliced

Dressing:
1 egg
¼ cup wine vinegar
½ teaspoon salt
¼ teaspoon pepper
1 clove garlic, peeled and minced
pinch of sugar
2 tablespoons fresh parsley,
   chopped
2 tablespoons fresh dill (or 1 to 2
   teaspoons dry dill weed)
1 teaspoon dried basil
1 cup salad oil

Prepare dressing by placing egg, vinegar, salt, pepper, garlic, sugar, parsley, dill and basil in electric blender (or food processor). Blend at mayonnaise speed. Add oil in pencil-thin stream until mixture thickens. Cook and drain macaroni. Mix with a portion of the prepared dressing while macaroni is still warm. In large bowl, toss pasta, chicken (or crabmeat) and vegetables with enough dressing to bind together. Chill at least 30 minutes before serving. Store remainder of dressing in refrigerator.

Alice Pearce

LINGUINE SALAD

Preparation: 20 minutes   Serves: 12

1 pound Linguine, cooked al denté,
   rinsed and drained
1 (8-ounce) bottle Italian dressing
   (not creamy type)
½ bottle McCormick Salad
   Supreme
1 Bermuda onion, sliced thin

May use any or all of the
   following: tomato (seeded and
   chopped); cucumber (seeded,
   but not peeled); broccoli,
   chopped; garlic salt to taste; 1
   tablespoon Parmesan cheese

Mix and refrigerate all ingredients overnight, or at least 7 hours. Keeps well in refrigerator. May add more Italian dressing or Salad Supreme to taste.

An attractive covered-dish selection for football games or picnics!

Betty Baxter

SPINACH NOODLE KUGGLE

Preparation: 15 minutes   Serves: 4 to 6
Cooking: 1 hour

1 package frozen chopped spinach,   3 eggs
    drained $^{1}/_{2}$ pint Coffee Rich or light cream
1 package Lipton Onion Soup $^{1}/_{2}$ pound fine noodles or fettucini
$^{1}/_{4}$ pound margarine or butter

Use 9 × 13 inch casserole, greased. Cook noodles and drain. Melt butter or margarine. Beat eggs, onion soup, Coffee Rich and melted butter together in blender. Add spinach, drained, and mix by hand. Add all ingredients to noodles. Mix together and place in baking dish. Bake 1 hour at 350 degrees.

Recipe doubles well for a large crowd.

Elaine Abrams

DIET ZUCCHINI LASAGNE

Preparation: 35 minutes   Serves: 6
Cooking: 30 minutes

$3^{1}/_{4}$ cups tomato sauce (see recipe)   Tomato Sauce:
$^{1}/_{2}$ cup shredded mozzarella cheese   3 cups tomatoes, peeled and
$^{1}/_{2}$ cup low-fat cottage cheese   chopped
3 cups cubed raw zucchini   1 clove garlic, minced
$^{1}/_{2}$ pound dry lasagne noodles   1 cup onions, chopped
2 tablespoons Parmesan cheese   2 tablespoons tomato paste
                                           $^{1}/_{4}$ teaspoon oregano
                                           $^{1}/_{4}$ teaspoon basil
                                           1 bay leaf
                                           $^{1}/_{4}$ teaspoon ground pepper

Combine all ingredients for tomato sauce in large pan over low heat and cook 30 minutes. Cook noodles according to directions on the box. Place $^{1}/_{4}$ cup of tomato sauce in the bottom of baking dish. Place a layer of noodles on top of the $^{1}/_{4}$ cup sauce. Sprinkle $^{1}/_{4}$ cup cottage cheese, $1^{1}/_{2}$ cups zucchini, 1 cup tomato sauce on top of the layer of noodles. Repeat with second layer. Place remaining noodles on top and tomato sauce and sprinkle Parmesan. Bake at 350 degrees for 30 minutes.

Recipe originated at a well known health resort.

Holly Lucas

GOURMET NOODLE PUDDING

Preparation: 20 minutes
Cooking: 40 minutes

Serves: 10

½ pound wide noodles
1 pound cottge cheese
1 pint sour cream or yogurt
½ pound cream cheese
¼ cup milk
¼ cup sugar
¼ pound butter, melted
½ cup raisins (optional)

5 or 6 eggs
1 teaspoon vanilla

Topping:
½ (7-ounce) box corn flakes
¼ pound butter, melted
1 cup brown sugar

Boil noodles in boiling salted water. When cooked, put noodles in strainer. Rinse under cold water and drain. Beat eggs with the sugar. Mash cream cheese with milk. Put thoroughly drained noodles in bowl and add all the ingredients. Butter oblong (9 × 13 inch) pan well and pour in noodle mixture. Crumble cornflakes with hands. Add brown sugar and melted butter and mix together. Spread cornflake mixture over the noodle pudding. Bake in 350 degree oven for about 40 minutes. (This dish may be prepared in advance and frozen.)

Lorraine Valitutto

CHEESE PASTA SOUFFLE

Preparation: 20 minutes
Cooking: 1 hour

Serves: 6

½ cup small elbow macaroni
1½ cup skim milk
6 ounces sharp process American
   cheese, grated
4 beaten egg yolks
1 cup soft bread crumbs (1½
   slices)

¼ cup chopped canned pimento
2 tablespoons chopped green
   onion
4 egg whites
¼ teaspoon cream of tartar
¼ teaspoon salt

Cook macaroni in boiling, salted water until tender. Drain. Combine milk, cheese and ¼ teaspoon salt. Stir over low heat until cheese melts. Stir small amount of hot mixture into egg yolks. Return to hot mixture. Blend well. Stir in macaroni, crumbs, pimento and onion. Beat egg whites and cream of tartar until stiff. Fold into macaroni mixture. Pour into ungreased 1½ quart souffle or baking dish. Bake at 325 degrees until knife inserted off center comes out clean, about 1 hour. Serve immediately.

Joanne Osteen

SPAGHETTI FOR TOMATO HATERS

Preparation: 15 minutes   Serves: 6

1/2 pound thin spaghetti or
   vermicelli
2 tablespoons basil, optional
2 tablespoons parsley flakes
1/4 cup butter or margarine
1 (8-ounce) package cream cheese

1/3 cup grated Parmesan cheese
1/4 cup olive or salad oil
1/2 teaspoon garlic salt
1/2 teaspoon pepper
2/3 cup boiling water

Cook spaghetti until tender. Do not overcook. Melt butter in saucepan. Add basil and parsley flakes. Blend in cream cheese, Parmesan cheese, oil, garlic salt and pepper. Stir in boiling water and blend well. Pour over drained spaghetti.

Anita Search

BACON AND SWISS CHEESE PUFF

Preparation: 30 minutes   Serves: 8 to 10
Cooking: 50 minutes

8 slices bacon
2 medium onions, sliced
12 slices white bread, quartered
1/2 pound Swiss cheese, shredded
8 eggs

4 cups milk
1 1/2 teaspoons salt
1/4 teaspoon pepper
Red pepper sauce or mustard to
   taste

Cook bacon until crisp. Remove from pan, drain, crumble. In bacon drippings, cook onions until soft. Arrange half the bread slices in single layer in bottom of greased 9 × 18 inch pan or casserole. Sprinkle with half the crumbled bacon, onions and cheese. Repeat layer with remaining bread, bacon, onions, cheese. Combine remaining ingredients. Pour over top layer in pan. (Casserole can be prepared to this stage in advance and stored in the refrigerator until an hour before serving time.) Bake in 375 degrees oven until mixture is set and top is puffed and golden, about 50 minutes.

Peggy Johnson

SPINACH CHEESE PUFF

Preparation: 30 minutes
Cooking: 1 hour

Serves: 12

12 slices day old bread
(square-shaped slices), crust
removed
2 cups (8-ounces) shredded sharp
cheddar cheese
1 (10-ounce) package frozen
chopped spinach, thawed
1 (4½-ounce) jar sliced
mushrooms, drained
5 eggs

2½ cups milk
2 to 3 tablespoons grated mild
onion
¼ teaspoon salt
½ teaspoon prepared mustard
1 teaspoon seasoned salt
Dash red pepper
Dash black pepper
Paprika

Arrange 6 slices bread in grease 9 × 13 inch casserole. Sprinkle cheese over bread. Drain spinach. Squeeze water out. Place spinach over cheese. Put mushrooms over spinach. Sprinkle onions over mushrooms. Cut each slice in half (to aid in serving). Place bread over onions. Combine remaining ingredients. Beat well. Pour over bread. Sprinkle paprika lightly. Cover and chill several hours or overnight. Bake at 325 degrees, uncovered, for one hour.

Carolyn O'Tuel

BREAKFAST STRATA

Preparation: 45 minutes
Cooking: 1 hour

Serves: 12 to 14

1 pound hot, spicy sausage, bulk,
or 1½ pounds link sausage, cut
in 1 inch pieces
1 pound bacon
12 slices bread, cubed
2½ to 3 cups sharp cheese, grated
8 eggs

Worcestershire sauce, to taste
1 teaspoon salt
1 teaspoon dry mustard
1 quart milk
1 tablespoon green onions, diced
1 tablespoon parsley, diced

Sauté sausage and bacon until lightly browned. Drain, dry and crumble and mix together. Butter a 10 × 14 inch large casserole dish. Place ½ bread cubes, ½ cheese and all sausage mixture in casserole. Cover with remaining bread cubes and cheese. Beat eggs and add a small amount of Worcestershire sauce, the salt, dry mustard and milk. Pour over casserole and refrigerate overnight. Bake 1 hour at 325 degrees.

Marian Ferrel

CHEESE GRITS

Preparation: 15 minutes
Cooking: 1 hour

Serves: 8

1 cup grits
4 cups water
1 teaspoon salt
3 to 4 eggs, beaten
1 cup sharp cheese, grated
1 cup milk

2 tablespoons Worcestershire
   sauce, optional
$1/2$ cup butter
Black pepper to taste
1 teaspoon garlic salt, optional

Cook grits in salted water until thick. Cool and add the beaten eggs, $3/4$ cup cheese, milk, Worcestershire sauce, butter, pepper, and garlic salt. Pour into a buttered baking dish and sprinkle the remaining cheese on top. Bake at 250 degrees for 1 hour. Sprinkle top with Parmesan cheese and paprika for color.

Marian Ferrel

SOUR CREAM SOUFFLE

Preparation: 20 minutes
Cooking: 30 to 35 minutes

Serves: 8

$1/2$ cup freshly grated Parmesan
   cheese
$1^{1/2}$ cups commercial sour cream
5 eggs, separated
1 generous teaspoon salt

2 tablespoons chopped chives
$1/2$ cup sifted flour
2 extra egg whites
$1/4$ teaspoon cayenne pepper

Butter a 2 quart souffle dish. Coat with parmesan cheese and refrigerate. Pour sour cream into a large bowl and sift flour into sour cream. Thoroughly whip together with a wire whisk. Add egg yolks one at the time, whipping briskly after each addition. Stir in salt, pepper, chives and remaining cheese. Beat egg whites until they hold firm, shiny peaks when beater is held straight up. Fold gently into yolk mixture with a rubber spatula. Mix well and place in preheated oven at 350 degrees. Bake 30 to 35 minutes.

Louise Glover

CHEESE STRATA

Preparation: 30 minutes   Serves: 8
Cooking: 35 minutes

12 slices white bread, crusts
    removed and cubed
1 pound sharp cheddar cheese,
    shredded

6 eggs, beaten
2 cups milk
1/4 cup melted margarine

Place cubed bread in 9 × 13 inch baking dish. Sprinkle cheese over bread. Mix eggs, milk and margarine together. Pour over bread and cheese. Cover with plastic wrap and refrigerate overnight. Bake uncovered and serve immediately.

Janie Grantham

POTATO SCRAMBLE

Preparation: 20 minutes   Serves: 6 to 8

1/4 cup butter
1 small onion, grated
8 eggs, beaten
3 tablespoons cream
1 cup chopped bacon or ham

Salt and pepper to taste
1 cup grated cheddar cheese
1/2 large package frozen grated
    potatoes

Melt butter in sauté pan and add potatoes and onion. Cook over medium heat until lightly browned. Combine next 5 ingredients. Pour over potatoes and cook as for scrambled eggs. Add cheese. Heat until melted. To serve, cut in pie wedges.

Linda Lee

PORTUGUESE EGGS

Preparation: 15 minutes   Serves: 6

6 tomatoes, ripe and juicy
Salt and pepper to taste

2 teaspoons basil
6 eggs

Cut off top of tomato, scoop out seeds and core. Season with salt, pepper and basil. Break an egg into the cavity. Bake 400 degree oven until egg is set.

Linda Lee

MEXICAN EGGS

Preparation: 45 minutes   Serves: 10 to 12
Cooking: 55 minutes

1 dozen eggs
1/2 cup flour
1 teaspoon baking powder
2 sticks margarine, melted
8 ounces green chiles, chopped, or
    two (4-ounce) cans Old El Paso
    brand

1 pound Monterey Jack cheese,
    grated
1 pint cottage cheese
1 1/2 pounds diced, cooked ham
1 (6-ounce) can Salsa, medium,
    not hot (optional)

Beat eggs slightly. Add flour and baking powder. (Mixture will be lumpy.) Add melted margarine, chopped chilies, ham, and cheeses. Blend gently. Pour into greased 9 × 13 inch baking dish. Bake at 400 degrees for 15 minutes. Reduce heat to 350 degrees for 35 to 40 minutes until eggs are set. Serve with Salsa, warmed, if desired.

Vivien Bauman

CHILI RELLENOS CASSEROLE

Preparation: 30 minutes   Serves: 10
Cooking: 35 minutes

1 (2-pound) can whole, peeled
    green chilies
2 (10-ounce) packages sharp
    cheddar cheese
3 eggs

3 tablespoons flour
1 (13-ounce) can evaporated milk
1 (8-ounce) can tomato sauce

Grease 9 × 13 inch baking dish. Remove seeds from chilies (you may want to wear rubber or plastic gloves when handling chilies!). Layer half of chilies in bottom of dish. Reserve 12 thin slices of cheese and grate remainder. Sprinkle grated cheese over chilies. Add remaining chilies. Beat eggs. Blend in flour and milk and beat until smooth. Pour over casserole and bake 25 minutes at 350 degrees. Remove from oven and pour tomato sauce over casserole. Arrange cheese squares in checkerboard fashion on top of sauce. Return to oven 5 to 10 minutes until cheese melts.

Locally, large-size cans of chilies are not easy to find. One may use Old El Paso Brand Green Chilies, available in 4 ounce size, to equal 2 pounds.

Vivien Bauman

EGG-STUFFED SPINACH ROLL

Preparation: 30 minutes   Serves: 10
Cooking: 15 minutes

3 (10-ounce) packages frozen   4 yolks, beaten
    chopped spinach   4 whites, beaten
6 tablespoons melted butter   Bread crumbs
Salt, pepper and nutmeg   Parmesan cheese

Thaw spinach and pour boiling water over spinach. Drain well and chop.
Mix in the butter, salt, pepper and nutmeg. Add the yolks. Fold in the beaten
egg whites. Pour into a jelly roll pan, 14 × 11 inch, lined with foil, buttered
and sprinkled with bread crumbs. Sprinkle with Parmesan cheese. Bake at
350 degrees for 15 minutes. Unmold. Fill with scrambled eggs, creamed
mushrooms or crabmeat. Roll up. Slice and serve.

Elizabeth West

EGGS IN HELL

Preparation: 5 minutes   Serves: 8
Cooking: 20 minutes

4 tablespoons olive oil   1/2 teaspoon crushed basil
1 clove garlic, crushed   1 teaspoon chopped parsley
1 onion chopped   Salt and pepper to taste
2 (16-ounce) cans tomato sauce   8 eggs
1/2 teaspoon crushed thyme   4 English muffins or Holland Rusk

Heat oil in sauté pan. Add onion and garlic, cooking until lightly browned
(yellow). Add tomato sauce and seasonings. Cook 15 minutes. Break eggs
into sauce, spooning sauce over eggs. Cover and cook slowly until desired
doneness. Remove eggs and serve on split toasted English muffins or
Holland Rusk. Spoon sauce over eggs.

Linda Lee

EGG AND SAUSAGE CASSEROLE

Preparation: 10 minutes   Serves: 6
Cooking: 30 minutes

8 hard boiled eggs, sliced   3/4 cup dry bread crumbs
1 pound hot sausage   2 cups sharp cheddar cheese,
2 cups sour cream   grated

Place eggs, layered in 2 quart greased casserole. Cook, drain, and crumble
sausage. Sprinkle over eggs. Whip sour cream, spoon over sausage.
Combine bread crumbs and cheese. Sprinkle over casserole. Heat until
thoroughly warm and cheese is melted.

Linda Lee

BRUNCH CASSEROLE

Preparation: 15 minutes
Cooking: 25 minutes

Serves: 10

18 hard cooked eggs, sliced
1 pound fried bacon

White sauce:
1/4 cup butter
1/4 cup flour

2 cups milk
3/4 pound cheddar cheese, grated
1/4 teaspoon thyme
1/4 teaspoon basil
1/4 teaspoon marjoram
Chopped, fresh parsley to taste
Bread crumbs

Melt butter. Add flour, stirring until smooth. Stir in milk gradually and cook until thickened. Add grated cheese and herbs. Layer bacon, egg, chopped parsley, white sauce in 13 × 9 × 2 inch casserole. Repeat layers. Top with buttered bread crumbs. Bake at 350 degrees until heated through, about 25 minutes.

Sandra Burns

FRENCHY FRENCH TOAST

Preparation: 15 minutes
Cooking: 45 to 60 minutes

Serves: 8

1 long loaf French bread, cut in
   1 1/2 inch thick slices (about 12
   to 14 slices. Fill pan.)
8 eggs
2 cups milk

1/4 cup brandy
1 teaspoon cinnamon
2 tablespoons sugar
1 tablespoon vanilla

Put bread slices in 13 × 9 inch buttered pan. Mix all ingredients well and pour over bread. Refrigerate overnight. After 6 to 8 hours turn bread over. Bake at 350 degrees for 45 to 60 minutes and let stand 15 minutes before serving.

Mary Twomey

ELEGANT CRAB QUICHE

Preparation: 10 minutes   Serves: 6
Cooking: 35 minutes

1 pound crab meat   ½ teaspoon salt
1 cup Swiss cheese, shredded   ⅛ teaspoon black pepper
5 eggs   ½ cup mushrooms
1¼ cups milk or half and half   1 (9-inch) unbaked pie shell

Sprinkle cheese into pie shell. Beat eggs, mix seasonings and milk. Pour over cheese. Sprinkle crab meat over ingredients. Bake 35 minutes at 375 to 400 degrees or until firm and knife comes out clean when inserted into center. Cut into wedges.

Pat Myrick

NANCY'S QUICHE

Preparation: 30 minutes   Serves: 10 to 12
Cooking: 1 hour

2 (9-inch) deep-dish pie shells,   10 to 12 ounces Swiss cheese,
   unbaked   grated
1 egg yolk   14 to 16 ounces medium sharp
1½ pounds hot sausage   cheddar cheese, grated
1 bunch green onions, chopped   1½ teaspoons grated Parmesan
6 eggs   cheese
1 cup milk   1½ teaspoons paprika
⅛ teaspoon nutmeg

Preheat oven to 350 degrees. Brush pie shells with egg yolk and bake 10 minutes, according to package directions. Sauté sausage and onions together until sausage is browned. Drain well. Combine eggs, milk, and nutmeg. Arrange layers of sausage mixture, Swiss cheese, and cheddar cheese in pie shells. Repeat layers. Pour egg mixture over all. Bake in preheated 350 degree oven for 45 minutes. Combine Parmesan cheese and paprika. Sprinkle over quiches. Bake 15 minutes longer. Remove from oven and allow to stand 10 minutes before slicing.

Nancy Brown

SPINACH AND MUSHROOM QUICHE

Preparation: 15 minutes
Cooking: 25 to 30 minutes

Serves: 6

1 (10-ounce) box frozen chopped
   spinach
4 tablespoons butter
2 teaspoons lemon juice
1/2 cup light cream
4 eggs
1 tablespoon salt
1 teaspoon pepper

4 ounces Swiss cheese, grated
1 (2 1/2-ounce) can mushroom
   pieces, drained
1 cup heavy cream
2 cloves minced garlic
1 10 inch pastry shell, partially
   baked

Preheat oven to 375 degrees. Thaw and drain spinach. Sauté the spinach in the butter. Add lemon juice and garlic. Make a batter by beating cream, eggs, salt and pepper together. Add cheese and mix well. To assemble, line partially baked pie shell with mushrooms and spinach. Pour batter over all and bake for 25 to 30 minutes.

Alice Radcliffe

HEARTY QUICHE

Preparation: 20 minutes
Cooking: 45 minutes

Serves: 4 to 6

1/2 pound bulk sausage
1/2 package frozen chopped
   spinach
1/2 package Pepperidge Farm
   Stuffing

1 cup Half-and-Half
3 eggs
1 cup grated sharp cheese
1 9-inch pie shell

Brown sausage. Drain well and crumble. Cook 1/2 package spinach and drain well. Mix together sausage and spinach. Add stuffing. Mix together eggs and half and half. Add sausage mixture to egg mixture. Set aside. Put 1 cup grated cheese in bottom of non-pricked, pre-baked pie shell. Pour mixture over cheese and bake for 45 minutes at 325 degrees.

Jo Smith

In the 1970's, thanks to the generosity of Mr. and Mrs. Joseph M. Bryan, Bryan Park and Enrichment Center were developed for the city of Greensboro. In addition to meetings and seminars of various clubs and organizations, sumptuous banquets and dinner dances are held in the spacious Center. Entrees featured on the following pages are perfect for the most intimate dinner to the grandest of gatherings.

Entrees

·BRYAN ENRICHMENT CENTER·

TOJO'S CHICKEN CURRY

Preparation: 2 hours   Serves: 8

4 chicken breasts (whole)
2 onions
6 tablespoons flour
1/4 teaspoon cinnamon
1 tablespoon real Indian curry
    powder
Chicken broth for correct
    consistency (approximately 2
    cups)

1/2 cup ketchup
1 tablespoon brown sugar
1/2 cup carrots, very finely minced
2 teaspoons Worcestershire sauce
Garlic, if desired
1/2 teaspoon salt if necessary
Rice

Prepare chicken in two cups of water to make broth. Strain. Remove meat from bones and skin. Sauté onions in small amount of shortening until soft. Add flour, cinnamon, curry powder. Gradually add chicken broth. Add ketchup and other ingredients with the exception of the chicken pieces which are added at the last minute. Heat through. Serve over boiled white rice, each grain separate and fluffy. Offer the following "boys" (at least 3):

Chutney
Mustard pickle
French fried onions (canned)
Crystallized ginger
Sieved hard-cooked egg yolk

Toasted coconut
Ground roasted peanuts
Slivered almonds
Crushed crisply cooked bacon

Kathryn Lambeth

SAVORY CHICKEN AND PIMENTO

Preparation: 30 minutes   Serves: 6 to 8
Cooking: 35 minutes

2 broilers, fryers (cut up)
Flour seasoned with salt and
    pepper
1/4 cup olive oil
1 clove garlic, mashed
1/4 cup chopped parsley
1/2 teaspoon poultry seasoning
1/3 teaspoon pepper
1 cup white wine

3/4 cup black olives
1 small jar mushrooms
1 jar (7-ounce) pimentos (drained
    and cut into large pieces)
1 (8-ounce) package thin spaghetti
1 teaspoon salt
Dash tabasco

Roll chicken pieces in seasoned flour, then brown in hot oil. Mix garlic, parsley, seasonings and wine. Pour over browned chicken, cover skillet and cook over moderately low heat about 35 minutes, or until chicken pieces are fork tender. Serve hot with parsley buttered spaghetti.

Martha Long

CRAB STUFFED CHICKEN BREASTS

Preparation: 20 minutes
Cooking: 45 to 60 minutes

Serves: 8 to 10

5 whole boned chicken breasts
    with skin (10 halves)
1 cup herb seasoned stuffing mix
1 can condensed mushroom soup
1 (6½-ounce) can crab meat,
    flaked and drained
¼ cup finely chopped green
    pepper

1 tablespoon lemon juice
2 teaspoons Worcestershire sauce
1 teaspoon prepared mustard
¼ teaspoon salt
3 tablespoons butter
½ teaspoon rosemary

Combine stuffing mix with ½ can mushroom soup, crab meat, green pepper, lemon juice, Worcestershire sauce, mustard and salt. Place a portion of mixture in center of each breast. Roll up and fasten with toothpicks or skewers. Brown in butter, turning to brown on all sides. To drippings in skillet add remaining soup and crushed rosemary. Pour sauce over chicken. Bake covered in preheated 375 degree oven for 45 to 60 minutes (depending on size of breasts). May be assembled and frozen ahead, then baked when needed. If only chicken breast halves are available, place stuffing in middle, bring ends up over and fasten with toothpick. Stuffing will be exposed on sides. Do not try to brown in butter. Instead, pour melted butter over top, then sauce. Bake as directed.

Donna Moore

CHICKEN BREASTS EN CHAMPAGNE

Preparation: 30 minutes

Serves: 4

4 boned and skinned chicken
    breasts
¼ cup flour
1 teaspoon salt
½ teaspoon pepper

½ cup butter
½ pound mushrooms, fresh, sliced
1 cup whipping cream
¼ cup champagne

Mix flour, salt and pepper. Roll chicken breasts in the mixture. Pat to shake off excess flour. Heat butter in large skillet. Cook breasts in butter over low heat until lightly browned on both sides. Drain off excess butter (keep and use in rice). Add 1 cup cream and simmer over low heat for 10 minutes. Transfer breasts to a warm platter. Add ¼ cup champagne to liquid in skillet. Bring to a rapid boil and cook until a creamy consistency. Spoon sauce over chicken breast.

Sally Miller, Nancy Wells

CHICKEN ROASTED WITH CARROTS AND ROSEMARY

Preparation: 30 minutes   Serves: 4
Cooking: 60 to 75 minutes

2 tablespoons butter
1 3-pound whole broiler chicken
1 teaspoon salt
1/2 teaspoon pepper

5 sprigs fresh rosemary or 2
   teaspoons dried rosemary
10 medium carrots
Sprigs of fresh rosemary or parsley
   for garnish

Grease a large ovenproof skillet or baking pan with 1 tablespoon butter. Rub the chicken inside and out with the salt and pepper. Put the 5 sprigs of rosemary in the body cavity. Close the neck and lower cavities with skewers. Tuck wings behind the body. Place chicken breast-side down in pan. Peel carrots and slice into 3-inch diagonal lengths. Arrange carrots around the chicken and dot with 1 tablespoon butter. Bake at 400 degrees for 15 minutes. Turn chicken breast-side up and stir carrots. Return to oven and bake for 45 to 60 minutes until done and juices run clear. Remove from oven and let rest for 5 minutes. Remove chicken skewers and cut into quarters. Discard rosemary from cavity. Serve chicken and carrots with pan juices spread over chicken.

Darlene Young

CHICKEN FLORENTINE CREPES

Preparation: 30 minutes   Yield: 12 to 18
Cooking: 10 to 15 minutes

12 to 18 crepes (see Index)
6 tablespoons butter
1 cup fresh mushrooms, sliced
1 cup chicken, diced
3 hard cooked egg yolks, mashed
1/3 cup sour cream
1 tablespoon fresh parsley,
   chopped

3/4 teaspoon salt
Pepper to taste
1/2 cup spinach, cooked and well
   drained
3 tablespoons Parmesan cheese,
   grated
Veloute Sauce (see Index)

Melt 1/2 butter (3 tablespoons). Sauté mushrooms. Remove from heat. Mix in chicken, yolks, sour cream, parsley, salt, pepper, and spinach. Fill crepes and roll tightly. Arrange in buttered baking dish. Sprinkle with cheese. Dot with remaining butter. Bake at 425 degrees for 10 to 15 minutes or until done. Serve with Veloute Sauce.

Marian Ferrel

COMPANY CHICKEN

Preparation: 10 minutes
Cooking: 45 minutes

Serves: 8

8 boned chicken breast halves
salt and pepper to taste
1 (10-ounce) jar Durkee sauce
$1/8$ cup white vinegar

$1/8$ cup lemon juice
$1/2$ cup sugar
2 tablespoons Worcestershire
 sauce
1 lemon, cut into slices

Preheat oven to 425 degrees. Season chicken. Arrange in baking dish (greased). Bake uncovered for 15 minutes. Drain any grease. Combine sauce ingredients (Durkee, white vinegar, lemon juice, sugar and Worcestershire sauce). Pour over chicken. Reduce oven temperature to 350 degrees. Cover chicken and bake for 25 minutes. Serve with slice of lemon on top of each piece.

Linda Lee

CORNISH HENS WITH ORANGE RICE

Preparation: 40 minutes
Cooking: 1 hour, 10 minutes

Serves: 6

6 Cornish hens
1 cup melted butter or margarine
1 cup apple jelly
$1/4$ cup cornstarch
$1^{1}/3$ cups Sauterne
$1/2$ cup orange juice
Salt to taste
2 cups seedless grapes

Orange Rice:
2 cups diced celery and leaves
6 tablespoons chopped onion
$1/2$ cup melted butter or margarine
2 cups uncooked regular rice
1 teaspoon salt
$2^{1}/2$ cups boiling water
$1^{1}/2$ cups orange juice
$1/4$ cup grated orange rind

Brown hens in butter. Remove from skillet and place in baking dish. Can do this the day before. Melt apple jelly over low heat. Set aside. Add cornstarch to skillet drippings. Blend well, stirring in jelly, Sauterne, orange juice and salt. Cook, stirring constantly until smooth and thickened. Pour sauce over hens. Bake uncovered 350 degrees for 1 hour. Add grapes and bake 10 additional minutes or until grapes are warm. Arrange hens on orange rice on platter. Garnish with grapes and parsley. Serve sauce with hens.
Orange Rice: Sauté celery and onion in butter until tender. Stir rice and salt into boiling water, cover and simmer 15 to 20 minutes. Add orange juice, orange rind and vegetables. Cover and cook 5 minutes until rice is done.

Jo Smith

EASY BAKE CHICKEN PIE

Preparation: 30 minutes   Serves: 4
Cooking: 1 hour

1 whole chicken or 4 chicken   1 1/2 cups Bisquick mix
   breasts   1 1/2 cups milk
1 can cream of celery soup   1 stick margarine
1/2 cup chicken broth

Boil or stew chicken. Take off bone and cut in bite size pieces. Put in bottom
of 2 quart glass baking dish. Mix broth with cream of celery soup and pour
over chicken. Mix Bisquick and milk (it will be lumpy) and add to top of
chicken. Melt margarine and pour over Bisquick mixture. Bake 350 degrees
for 1 hour.

Mary Henrie French

DUCKLING ORANGE ROSE

Preparation: 15 minutes   Serves: 2 to 4
Cooking: 3 hours

1 duckling, 4 to 4 1/2 pounds   1 jar (12 to 16 ounce) good quality
Salt   orange marmalade
Pepper   1/2 cup rose wine

Season the duckling with salt and pepper and place on a large piece of foil
in a baking pan. Coat the duckling generously with the marmalade. Pour
the rose wine over meat. Wrap the foil completely around the duckling and
seal. Roast at 350 degrees for 2 1/2 hours. Uncover and baste well. Roast,
uncovered, for 30 minutes longer or until crisp and golden.

Darlene Young

HONEY BAKED CHICKEN

Preparation: 10 minutes   Serves: 4
Cooking: 1 hour

1/3 cup honey   1 teaspoon curry
1/3 cup butter   Dash salt
2 tablespoons mustard   4 chicken breasts, skinned

Bring first 5 ingredients to a boil. Cover chicken with the sauce. Bake at
350 degrees for 1 hour. Baste every 15 minutes. Can freeze.

Alice Radcliffe

BRAISED QUAIL WITH WINE AND SHALLOT SAUCE

Preparation: 40 minutes
Cooking: 30 minutes

Serves: 3

6 quail
Salt and pepper
3 tablespoons butter
1½ tablespoons parsley, minced
3 shallots, minced
2½ tablespoons flour
¾ cup white wine

½ cup lightly salted water
1 bay leaf
Sprig thyme
6 "croutés"*
4 tablespoons butter
Salt and pepper
Juice of ½ lemon

Dress and truss the quail. Season with salt and pepper. Melt butter in a heavy Dutch oven. Place quail, parsley, and shallots in sizzling butter and brown birds on all sides. Sprinkle with flour, stirring to coat birds and vegetable well, and add wine and salted water. Place bay leaf and thyme in Dutch oven. Bring to a boil, reduce heat, cover, and simmer gently for 30 minutes. Fry "croutés" in butter, lightly salt and pepper and reserve. When quail are done, remove from Dutch oven and keep warm. Add juice of ½ lemon to the sauce. Taste and adjust seasonings. To serve: Arrange birds on top of "croutés" on a warmed serving platter. Strain sauce over. Garnish with parsley, if desired.
*"Croutés" — thin white bread with edges trimmed. May be cut any shape you desire.

Trish Green

SHORT CUT COQ AU VIN

Preparation: 45 minutes
Cooking: 45 to 60 minutes

Serves: 4 to 5

4 slices bacon
2 pounds chicken (leg/thigh/breast)
½ to 1 pound mushrooms
1 clove garlic, minced
2 tablespoons flour

1 package onion soup mix
1 cup water
1 cup red wine
2 tablespoons parsley
⅛ teaspoon thyme
1 bay leaf

Cook bacon until crisp. Remove from skillet and crumble. Pour off all fat except 2 tablespoons. Brown chicken in fat. Remove from skillet. Sauté mushrooms, garlic (may have to add margarine to pan). Stir in flour, soup mix and remaining ingredients. Cook until thickened (may need a bit more flour). Put chicken in a serving dish. Pour sauce over and cover with foil. Bake at 350 degrees for 45 to 60 minutes. Check while baking for consistency desired. Top with bacon.

Mary Twoney

CHICKEN PAPRIKASH

Preparation: 30 minutes
Cooking: 1 hour

Serves: 10

2 (3-pound) chickens, cut into
  serving pieces (or equal parts of
  just breast or thigh and legs or
  combination)
Salt and freshly ground pepper
2 tablespoons oil
2 tablespoons butter
4 cups chopped onion

5 tablespoons sweet paprika
  (preferred imported Hungarian)
2 cups sour cream
(optional) 2 cubes Knorr Swiss
  instant chicken flavor bouillon
  cubes or 4 cubes Maggi chicken
  bouillon cubes

Sprinkle chicken pieces with salt and pepper to taste and set aside. Heat butter and oil in large pot or casserole and add onions. Cook, stirring until wilted. Cook until most liquid from onions evaporate. Do not let onion get brown. Add chicken pieces and stir briefly. Cover and cook gently over low heat about 10 to 15 minutes. Sprinkle with paprika. Make sure all chicken is covered. Cover and cook at 325 degrees for 1 hour or until chicken is tender. Remove from heat. Pour liquid from chicken in bowl and skim off fat. Add sour cream and bouillon cubes. Stir until bouillon cubes are dissolved. Do not boil. Pour sauce over chicken and serve.

Evelyn Sturm

CHICKEN BREASTS HAWAIIAN

Preparation: 15 minutes
Cooking: 20 to 25 minutes

Serves: 8

4 whole chicken breasts, split,
  skinned and boned
2 eggs, beaten
3 cups finely grated bread crumbs
2 teaspoons salt
4 tablespoons butter

2 cups pineapple juice
4 tablespoons lemon juice
2 tablespoons cornstarch
2 teaspoons curry powder
2 tablespoons sugar
Slivered almonds

Dip each half-breast in the beaten egg. Then roll in the bread crumbs that have been mixed with the salt. Melt the butter in a large skillet and sauté the chicken until lightly browned. Combine juices, cornstarch, curry powder, and sugar. Pour over the chicken. Cover the pan and cook over low heat for 20 to 25 minutes. Serve topped with slivered almonds.

Darlene Young

POULET DORE
(GOLDEN CHICKEN)

Preparation: 30 to 45 minutes   Serves: 6
Cooking: 45 minutes

1 fryer, cut into serving pieces
6 tablespoons chopped almonds
1½ cups crushed grapenut flakes
1½ teaspoons celery seed
½ teaspoon salt
¼ teaspoon pepper

¼ teaspoon garlic salt
4 teaspoons chopped parsley
1 egg, beaten
2 tablespoons milk
½ cup pancake mix
4 tablespoons margarine

Steam chicken for ½ hour. Mix almonds, grapenut flakes, celery seed, salt, pepper, garlic salt and parsley together. Mix egg with milk. While chicken is hot, coat each piece with dry pancake mix. Then dip in egg wash and finish rolling in the grapenut mixture. Melt margarine in a casserole. Place chicken in one layer only. Cover and bake at 375 degrees for 45 minutes.

Gini Legare

CHICKEN, RICE AND BROCCOLI CASSEROLE

Preparation: 30 minutes   Serves: 10
Cooking: 30 minutes

1 chicken (3½ pounds) cooked
    whole or 3 cups cubed chicken
    or turkey
2 boxes frozen broccoli (chopped
    or spears)
1 stick butter
1 cup washed long grain rice
1 can beef consomme
1 can onion soup
1 can (medium) sliced mushrooms

¼ teaspoon garlic powder
1 cup cheddar cheese

Sauce ingredients:
1 can cream of mushroom soup
½ can milk
¼ cup mayonnaise
¼ teaspoon Worcestershire sauce

Cook chicken and remove meat from bones. Cook broccoli until done but still crisp. Cook rice as follows: Melt 1 stick butter in 3 quart flat glass casserole. Add and mix together the consomme, onion soup, mushrooms. Add garlic. Cook covered in 325 degree oven for 1 hour or until done. Make sauce: Mix sauce ingredients and heat until warm. Put casserole together: Place broccoli on rice. Put chicken on top of broccoli. Pour (or spoon) sauce over all. Grate cheese on top. Heat in 375 degree oven until hot (about 20 or 30 minutes).

Nell Abels

EAST AND WEST CHICKEN LIVERS

Preparation: 40 minutes   Serves: 4

1 pound chicken livers
1/3 cup chopped onion
1/2 cup chopped celery
1/4 cup chopped green pepper
1 small clove garlic, minced
2 tablespoons cooking oil
2 teaspoons corn starch

1/2 teaspoon salt
1/2 cup cold water
1/4 cup dry white wine
1 teaspoon soy sauce
Dash of curry powder (optional)
Hot cooked rice

Halve chicken livers. Drain well. In large skillet cook onion, celery, green pepper and garlic in hot oil until tender, but not brown. Remove and set aside. In same skillet cook chicken livers quickly until lightly browned. Do not overcook. Return vegetables to skillet. Combine cornstarch, salt, pepper, curry powder, cold water, wine and soy sauce. Add to chicken liver mixture in skillet. Cook, stirring constantly, until mixture thickens and bubbles. Serve mixture immediately over hot, cooked rice. Garnish with green pepper rings, if desired.

Laurie Southworth

CHICKEN RICE CASSEROLE

Preparation: 20 minutes   Serves: 6
Cooking: 1 hour

10 to 11 chicken breasts, deboned
9 cups water
3 packages dry Lipton Chicken
    Noodle Soup Mix
2 cups raw rice
1 pound hot sausage
1 bell pepper, chopped

1 large onion, chopped
1 cup celery, chopped
Salt to taste
2 cans mushroom soup, undiluted
1/2 cup slivered almonds, toasted in
    melted butter

Cut chicken breasts into pieces. Set aside. To boiling water add soup mix and rice. Boil 9 minutes uncovered. Fry sausage. Remove from skillet and drain. In the sausage drippings, brown bell pepper, onion, and celery. Add with sausage to soup mixture, seasoning with salt. Add mushroom soup and chicken pieces. Place mixture in casserole and bake for 45 minutes at 350 degrees. Top with toasted almonds and bake 15 additional minutes. May be prepared and frozen, thawed and baked.

Beverly Stocks

CHICKEN AND ARTICHOKE DIVINE

Preparation: 15 minutes
Cooking: 1 hour

Serves: 6

6 boned chicken breasts
1 can artichoke hearts, chopped, drained
$1/2$ cup green onions, chopped, including tops
2 to 3 stalks celery, chopped, including leaves
1 (4-ounce) jar chopped pimento, drained

1 to 2 cans cream of celery soup (depending on how much sauce you want)
$1/2$ soup can white wine
1 clove garlic, minced
Salt and pepper
2 tablespoons parsley

Brown chicken breasts in 2 tablespoons salad oil. Place in 13 × 9 inch pan. Add onions, celery, artichoke hearts, garlic, salt and pepper and parsley to pan and sauté for 1 to 2 minutes. Spread over chicken along with pimento. Add soup and wine to pan and bring to boil. Pour over chicken and vegetables. Cover pan with aluminum foil and bake at 350 degrees for 1 hour. Can be uncovered the last $1/2$ hour.

Dawn Long

CHICKEN CACCIATORE

Preparation: 30 minutes
Cooking: 1 hour

Serves: 4

$1/4$ cup olive oil
1 medium chicken (or 6 pieces)
2 medium onions, chopped
2 garlic cloves, minced
1 (16-ounce) can tomatoes
1 (8-ounce) can tomato sauce
1 teaspoon salt

$1/4$ teaspoon pepper
$1/2$ teaspoon celery seed
1 teaspoon oregano
1 or 2 bay leaves
$1/4$ cup Sauterne wine — can use Chablis

Heat oil in skillet, add chicken and brown slowly. Remove chicken. Cook onion and garlic in oil until tender, but not brown. Combine remaining ingredients, except wine. Return chicken to sauce mixture. Cover and simmer 45 minutes. Stir in wine and bring to boil. Simmer about 10 minutes uncovered. Serve over egg noodles.

Pat Haley

MEL'S MARSALA CHICKEN

Preparation: 1½ hours
Cooking: 30 minutes

Serves: 3

2 whole boneless, skinned chicken
   breasts (cut in half)
1 cup flour
Salt
Pepper

4 tablespoons butter
1 clove garlic, crushed
½ pound sliced mushrooms
½ cup Marsala cooking wine

Preheat oven 350 degrees. Beat chicken breast pieces with smooth side of mallet until they are about ⅛ to ¼ inches thin. Salt and pepper chicken to taste and dredge in flour. Melt 3 tablespoons butter in skillet, and brown 1 crushed garlic clove. Add chicken, browning quickly on both sides. Remove chicken to 13 × 9 pyrex baking pan that has been sprayed with Pam. Add 1 tablespoon butter to skillet and brown mushrooms. Add ½ cup Marsala cooking wine and bring to boil. Simmer approximately 2 minutes to blend flavors. Pour wine-mushroom sauce over chicken. Cover pan and bake approximately 30 minutes (or longer if needed) at 350 degrees.

Melissa Block

FAVORITE CHICKEN CASSEROLE

Preparation: 45 minutes
Cooking: 35 minutes

Serves: 10 to 12

8 chicken breast halves, cooked
   and cubed
1 cup rice cooked in chicken broth
   (2 cups)
1 cup celery, diced
¾ cup mayonnaise
1 cup fresh mushrooms, sliced
1 teaspoon lemon juice
1 teaspoon salt

1 (10¾-ounce) can cream of
   chicken soup
4 ounces water chestnuts, drained
   and sliced
1 teaspoon onion chopped
½ cup butter
½ cup sliced or slivered almonds
1 cup corn flakes

Mix all ingredients together except butter, almonds and corn flakes. Put in a 2 quart casserole. Melt butter. Add almonds and corn flakes. Sprinkle on top of casserole and bake in 350 degree oven for 35 minutes.

Nancy Beard

CHICKEN ITALIANO

Preparation: 20 minutes   Serves: 8
Cooking: 45 minutes

8 to 12 halves boned chicken $1/4$ teaspoon paprika
  breast $1/3$ cup butter
2 eggs, slightly beaten   1 package (6 ounces) Mozzarella
$3/4$ cup Italian bread crumbs   cheese
$3/4$ cup Parmesan cheese   1 small can tomato sauce

Dip chicken breasts in slightly beaten egg, and then into mixture of bread
crumbs mixed with Parmesan cheese and paprika. Brown in $1/3$ cup butter
until nicely browned on both sides. Remove from pan and place in pyrex
dish. Top with sliced Mozzarella cheese. Pour tomato sauce over all. Cover
tightly with foil. Bake at 350 degrees for 45 minutes.

Carolyn Pokela

BAJA CALIFORNIA CHICKEN

Preparation: 40 minutes   Serves: 8

8 boned chicken breasts   4 tablespoons olive oil
Seasoning salt and pepper, to taste 4 tablespoons tarragon vinegar
2 cloves garlic, crushed $2/3$ cup dry sherry

Sprinkle chicken with seasoning salt and pepper. Crush garlic into oil and
vinegar in a skillet. Sauté chicken pieces until golden brown, turning
frequently. Remove. Place in a baking dish. Pour sherry over pieces and
place in 350 degree oven for 10 minutes.

Nancy Reagan

Nancy Reagan

CRUNCHY CHICKEN IMPERIAL

Preparation: 30 to 45 minutes   Serves: 8
Cooking: 1 to $1^{1/2}$ hours

$1/2$ pint sour cream $1/2$ teaspoon salt
2 tablespoons lemon juice $1/8$ teaspoon pepper
2 teaspoons Worcestershire sauce   8 boned chicken pieces
1 teaspoon celery salt   1 package Pepperidge Farm
1 teaspoon paprika   Stuffing
$1/2$ teaspoon garlic salt $1/2$ cup butter, melted

Mix first 8 ingredients. Dip 8 boned chicken pieces in above mixture. Chill 4
to 5 hours or overnight. Roll in 1 package Pepperidge Farm stuffing ground
finely with rolling pin. Pour $1/2$ cup melted butter or more over all, and bake
uncovered in 350 degree oven until chicken is brown (1 to $1^{1/2}$ hours).

Mary Jane Sevier, Joan Shumate

CHICKEN DESIRÉE

Preparation: 10 minutes
Cooking: 55 minutes

Serves: 8

4 whole chicken breasts, split,
   skinned and boned
8 (4 × 4 inch) slices Swiss cheese
1 (10½-ounce) can cream of
   chicken soup

¼ cup dry white wine
1 cup herb-seasoned stuffing mix
¼ cup melted butter or margarine

Arrange chicken in lightly greased 13 × 9 × 2 inch baking dish. Top with cheese slices, sprinkle a little pepper and garlic powder on top of chicken. Combine undiluted soup and wine, stirring well. Spoon over chicken, sprinkle with stuffing mix. Drizzle butter over crumbs and bake uncovered at 350 degrees for 55 minutes.

Elaine Abrams

BAKED TURKEY ROAST

Cooking: 4 hours

Serves: 6

2½ pound frozen, boneless, rolled
   turkey roast (without gravy)
1 cup plum preserves
½ cup Italian salad dressing

½ envelope (¼ cup) dry onion
   soup mix
1 tablespoon cornstarch
2 tablespoons water

Remove roast from foil pan and wrap in heavy foil. Place in shallow pan and roast in 350 degree oven for 2 hours. Combine plum preserves, salad dressing, and soup mix. Loosen foil. Pour sauce over turkey and reseal foil. Roast 1¾ to 2 hours more or until meat thermometer registers 185 degrees. Transfer roast to serving plate. Reserve drippings. In saucepan, combine cornstarch and water. Stir in drippings. Cook and stir until thickened and bubbly. Spoon some sauce over turkey. Reserve remainder until serving time.

Hazel Blackwelder

FLOUNDER STUFFED WITH SHRIMP

Preparation: 35 minutes   Serves: 6
Cooking: 25 minutes

6 flounder filets
1/4 cup chopped green onion
3 tablespoons margarine
1 (4-ounce) can sliced mushrooms
1 pound shrimp
1/2 cup bread crumbs, fresh
2 tablespoons chopped fresh
    parsley
Salt and pepper

Sauce:
2 tablespoons margarine
2 tablespoons flour
1 tablespoon lemon juice
1 cup milk
1 egg, beaten
Paprika
1/4 cup white wine

Cook onion in margarine until tender. Add mushrooms and shrimp. Stir until shrimp turn pink. Add bread crumbs, parsley, salt and pepper. Put large rounded tablespoon of shrimp stuffing at one end of each filet and roll up. Place seam side down in buttered baking dish.
Sauce: Heat margarine, stir in flour, cook one minute. Add lemon juice and milk, stirring after each addition. Pour sauce slowly into egg so as to prevent curdling. Add remaining stuffing to sauce and pour over filets. Sprinkle with paprika. Bake 25 minutes in preheated 350 degree oven.

Sonja Andrew

FLOUNDER MARINATA

Preparation: 25 minutes   Serves: 4

Flounder, 2 or 3 pounds
Lemon Marinade:
1/2 cup vegetable oil
5 tablespoons lemon juice
1/2 teaspoon prepared mustard
    (optional)

1 clove garlic crushed
1 teaspoon oregano
1/2 teaspoon salt
1/4 teaspoon pepper

Flounder: Cut 3 or 4 gashes through skin. Combine marinade ingredients with wisk or fork. Pour over fish in shallow dish. Refrigerate at least one hour. Place on greased broiler pan. Broil until easily flaked with fork. Brush once or twice with marinade. (If fish is too large, do not turn.) Remove to large platter, pour remaining marinade over fish.
Variation: For anchovy dressing, add 2 teaspoons anchovy paste to lemon marinade. Substitute chopped parsley for oregano.

Titsa Dermatas

LENTEN MACKEREL STEAKS

Preparation: 10 minutes
Cooking: 20 to 25 minutes

Serves: 4

4 medium tomatoes, skinned
1 small onion, thinly sliced
4 peppercorns
4 strips of lemon peel
4 thick mackerel steaks

1/2 teaspoon powdered thyme
1 teaspoon fennel
Salt to taste
1/4 cup water
3/4 cup dry white wine

Slice tomatoes. Arrange tomato slices and onion slices in a well buttered shallow baking pan. Add peppercorns and lemon peel. Arrange mackerel steaks over the tomato mixture. Sprinkle with thyme and fennel leaves and season with salt. Pour water and wine in baking pan. Cover with foil. Bake in pre-heated 325 degree oven 20 to 25 minutes or until mackerel flakes when pierced.

Jimmie Johnson

SHRIMP-ARTICHOKE DELIGHT

Preparation: 1 hour
Cooking: 30 minutes

Serves: 6

3 scallions
6 sprigs parsley or 3 tablespoons
    dried parsley
4 chives or 2 tablespoons dried
    chives
4 basil leaves or 1 teaspoon dried
3 sprigs dill or 1 teaspoon dried
4 ounces cheddar cheese
2 (20-ounce) cans artichoke
    hearts, drained

1 1/2 to 2 pounds cooked shrimp
1 1/2 cups tomato juice
1 tablespoon lemon juice
2 tablespoons olive oil
1 teaspoon salt
1/2 teaspoon pepper
2 ounces Parmesan cheese
6 to 8 cups cooked rice

Preheat oven to 350 degrees. Using steel blade of food processor, chop together the scallions, parsley, chives, basil and dill. Leave the above in food processor bowl and insert the shredding disk. Shred the cheddar cheese. Line greased casserole dish with artichoke hearts. Sprinkle the herb-cheese mixture over the top. Layer the shrimp over the herb-cheese mixture. Mix well the tomato juice, lemon juice, oil, salt and pepper. Pour over the shrimp. Sprinkle Parmesan cheese on the top. Bake until bubbly, about 30 minutes at 350 degrees. Serve over cooked rice.

Doris Bradley

POACHED FISH WITH BEURRE BLANC SAUCE

Preparation: 30 minutes   Serves: 6 to 8

8 fish filets
6 tablespoons chopped shallots
Salt and pepper, to taste
1 cup white wine

Sauce:
6 tablespoons chopped shallots
1½ cups dry white wine
¼ cup heavy cream
½ pound cold butter

Place fish in baking dish. Scatter shallots over it. Salt and pepper to taste and pour wine over top. Cover with buttered paper and bake at 375 degrees for 7 minutes for every inch of depth. Remove to a heated platter and serve with sauce.
Sauce: Combine shallots, wine and cream in saucepan over medium heat. Reduce to ½ cup. Whisk in butter, bit by bit. Salt and pepper to taste.

Elizabeth West

CHINESE SHRIMP AND PORK

Preparation: 30 minutes   Serves: 4
Cooking: 10 minutes

½ pound cauliflower
1 carrot
1 green pepper
1 red pepper
8 ounces pork
½ teaspoon cornstarch
1 tablespoon water

8 ounces medium size shrimp
2 onions sliced finely
2 tablespoons cooking oil
1 teaspoon sugar
1 teaspoon monosodium glutamate
1 teaspoon soy sauce
Salt, pepper and monosodium
    glutamate to taste

Cut cauliflower, green and red peppers into small pieces. Slice carrot thinly. Remove shells from shrimp and de-vein. Put cauliflower and carrot in hot boiling water and simmer for 2 minutes. Strain and leave aside. Slice pork thinly. Mix shrimp and pork with sugar, 1 teaspoon monosodium glutamate, and soy sauce. Heat 1 tablespoon cooking oil in pan. Fry onions. Put in shrimp and pork and fry for 3 minutes. Set aside. Heat 1 tablespoon cooking oil in pan. Put in cauliflower, carrot, green and red pepper. Add salt, pepper, and monosodium glutamate (optional) to taste. Put in shrimp and pork. Mix cornstarch and water and add to ingredients. Stir-fry quickly.

Irene Snowberger

SHRIMP CASSEROLE

Preparation: 25 minutes
Cooking: 50 minutes

Serves: 8 to 10

1½ pounds shrimp, cooked and
   shelled
1 pound New York State sharp
   cheese
1 cup rice, cooked 10 minutes
1 cup celery and green pepper,
   chopped together

1 large onion, chopped fine
23 ounces tomato sauce
8 ounces chopped mushrooms
   with juice
1 teaspoon Worcestershire sauce
Salt and pepper to taste

Cook celery, pepper and onions in 2 tablespoons butter. Combine with other ingredients. Add ¾ cheese but save ¼ for topping. Bake at 325 degrees for 50 minutes. Add cooked shrimp last 10 minutes of cooking time.

Nancy Beard

CRAB-SHRIMP CASSEROLE

Preparation: 30 minutes
Cooking: 30 minutes

Serves: 8

1 cup mayonnaise
2 teaspoons Worcestershire sauce
2 tablespoons prepared mustard
½ cup good sherry
1 teaspoon salt
Dash of cayenne pepper
1 teaspoon curry powder (paprika
   may be substituted)
2 tablespoons parsley

½ cup onion, chopped
½ cup celery, chopped
2½ cups bread crumbs
1 can cream of mushroom soup
2 (6-ounce) packages frozen snow
   crab meat, cooked
2 pounds shrimp, cleaned and
   cooked

Combine all ingredients in baking dish. Bake at 350 degrees for about 30 minutes. Can be served plain, in patty shells, or on toast points. Lobster can be added, if desired.

June Rutherford

SHRIMP AND WILD RICE CASSEROLE

Preparation: 20 minutes

Serves: 8

Cooking: 1 hour

2 cups chopped onions
2 cups chopped celery
2 green peppers, chopped
1/4 cup margarine
1 package wild rice, cooked
according to directions on
package
1 cup white rice, cooked

2 1/2 pounds shrimp, peeled and
deveined
3 cans cream of mushroom soup,
undiluted
2 (2-ounce) jars pimento, drained
2 (4-ounce) cans drained
mushrooms
Bread crumbs for top, if desired

Sauté vegetables in margarine until tender. Do not brown. Add remaining
ingredients except crumbs. Stir well. Spoon into two 2-quart casseroles.
Sprinkle with crumbs, if desired. Bake at 350 degrees for one hour.

Subette Strand

SCALLOPED SEAFOOD CASSEROLE

Preparation: 40 minutes

Serves: 6 to 8

Cooking: 12 to 15 minutes

1 (15-ounce) can artichokes,
halved and drained
1 (4-ounce) can mushrooms (may
use more)
1 pound crab meat
1 pound shrimp, cleaned
1 pound scallops, (bay or sea cut
into quarters)
1/4 cup butter or margarine

1/4 cup flour
1/2 teaspoon salt
Dash of cayenne pepper
1 1/2 cup half and half
1 cup sherry
2 tablespoons cereal crumbs
1 tablespoon Parmesan cheese
Paprika to taste

Place artichokes in well greased shallow 1 1/2 to 2 quart casserole. Cover
with mushrooms, crabmeat, shrimp and scallops. Melt margarine, blend in
flour and seasonings. Add cream gradually. Cook until thick, stirring
constantly. Stir in sherry. Pour sauce over seafood mixture. Combine
crumbs and cheese. Sprinkle over sauce. Sprinkle with paprika. Bake at
450 degrees 12 to 15 minutes or until bubbly.

Nancy Smith

SHRIMP DIJON

Preparation: 20 minutes   Serves: 6 to 8

2 pounds shrimp, peeled and
   cleaned
4 tablespoons butter
1/2 cup shallots or green onions,
   chopped

2 teaspoons tarragon, chopped
1/4 cup dry sherry
1 1/2 cups heavy cream
2 tablespoons butter, softened
1 tablespoon Dijon mustard

Melt butter. Add shrimp and sauté 1 minute on each side. Remove shrimp
from pan. Add shallots and tarragon. Stir and cook for 2 to 3 minutes.
Deglaze pan with sherry and reduce to half. Add cream and reduce to half
again. Swirl in butter and mustard. Pour over shrimp which have been
arranged on a serving dish.

Elizabeth West

PAELLA

Preparation: 1 hour   Serves: 10
Cooking: 25 minutes

2 cloves garlic
1/4 cup Spanish olive oil
1 uncooked chicken breast, boned,
   cut in 1 inch pieces
1 pimento, diced
1 medium onion, thinly sliced
1 cup uncooked rice
1 teaspoon salt
1/2 teaspoon saffron

2 1/2 cups boiling water
1 (8-ounce) can minced clams with
   juices
1 cup green beans, cut in 1 inch
   pieces
2 lobster tails cut in thirds
   (undershell removed)
1 tablespoon minced parsley
1/2 pound cooked shrimp

In heavy 10 inch skillet, heat garlic in olive oil until brown. Discard garlic
clove. Sauté chicken quickly and remove from pan. Add pimento and onion
to skillet, cooking until onion is soft. Add rice, salt and saffron. Stir to coat
rice with oil. Add boiling water, clams and juice, beans, and lobster pieces.
Bring to boil, lower heat, and cook uncovered for 15 minutes. (The mixture
should boil steadily but moderately.) Remove from heat. Stir in shrimp.
Sprinkle parsley over top, cover and set aside for 10 minutes to allow
absorption of remaining liquid.

Sallie Nolan

JAMBALAYA

Preparation: 1 hour
Cooking: 30 minutes

Serves: 8

4 bacon slices
1½ cups chopped celery
2 medium chopped onions
1 small garlic bud, minced
2 medium green peppers, chopped
   in large pieces
2 (28-ounce) cans whole tomatoes
1 cup water

1½ tablespoons all purpose flour
1½ teaspoons salt
1½ cups cleaned, cooked shrimp
1 pound bay scallops (cut up large
   ones)
12 fresh clams in shells, steamed
   open
1 cup rice

Fry bacon in large frying pan and chop. Stir in celery, onion, garlic, and green pepper. Simmer 5 minutes, stirring. Add water mixed with flour, tomatoes and juice and salt. Mix well. Bring to a boil. Simmer 20 minutes, stirring occasionally. Can do ahead to this point. When ready to serve, add shrimp and scallops and just let get hot. Serve over rice with opened clams in shells on top.

Pat Haley

SEAFOOD DELIGHT

Preparation: 20 minutes
Cooking: 40 minutes

Serves: 6

1½ pounds asparagus or 2 cans
½ cup water
1 teaspoon salt
½ pound sharp cheese, grated
1 (5-ounce) can lobster
1 (6½-ounce) can crabmeat
1 (4½-ounce) can shrimp

2 (4-ounce) cans sliced
   mushrooms, not drained
2 cans mushroom soup, undiluted
½ cup fine fresh bread crumbs
½ cup slivered almonds
Paprika

Place asparagus, water, and salt in a heavy pan. Cover and cook to boiling. Lower heat and cook for 5 minutes. Drain. Place asparagus in a buttered shallow casserole. Sprinkle half of cheese on top. Drain and flake lobster, crabmeat, and shrimp. Place over cheese. Blend mushrooms and liquid with soup. Spread on top. Cover with bread crumbs, remaining cheese, and almonds. Sprinkle paprika on top. Cover dish with foil. Bake at 350 degrees for 40 minutes.

Pat Blythe

ELEGANT SEAFOOD CREPES

Preparation: 30 minutes
Cooking: 10 minutes

Serve: 4 to 6

8 crepes (see Index)
3 tablespoons flour
3 tablespoons butter
2 tablespoons chopped chives
¼ teaspoon salt
3 tablespoons sherry

1 (7-ounce) package frozen
    crabmeat (thawed, flaked, and
    drained)
1 (10-ounce) package frozen,
    cooked shrimp (thawed and
    drained)

Melt butter in saucepan. Blend in flour, chives and salt. Gradually add milk and sherry. Cook over medium heat, stirring constantly until thickened. Add crabmeat and shrimp. Cook over low heat, stirring occasionally until heated thoroughly. Spread ¼ cup filling down center of each crepe. Roll up, overlapping on top. Place in 9 x 13 inch baking dish. Spoon remaining filling down center of each crepe. Bake in preheated 350 degree oven for 10 minutes. Garnish with parsley.

Lucy Majors

BISCAYNE BAY SOUFFLE

Preparation: 30 minutes
Cooking: 1½ hours

Serves: 8

2 tablespoons breadcrumbs
8 slices white bread, cubed, crust
    removed
8 ounces fresh crabmeat (or
    cooked shrimp)
½ pound sliced mushrooms
¼ cup sliced green onions

8 ounces medium cheddar cheese
2½ cups milk
4 eggs, beaten
½ teaspoon salt
½ teaspoon dry mustard
Cayenne pepper, to taste

Butter a 2 quart souffle dish (or 6 × 10 inch baking dish) and dust with breadcrumbs. Combine milk, eggs, salt, mustard, pepper and cheese in blender. Blend until smooth. (May need to be prepared in two batches.) Make several layers of bread cubes, crabmeat, mushrooms, green onions, and cheese mixture. Refrigerate at least 4 hours. Bake in preheated oven at 350 degrees for 1½ hours until golden and firm and knife inserted in middle comes out clean. (Reduce time to 1 hour in using 6 × 10 inch baking dish.)

Patsy Hoffman

MRS. TAYLOR'S CRABMEAT

Preparation: 20 minutes   Serves: 8
Cooking: until light brown

1 pound crabmeat
2 cups bread crumbs
1 teaspoon chopped onion
4 hard cooked eggs, chopped very
 fine

1/2 cup milk
1 cup mayonnaise
1 tablespoon chopped parsley
Red pepper and salt to taste

Flake crabmeat. Add onion, egg and parsley. Marinate with mayonnaise and seasonings until stiff enough to mold, then thin with milk. Put in shell baking dishes and cover with buttered bread crumbs. Bake at 350 degrees until light brown.

Nancy Beard

MARYLAND CRAB

Preparation: 15 minutes   Serves: 4
Cooking: 15 minutes

1/2 cup mayonnaise
1 egg, slightly beaten
1/2 cup green pepper, finely chopped
1 teaspoon dry mustard
1 tablespoon pimento, finely chopped

1/2 teaspoon salt, dash pepper
1 pound fresh or frozen lump
 crabmeat
Mayonnaise and paprika for garnish

Thoroughly combine mayonnaise, green pepper, egg, dry mustard, salt and pepper. Add crabmeat. Stir to coat. Divide mixture between 4 cleaned crab shells. Top with thin coating of mayonnaise. Sprinkle with paprika. Bake at 350 degrees for 15 minutes.

Anne Bodner

OYSTERS ROCKEFELLER CASSEROLE

Preparation: 15 minutes   Serves: 8 to 10
Cooking: 30 minutes

1 quart raw oysters, thoroughly
 drained
1 stick butter, melted
1 rib celery, chopped
1 tablespoon onion, finely chopped
1/2 cup parsley, chopped

1 package frozen chopped spinach,
 thawed and thoroughly drained
1/4 teaspoon anise seed (optional)
1/4 cup Worcestershire sauce
1/2 cup breadcrumbs
1 cup grated cheddar cheese
Salt and pepper to taste

Sauté celery, onions, and parsley in butter. Add spinach, anise, Worcestershire, breadcrumbs, salt and pepper. Arrange oysters in single layer in 9 × 13 inch dish. Cover with Rockefeller mixture. Bake 20 minutes at 350 degrees. Do not overcook. Sprinkle with grated cheese. Return to oven for approximately 10 minutes to brown.

Ann Rives

SCALLOPS THERMIDOR

Preparation: 30 minutes   Serves: 6
Cooking: 10 to 15 minutes

1 pound cooked scallops
1 (4-ounce) can mushroom stems
   and pieces, drained
1/4 cup butter or margarine, melted
1/4 cup flour
1 teaspoon salt
1/2 teaspoon powdered mustard

Dash cayenne pepper
2 cups milk
2 tablespoons chopped parsley
Grated Parmesan cheese
Paprika

Cut large scallops in half. Sauté mushrooms in butter for 5 minutes. Blend in flour and seasonings. Add milk gradually and cook until thick, stirring constantly. Add scallops and parsley. Place in 6 well-greased casseroles or shells. Sprinkle with cheese and paprika. Bake 400 degrees for 10 to 15 minutes or until cheese browns.

Debbie Bielski

SCALLOP MOUSSE

Preparation: 10 minutes   Serves: 6 to 8
Cooking: 20 to 30 minutes

2 pounds scallops
2 eggs
Salt, to taste
Cayenne pepper, to taste
Nutmeg, to taste
3 cups whipping cream,
   unwhipped

Dill Sauce:
2 tablespoons butter
1/4 cup chopped shallots
1 cup clam juice
1 1/2 cups chopped tomatoes
2 tablespoons tomato paste
1 cup whipping cream, unwhipped
Salt and pepper to taste
1 to 2 tablespoons chopped, fresh
   dill (or 1 to 2 teaspoons dried)

Process scallops in food processor or blender. Add eggs, salt, cayenne, and nutmeg. Add cream and process to mix. Pour into buttered individual soufflé dishes. Cover with foil. Bake in a bain marie at 375 degrees for 20 to 30 minutes. Unmold and serve with Dill Sauce: Heat butter. Add shallots. Cook 2 minutes. Add clam juice and cook until almost evaporated. Puree the tomatoes and paste. Add to pan. Add cream and cook until thick. Season with salt, pepper, and dill. Serve over mousse.

Elizabeth West

CHERRY-ALMOND GLAZED PORK

Preparation: 15 minutes
Cooking: 2 to 2½ hours

Serves: 8

1 (3-pound) boneless pork loin
   roast
salt and pepper
1 (12-ounce) jar cherry preserves
¼ cup red wine vinegar

2 tablespoons light corn syrup
¼ teaspoon (each) ground
   cinnamon, ground nutmeg
⅛ teaspoon ground cloves
¼ cup slivered almonds, toasted

Rub roast with a little salt and pepper. Place on rack in shallow roasting pan. Roast uncovered at 325 degrees for 2 to 2½ hours. Meanwhile, combine preserves, vinegar, syrup, spices, and ½ teaspooon salt. Heat and stir until boiling, then simmer for 3 minutes. Add almonds to mixture. Spoon sauce over roast. Return to oven and continue basting with sauce several times. When serving, pass remaining sauce with roast.

Jan Lee, Donna Tibbals

HAM BAKED IN RASPBERRY GRAND MARNIER SAUCE

Preparation: 15 minutes
Cooking: 1½ to 2 hours

Serves: 15

½ fully cooked bone-in ham,
   shank or butt (about 6 pounds)
Whole cloves
½ cup prepared yellow mustard
1 cup firmly packed dark brown
   sugar
1 cup cream sherry

Sauce:
1 orange, unpeeled, diced
1 cup firmly packed dark brown
   sugar
2 cups raspberry preserves or jam
2 tablespoons prepared yellow
   mustard
1 tablespoon Worcestershire Sauce
1 cup cream sherry
½ cup Grand Marnier

To Cook Ham: Score fat surface of ham. Stud with whole cloves. Combine mustard, and brown sugar. Spread over ham. Place ham in baking pan. Add sherry to pan. Bake at 325 degrees for 1½ to 2 hours or until meat thermometer registers 130 degrees. About half an hour before ham is heated through, pour sauce over ham and finish cooking, basting several times with sauce. To serve, slice ham and pour sauce over slices. Allow ⅓ to ½ pound of bone-in ham per person.
Prepare Sauce as follows: Combine all ingredients. Puree in blender. A half hour before ham is finished cooking, pour sauce over ham as directed.

Donna Tibbals

LUNCHEON ROLLUPS

Preparation: 30 minutes   Serves: 8
Cooking: 15 minutes

1 cup cooked wild rice
1 cup finely chopped cooked
   chicken
8 (6½ × 4½ inch) ham slices

Mushroom Cheese Sauce:
¼ cup butter or margarine
1 cup sliced fresh mushrooms
¼ cup all-purpose flour
1 cup chicken broth
1 cup Half-and-Half
1 cup (4 ounces) shredded sharp
   cheddar cheese
Dash of salt

To make sauce, melt butter in a heavy saucepan over low heat. Add mushrooms, and sauté until tender. Add flour, stirring until mushrooms are coated. Add chicken broth and half-and-half. Cook 1 minute, stirring constantly, until thickened and bubbly. Add cheese and salt. Stir until cheese melts. Rollups: Combine rice and chicken. Place ¼ cup rice mixture in center of each ham slice. Roll up, and place seam side down in a lightly-greased 13 x 9 x 2 inch baking dish. Spoon mushroom-cheese sauce over ham rolls. Bake 350 degrees for 15 minutes or until the sauce is bubbly. (May be heated in a microwave on medium power, until bubbly and heated through.) Sprinkle with paprika and parsley (fresh or dried) before serving.

Sally Miller

HAM LOAF WITH ORANGE SAUCE

Preparation: 20 minutes   Serves: 10 to 12
Cooking: 2 hours

Ham Loaf:
2 pounds fresh pork, ground
2 pounds cured ham, ground
2 eggs
20 ritz crackers, crushed

Orange Sauce:
1 cup light brown sugar
2 tablespoons cornstarch
½ teaspoon salt
½ cup water
4 tablespoons orange peel, grated
2 cups fresh orange juice

Mix pork, ham, eggs, and crackers together. Form into loaf. Place in baking pan. Bake at 350 degrees, skimming fat from pan every thirty minutes. Orange Sauce: Combine sugar, cornstarch and salt. Stir in orange peel, juice and water. Cook over low heat, stirring constantly, until thickened and transparent. Brush sauce on ham loaf and baste frequently with pastry brush during last hour of cooking. Do not cover.

Elaine Wright

BEER BASTED SUMMER BAKED HAM

Preparation: 30 minutes   Serves: 16
Cooking: 3 1/2 hours

10 to 12 pound fully cooked,   4 sprigs parsley
    bone-in ham   6 whole cloves
1 cup sliced onion   3 whole black peppers
2 bay leaves   1 pint beer
1/4 cup brown sugar, packed

Glaze:
1/2 cup brown sugar, packed   Whole cloves
1/4 cup honey

Preheat oven to 325 degrees, place ham, fat side up, in shallow roasting pan. Place onion and bay leaves on ham, sprinkle with sugar, parsley, cloves and pepper. Insert meat thermometer in center of thickest part, away from bone. Pour beer into pan around ham. Cover pan tightly with foil. Bake, basting every 30 minutes with beer in pan, about three hours or until thermometer registers 130 degrees. Remove ham from oven. Remove foil, baste. Make glaze. When ham is done, remove it from pan, and pour off all fat and drippings. Reserve 2 tablespoons of drippings (not fat). Combine with brown sugar and honey. Return ham to raosting pan. Increase oven temperature to 400 degrees. With sharp knife carefully remove any remaining skin. Score fat. Stud with whole cloves and brush with 1/2 glaze and bake 30 minutes longer, basting every 10 minutes with more of the glaze.

Louise Glover

ROAST LOIN OF PORK POLYNESIAN

Preparation: 20 minutes   Serves: 6 to 8
Cooking: 2 1/2 hours

1 loin of pork chops (10 chops, 4 1/2   1 tablespoon ground ginger
    to 5 pounds)   1 clove garlic, put through garlic
Salt and pepper to taste   press
1 cup orange juice   2 tablespoons soy sauce
1/2 cup brown sugar

Preheat oven to 325 degrees. Season the pork with salt and pepper. Place the pork fat side up, in a roasting pan. Roast for 2 1/2 hours, basting it with the following sauce every 15 minutes: In a small sauce pan combine the orange juice, brown sugar, ginger, garlic, and soy sauce, and simmer for 15 minutes.

Kitty Robison

117

HAM AND APPLE CASSEROLE

Preparation: 10 minutes   Serves: 6 to 8
Cooking: 40 to 50 minutes

2 cups cooked ham   ½ cup flour
4 cups thinly sliced apples, peeled ⅔ cup sugar
3 tablespoons sugar   ½ cup margarine
2 teaspoons lemon juice   ½ cup grated Parmesan
¼ teaspoon salt   ½ cup American cheese

Place ham in dish. Cover with apples. Blend sugar and lemon together. Spoon evenly over apples. In another bowl mix salt, flour, and sugar. Cut in butter until crumbly. Add cheese and stir. Sprinkle over apples. Cover top with cheese and bake at 350 degrees for 40 to 50 minutes.

Anne Jones

BEST WAY TO COOK COUNTRY HAM

Preparation: 10 minutes

1 (6-ounce) can orange juice
1 (6-ounce) can of water
1 (6-ounce) can of white vinegar

Scrub ham and remove hock. Mix all ingredients together and pour over ham after placing it in heavy duty aluminum foil. Secure the aluminum foil very tightly. Bake country ham for 30 minutes a pound at 250 degrees. Do not remove from oven or open door until next morning.

Beverly Gwinn

HAM CREPES

Preparation: 20 minutes   Serves: 10
Cooking: 15 minutes

20 crepes (see Index)   2 cups whipping cream
20 pieces baked ham, thinly sliced   2 egg yolks
1 cup Swiss cheese, grated

Place ham on crepes. Sprinkle with ½ cup cheese. Roll like a diploma. Place in shallow buttered baking dish (large enough to hold crepes flat). Beat cream until stiff. Stir in slightly beaten yolks and spoon over crepes. Sprinkle with remaining cheese. Bake at 450 degrees for 15 minutes.

Marian Ferrel

PORK CHOP CASSEROLE

Preparation: 15 minutes
Cooking: 45 minutes

Serves: 3

Salt
Pepper
3 pork chops
3 bouillon cubes
1/2 cup uncooked rice

1/4 cup celery, diced
Dash Tabasco
3 onion rings
3 slices green pepper, or chopped
3 slices tomato, or canned

Salt, pepper, and brown pork chops. Melt bouillon cubes in 1 1/2 cups boiling water. Stir until dissolved. Add rice, celery and Tabasco. Stir (it will be soupy). Place browned chops on rice. Place onion ring, green pepper, and tomato on top of each chop. Cover. Cook 45 minutes at 325 to 350 degrees.

Janet Sheffield

PORK CHOP ONION-RICE BAKE

Preparation: 20 minutes
Cooking: 45 minutes

Serves: 6

6 pork chops
2 tablespoons shortening
1 cup uncooked rice
1 envelope onion soup mix

1 (4-ounce) can sliced mushrooms
2 tablespoons diced pimento
Hot water

Brown chops in shortening. Spread rice in bottom of rectangular baking dish. Reserve 1 tablespoon of seasoning from envelope of onion soup mix and sprinkle remaining seasoning and bits of onion over rice. Drain mushrooms, reserve liquid, and distribute mushrooms and pimento over rice. Add hot water to reserved mushroom liquid to total 3 cups liquid and pour over rice. Arrange browned chops on top of rice mixture and sprinkle chops with reserved seasoning. Cover with foil and bake in 350 degree oven 45 minutes. Remove foil for last 10 minutes of cooking.

Vicky Purgason

HONG KONG PORK CHOPS

Preparation: 25 minutes   Serves: 8
Cooking: 50 minutes or until done

8 loin pork chops   1/4 teaspoon garlic powder
Salt to taste   1/2 large green pepper, cut into
2 to 3 tablespoons salad oil   rings
1 medium onion, thinly sliced   1/4 cup sliced water chestnuts
1/4 cup soy sauce   1 lemon, thinly sliced
2 tablespoons lemon juice   1/4 cup orange juice
1/2 teaspoon ground ginger   1 (4-ounce) can sliced mushrooms

Season chops with salt. Brown on both sides in hot oil. Place in a shallow 2 quart casserole dish. Cover with onion slices. Combine soy sauce, orange juice, lemon juice, mushrooms, ginger and garlic powder, blend well. Pour over chops, cover and bake at 350 degrees for 35 minutes. Add green pepper, water chestnuts and lemon slices. Bake uncovered an additional 15 minutes. The initial cooking time may vary depending on the thickness of the chops.

Marge Monroe

LAMB FRICASEE WITH ARTICHOKES

Preparation: 1 hour   Serves: 8 to 10
Cooking: 1½ hours

2 pounds lamb (cubed)   2 (14-ounce) cans of artichokes
1/2 cup green onions   (cut in halves)
1 clove crushed garlic   1 tablespoon dill, fresh
2 tablespoons butter   1 tablespoon fresh chopped
2 teaspoons salt   parsley
1/4 teaspoon pepper   1/2 cup water
                                           1/2 cup fresh squeezed lemon juice

Egg Lemon Sauce:
3 eggs, separated   1 cup chicken broth or stock
Juice of 2 lemons   1 tablespoon cornstarch

Brown meat with chopped onions and garlic. Season with salt and pepper. Add lemon, water, dill, parsley. Simmer, covered for 1½ hours or until tender. Add artichokes and cook until done. Add water if necessary. Prepare Egg Lemon Sauce as follows and pour over lamb. Beat egg whites until stiff. Add yolks and continue beating. Add lemon juice very slowly, beating constantly to avoid curdling. Thicken with cornstarch dissolved in a little hot water. Slowly add boiling stock to egg mixture, beating constantly until smooth and creamy. Serve over lamb.

Iris O'Donnell

TEN BOY LAMB CURRY

Preparation: 1 hour
Cooking: 3 to 3½ hours

Serves: 8 to 10

1 large leg of lamb, boned and cut in ½ inch cubes
lamb bones
3 teaspoons salt
15 teaspoons curry powder (or, to taste)
¼ cup oil
3 tablespoons butter
8 medium onions, finely chopped
3 cloves garlic, mashed
milk from 2 coconuts, approximately 28 ounces

3 teaspoons sugar
2 cups broth from bones
1 cup cream
8 cooking apples, chopped fine
2 cups Hubbard squash, chopped fine (substitute eggplant or acorn squash if necessary)
½ cup seedless raisins
7 heaping tablespoons grated coconut
Juice of 1 lemon
Rice

Ten Boy Condiments: About 1½ cups of each
1. Freshly grated coconut
2. Finely chopped peanuts
3. Crisp bacon, crumbled
4. Chutney
5. Hard-boiled egg white, finely chopped
6. Hard-boiled egg yolks, sieved
7. Green pepper, finely chopped
8. Firm tomatoes, seeded and finely chopped
9. French fried onions, crushed or chopped scallions
10. Sliced mushrooms sautéed in butter

After removing meat, cook bones in 3 cups of water 1 to 2 hours. Reserve broth. Cube meat and sprinkle with salt and curry powder. Mix with hands to coat evenly. In skillet, heat oil and brown meat, stirring frequently. Set aside. Melt butter in skillet, add onions and garlic, sautéing 10 minutes. This much can be done 1 or 2 days ahead, covered and refrigerated. In large heavy pot put meat, onions, coconut milk, sugar, 2 cups of broth and cream. Cover and simmer ½ hour. Add apples, squash, raisins, coconut and lemon juice, cooking gently for 2 hours. Add more curry if you like. May be refrigerated for serving the next day. Reheat slowly to prevent burning. The apples and squash are natural thickeners. Serve over rice. Sprinkle condiments on top as desired.

Nancie LaRoche

BUTTERFLY LEG OF LAMB

Preparation: 20 minutes   Serves: 6 to 8
Cooking: 50 minutes

6 to 7 pound leg of lamb, $1/2$ teaspoon fresh parsley, chopped
   butterflied $1/2$ teaspoon sweet dried basil
Dijon mustard $1/2$ teaspoon ground black pepper
Juice of one lemon   1 teaspoon Worcestershire
3 to 4 garlic cloves, finely chopped $1/4$ cup olive oil
                                    $1/4$ cup Wesson oil

Have butcher butterfly leg of lamb. (Bones are removed and meat is split lengthwise and spread flat like a thick steak.) Combine all ingredients and pour over meat. Let marinate all day or over night, covered. Turn at least twice. Place on grill over medium hot coals. Reserve marinade. Cook about 50 minutes, turning every 10 to 15 minutes. Brush occasionally with marinade. To serve: Cut crosswise in thin slices. May be baked in 350 degree oven for 15 to 20 minutes per pound, if desired.

Elaine Abrams

ROYAL LEG OF LAMB

Preparation: 10 minutes   Serves: 8 to 10
Cooking: $2^{1}/_{2}$ to 3 hours

1 (6-pound) leg of lamb, deboned $3/4$ cup red currant jelly
   and tied $3/4$ cup ketchup
Salt and freshly ground pepper to $1/2$ teaspoon crushed marjoram
   taste
$3/4$ cup dry sherry

Sprinkle lamb with salt and pepper and place on rack in a shallow roasting pan. Roast in preheated 300 to 325 degree oven for 2 hours. Combine sherry, jelly, ketchup and marjoram in a small saucepan and heat, stirring constantly, until the jelly is melted. Brush on lamb and roast for 30 to 60 minutes longer or 170 to 180 degrees on meat thermometer, depending on desired degree of doneness. Brush with sauce occasionally. Place lamb on a platter and garnish with parsley and lemon wedges. Heat the remaining sauce and serve with the lamb.

Lucy Major, Rosli Clark

THICK LAMB STEW WITH PARSLEY NOODLES

Preparation: 30 minutes   Serves: 6
Cooking: 1 1/2 hours

1 1/2 pounds cubed lamb shoulder
1 cup chopped onions
3 tablespoons all-purpose flour
1 1/2 teaspoons salt
1/2 teaspoon pepper
1/2 teaspoon mace
1 cup chicken stock or chicken
   bouillon
1 cup diced carrots

1/2 cup chopped green pepper
1 cup lima beans
1 tablespoon salt
3 quarts boiling water
8 ounces wide egg noodles (about
   4 cups)
1/4 cup melted butter or margarine
1/4 cup chopped parsley

Combine lamb and onions. Cook over low heat until lamb is browned on all sides. Add flour, 1 1/2 teaspoons salt, pepper and mace. Blend gradually, add stock or bouillon, and cook until thickened, stirring constantly. Add carrots, green pepper and beans. Cover and cook over low heat 1 1/2 hours, stirring occasionally. Meanwhile, add 1 tablespoon salt to rapidly boiling water. Gradually add noodles so that water continues to boil. Cook uncovered, stirring occasionally, until tender. Drain in colander. Combine noodles, butter or margarine and parsley. Mix well. Serve noodles with lamb stew.

Betty Geraci

VEAL IN WINE AND LEMON SAUCE

Preparation: 30 minutes   Serves: 4
Cooking: to taste

1 pound veal scallops
1/4 cup flour
1 1/2 teaspoons salt
1/4 teaspoon black pepper (freshly
   ground)
2 tablespoons olive oil

1/2 stick creamery butter
Juice of 1 large lemon
1/2 to 1 cup mushrooms (optional)
2 tablespoons minced parsley
1/2 cup white wine (optional)

Pound veal very thin. Dip slices in mixture of flour, salt and pepper. Heat oil in a large frying pan, and brown veal on both sides. When tender, remove from pan and pour off oil. Add butter to pan and melt. Add wine and lemon juice. Return veal to pan. Add mushrooms and parsley. Heat.

Frances Pulliam

ROAST LAMB WITH WALNUT STUFFING

Preparation: 2 hours   Serves: 8
Cooking: 35 minutes per pound

1 leg of lamb, boned (5 to 7   1 clove garlic
   pounds)   Juice of 1 or 2 lemons
Salt, pepper   Oregano, optional

Stuffing:
1½ cups walnut halves   1 teaspoon salt
¾ cup onion, minced   ¼ teaspoon pepper
2 cloves garlic, crushed   1 cup bread crumbs
2 tablespoons butter   ⅓ cup dry red wine
2 cups chopped mushrooms   2 eggs, slightly beaten
2 tablespoons chopped parsley

Blanch walnuts for 3 minutes in boiling water. Drain well. Place on cookie sheet to toast in 350 degree oven until golden brown, stirring often. Cool and chop medium fine. In large skillet, sauté onion and garlic in butter until golden. Add mushrooms. Stir over moderate heat for about 5 minutes. In large bowl, combine mushroom mixture, seasonings, and chopped nuts. Moisten bread crumbs with wine. Add to mixture. Stir in beaten eggs. Blend thoroughly. Place stuffing inside lamb. Roll up tightly, and secure with string. Rub meat with salt and pepper, a minced garlic clove, oregano and lemon juice. Place in roasting pan with 1 cup water. Brown in 450 to 500 degree oven on both sides. Cover. Lower heat to 325 degrees and bake until tender (35 minutes per pound). Remove cover and bake 10 minutes longer. Remove from oven. Let stand 10 minutes. Remove string from meat and serve.

Titsa Dermatis

VEAL SUPREME

Preparation: 45 minutes   Serves: 10 to 12
Cooking: 1½ hours

3 pounds stew veal   1 diced tomato
3 tablespoons butter   2 cans cream of mushroom soup
1 pound sliced mushrooms   ¼ cup sherry or white wine
2 sliced medium onions   1 pint sour cream
1 sliced zucchini

Brown veal in 3 tablespoons butter and remove to large casserole. Brown sliced mushrooms, onions, zucchini and tomato in same pan. Add vegetables to veal in casserole. Add soup, wine and sour cream to casserole. Bake at 350 degrees for 1½ hours. Serve over rice.

Joan Shumate

OSSOBUCO

Preparation: 30 minutes
Cooking: 45 minutes

Serves: 8

1/4 cup butter or margarine
1 1/2 cups chopped onions
1 cup finely chopped carrots
1 cup finely chopped celery
1 clove garlic
4 pounds veal cut in 2 inch cubes
   (or veal shanks)
1 cup dry white wine

1/2 teaspoon basil
3/4 cup chicken stock or canned
   broth
3 cups drained tomatoes
1 tablespoon lemon peel
3 tablespoons finely chopped
   parsley

Melt butter in heavy casserole. Add chopped onions, carrots, celery and garlic. Cook over medium heat until vegetables are tender. Season veal with salt and pepper. Roll in flour and brown in shortening. Transfer to casserole and drain all fat from skillet. Add wine and boil briskly. Stir in basil, stock, tomatoes, parsley, bay leaf and bring to boil. Return veal to skillet and bring again to boil. Cover all in heavy casserole and bake 1 1/2 hours at 350 degrees. When serving, sprinkle with lemon peel.

Carolyn Maness

GRILLED CURRY LAMB CHOPS

Preparation: 2 to 3 hours

Serves: 4

8 lamb chops about 3/4 inch thick
1 tablespoon curry powder
1/2 teaspoon ground ginger

1 clove crushed garlic
3/4 cup soy sauce

Mix all ingredients except lamb. Put chops in a bowl and pour marinade over top. Marinate in the refrigerator 2 to 3 hours, turning chops several times. Broil on grill to desired doneness.

Judy Murray

VEAL ELEGANTE

Preparation: 15 minutes
Cooking: 15 minutes

Serves: 6

3 tablespoons butter or margarine
6 thin sliced veal scallops
3 or 4 shallots, finely chopped
8 ounces fresh mushrooms, sliced
1/4 cup sherry, dry

1/2 pint cream or crème fraiche (1
   tablespoon buttermilk to 1
   carton of cream)
Salt and pepper to taste
Chopped fresh parsley for garnish

Finely chop shallots and sauté in butter until soft. Add veal slices and cook on each side for a minute or two until veal becomes a light, pale color (not brown). Remove veal and set aside. Add sliced mushrooms and sauté until soft. Deglaze pan with sherry. Return veal to pan, cover, and cook for 5 minutes. Add cream just before serving. Salt and pepper to taste. Serve veal with sauce. Garnish with chopped parsley.

Rose McConnell

GEORGE'S VEAL MARSALA

Preparation: 10 minutes   Serves: 4
Cooking: few minutes

1 pound scallops of veal cut about $\frac{1}{4}$ cup water
   $\frac{1}{4}$ inch thick $\frac{1}{3}$ cup fresh mushrooms, thinly
$\frac{1}{2}$ stick unsalted butter   sliced
$\frac{1}{3}$ cup Marsala wine   Fresh chives for garnish
$\frac{1}{4}$ cup chicken stock   Salt and pepper to taste

Pound veal until it is about $\frac{1}{8}$ inch thick. Cut into strips $2\frac{1}{2}$ to 3 inches wide. In large skillet, melt $\frac{1}{2}$ the butter over medium high heat and quickly cook veal, turning once. Add more butter as needed. (Note: the veal will cook very quickly and can become tough.) Have a large warm serving plate ready, as it will take 2 or 3 batches to cook all the veal. When all of the veal has been removed from the skillet, turn heat to high and rapidly boil the chicken stock, Marsala wine, water, mushrooms, and salt and pepper until the liquid is reduced by about $\frac{2}{3}$. Pour this remaining liquid over the veal. Garnish with a little fresh chives. Serve immediately.

Doris Egerton

VEAL WITH ARTICHOKES

Preparation: 20 minutes   Serves: 2
Cooking: approximately 10 minutes

1 pound veal cutlet   1 teaspoon salt
1 cup sliced mushroooms   2 teaspoons white pepper
8 artichoke hearts   6 ounces clarified butter
$\frac{1}{2}$ pint heavy cream   1 cup flour
2 ounces lemon juice $\frac{1}{4}$ cup chopped parsley
$\frac{1}{2}$ cup white wine

Pound veal using flat side of meat mallet. Add salt and pepper to flour and sift. Dredge veal in seasoned flour, lightly coating both sides. Heat butter in large sauté pan. Place veal in pan and cook slightly on each side. Remove to a plate. Add wine, mushrooms, and lemon juice to pan and sauté mushrooms. Add artichoke hearts and enough cream to thicken. Add parsley. Return veal to pan and simmer 2 minutes. Place veal on serving plate or platter and cover with sauce.

This recipe shared by Chef Patrick Kelley of Greensboro Country Club

VEAL CHOPS IN WHITE WINE

Preparation: 30 minutes   Serves: 6
Cooking: 15 minutes

6 veal chops (rib or loin)   1/2 cup (1 stick) butter
3/4 teaspoon salt   1/2 cup dry white wine
1/8 teaspoon black pepper   6 slices bread fried in butter
Flour

Rub chops with salt and pepper. Dredge in flour. Brown in butter on both sides, over moderate heat. Add wine. Cover and simmer 15 minutes. Cut slices of bread to fit chops and fry in butter. Serve the chops on the bread on a hot platter. Garnish with vegetables as desired: Cauliflower, green beans, peas, carrots.

Dorothy Frank

LOBSTER-STUFFED TENDERLOIN OF BEEF

Preparation: 20 minutes   Serves: 8 to 10
Cooking: 45 to 50 minutes

3 to 4 pound whole beef tenderloin   6 slices bacon, partially cooked
2 (4-ounce) frozen lobster tails   1/2 cup sliced green onions
1 tablespoon butter or margarine,   1/2 cup butter or margarine
   melted   1/2 cup dry white wine
1 1/2 teaspoons lemon juice   1/8 teaspoon garlic salt

Preheat oven to 425 degrees. Cut beef tenderloin lengthwise to within 1/2 inch of bottom to butterfly. Place frozen lobster tails in boiling salted water to cover. Return to boiling. Reduce heat and simmer 5 to 6 minutes. Carefully remove lobster from shells. Cut in half lengthwise. Place lobster, end to end, inside beef. Combine the 1 tablespoon melted butter or margarine and lemon juice. Drizzle on lobster. Close meat around lobster. Tie roast together securely with string at intervals of 1 inch. Place on rack in shallow roasting pan. Roast in 425 degrees oven for 45 to 50 minutes for rare doneness. Lay bacon slices on top. Roast 5 minutes more. Meanwhile, prepare wine sauce. In sauce pan, cook green onion in the remaining butter over very low heat until tender, stirring frequently. Add wine and garlic salt and heat through, stirring frequently. To serve, slice roast and spoon on wine sauce. Garnish platter with fluted whole mushrooms and watercress or parsley, if desired.

Nancy Brown

BEV'S FILET OF BEEF

Preparation: 10 minutes
Cooking: 40 to 60 minutes

Serves: 8

3 to 5 pound tenderloin of beef
2 tablespoons olive oil
1 teaspoon salt
1/2 teaspoon cayenne pepper
1 teaspoon freshly ground pepper

1 carrot, sliced
1 small onion, chopped
4 tablespoons lemon juice
3 cups beef stock

Rub tenderloin with oil, salt, cayenne and freshly ground pepper. Place in pan on top of carrots and onions. Pour on lemon juice and let stand for 2 to 3 hours. Preheat oven to 500 degrees. Pour stock over meat and bake for 5 minutes at 500 degrees. Reduce oven to 350 degrees and cook to desired doneness; 40 minutes for rare, 15 to 20 minutes longer for medium, and another 15 to 20 minutes for well done. Remove and keep warm until ready to serve. Serve with Madeira sauce. (See Index)

Glenda Johnson

INDIVIDUAL FILETS OF BEEF IN WINE SAUCE

Preparation: 20 minutes
Cooking: 9 to 12 minutes

Serves: 4

4 lean individual filets of beef, about 6 ounces each
Salt, if desired, and freshly ground pepper to taste
1 tablespoon peanut oil or vegetable oil

3 tablespoons finely chopped shallots
2 tablespoons butter
3/4 cup dry red wine, preferably a mellow Burgundy type

Gently flatten each filet. Sprinkle both sides with salt and pepper. Heat oil in heavy skillet and add meat. Cook over moderately high heat 3 minutes. Turn and cook 3 minutes. Continue cooking and turning every 3 minutes for a total cooking time of 9 to 12 minutes for rare. Remove meat to warm serving dish and pour fat from pan. Add shallots and half the butter. Cook, stirring, 30 seconds. Add wine and bring to boil, stirring to dissolve brown particles that cling to skillet. Cook about 4 minutes or until liquid is reduced to 1/3 cup. Swirl in remaining butter. Strain sauce over filets and serve.

June Rutherford

TERIYAKI STEAK

Preparation: 20 minutes

Serves: 6 to 8

Cooking: To taste

3/4 cup cooking oil
1/4 cup soy sauce
1/4 cup honey
2 tablespoons cider vinegar

2 tablespoons chopped green
   onion
1 large garlic cove, minced
1 1/2 teaspoons ground ginger
2 pounds top round steak or
   London broil

Combine all ingredients and pour over meat. Cover and let marinate at least 24 hours, turning occasionally. Broil or grill to taste, basting with the marinade. May heat marinade and serve on the side.

Madelyn Phillips

STROGANOFF STEAK SANDWICH

Preparation: 30 minutes

Serves: 6

Cooking: 5 to 7 minutes

2/3 cup beer
1/3 cup vegetable oil
1 teaspoon salt
1/4 teaspoon pepper
1/8 teaspoon garlic powder
2 pounds flank steak, 1 1/2 inches
   thick
2 tablespoons butter

1/2 teaspoon paprika
4 cups sliced onion
1 cup sour cream, warmed
1/2 teaspoon horseradish
1 pound fresh mushrooms, sliced
12 slices French bread, toasted
Paprika

In a shallow dish combine beer, oil, salt, garlic powder and pepper. Place flank steak in marinade, cover. Marinate overnight in refrigerator or several hours at room temperature. Drain. Broil flank steak 3 inches from heat or prepare on charcoal grill for 5 to 7 minutes for medium rare. In saucepan, melt butter, blend in paprika and dash salt. Add onion and mushrooms and cook until tender. Add sour cream and horseradish to onion and mushroom mixture, heat thoroughly. Toast bread slices. Arrange bread on serving plate. Arrange layers of meat on bread. Top with sour cream and mushroom sauce. Sprinkle with paprika.

Nan Fogel

REUBEN CASSEROLE

Preparation: 15 minutes
Cooking: 30 minutes

Serves: 8

1³/₄ cups fresh or canned
   sauerkraut, drained
¹/₂ pound thinly sliced cooked
   corned beef
2 cups (¹/₂ pound) shredded Swiss
   cheese
3 tablespoons thousand island
   dressing

2 medium tomatoes, thinly sliced
   (or 2 cups canned tomatoes)
2 tablespoons butter
¹/₂ cup (1 stick) butter
1 cup crumbled, seasoned rye
   wafers
¹/₄ teaspoon caraway seeds

Preheat oven to 425 degrees. Layer sauerkraut in buttered 1¹/₂ quart casserole. Top with sliced corned beef, cheese and dressing. Add tomatoes and dot with 2 tablespoons butter. Melt butter and sauté rye wafers and caraway seeds. Spread on top. Bake 30 minutes or until bubbly.

Pat Blythe

FRENCH ONION BEEF AU JUS

Preparation: 1 hour
Cooking: 3 hours

Serves: 8

3¹/₂ pounds fresh beef brisket
¹/₂ cup soy sauce
2 tablespoons oil
1 clove of garlic
1¹/₂ teaspoons browning sauce
1 teaspoon Beau Monde seasoning
1¹/₄ ounce package onion soup mix

5 cups water
2 large sweet onions, cut ¹/₄ inch
   slices separated in rings
¹/₄ cup butter
2 cups water
4 French rolls, sliced lengthwise
   buttered
Grated Gruyere or Swiss cheese

Combine soy sauce, oil, garlic, browning sauce and Beau Monde seasoning in blender. Blend on medium until smooth. Add onion soup mix and 5 cups water. Blend on low until just mixed. Place brisket in 3¹/₂ to 4 quart baking casserole or Dutch oven. Pour soy sauce mixture over beef. Cover tightly and cook in 350 degree oven for 2 hours. Meanwhile lightly brown onion rings in butter. Add to beef. Continue cooking covered 1 hour or until beef is tender. Remove brisket from cooking liquid and let stand 20 minutes before carving. Add 2 cups water to cooking liquid. Keep hot. Carve brisket across grain into thin slices. Return slices to cooking liquid. Toast roll halves in broiler. To serve, place hot beef slices and liquid on top of rolls. Sprinkle with cheese and broil just until cheese melts.

Nancy Durham

GOLFER'S SPECIAL

Preparation: 15 minutes
Cooking: 4 hours

Serves: 8

1½ pound stew beef
1 medium onion, diced
4 carrots
4 potatoes, sliced (large)
½ teaspoon lemon pepper

½ teaspoon salt, or to taste
1 teaspoon sugar
1 tablespoon cornstarch
1 (12-ounce) can V-8 juice

Cut meat into small pieces, cutting off fat. Put meat into bottom of greased casserole. Layer onions, carrots, and potatoes on top. Add lemon pepper and salt. Sprinkle with sugar and cornstarch. Pour V-8 juice over all. Cover with foil. Bake 4 hours at 250 degrees.

Cooks while you play a round of golf!

Sybil Sullivan

ORIENTAL STIR-FRY

Preparation: 25 minutes
Cooking: 10 minutes

Serves: 6

1½ pounds boneless round steak
¼ cup firmly packed brown sugar
¼ cup water
¼ cup soy sauce
2 tablespoons Worcestershire
    sauce
½ teaspoon minced garlic
1 tablespoon vegetable oil

1½ cup diagonally sliced carrots
1½ cup diagonally sliced celery
1 cup chopped onion
1 tablespoon vegetable oil
1 tablespoon cornstarch
1 cup uncooked regular rice,
    cooked

Slice thinly across grain of partially-frozen steak. Combine next 5 ingredients, mixing well. Pour into bowl. Add steak and cover. Marinate 4 to 6 hours in refrigerator. Stir occasionally. Pour 1 tablespoon oil around top of preheated wok, coating sides. Heat on medium for 2 minutes. Add carrots, celery, and onion. Stir fry 4 minutes. Remove and set aside. Add 1 tablespoon oil to wok. Drain steak, reserving marinade. Add steak to wok. Stir fry just until browned. Combine cornstarch and marinade. Stir into steak. Cook, stirring constantly until thickened. Combine vegetables and meat, tossing gently. Place on serving dish. Spoon steak mixture over rice.

Juanita Linton

BUSHILONA
(STUFFED ROUND STEAK)

Preparation: 45 minutes
Cooking: 1½ hours or more

Serves: 8

1 large onion, chopped
¼ cup chopped parsley
¼ cup chopped celery
2 cloves of garlic, minced
½ cup Parmesan cheese
¼ cup dry bread crumbs

2 round steaks, thinly sliced
Salt and pepper, to taste
2 (6-ounce) cans tomato paste
3 tablespoons sugar
1 (8-ounce) can tomato sauce

Sprinkle onion, parsley, celery, garlic, cheese and crumbs over steaks. Salt and pepper to taste. Pound steaks with a mallet or use tenderizer to insure tenderness. Roll steaks. Tie with twine or secure with poultry pins. Brown evenly in a small amount of hot fat. Remove from fat. Cook tomato paste in hot fat for 5 minutes. Add sugar and cook for 15 minutes. Add tomato sauce. Stir thoroughly. Return steaks to skillet immersing in tomato sauce. Cook for one hour and thirty minutes or until tender. Add water if needed.

Elissa Fuchs

RIBEYE ROAST

Preparation: 20 minutes
Cooking: 60 minutes

Serves: 8

6 to 8 pound rib eye roast
8 to 10 thick slices fresh ginger
  root
3 or 4 tablespoons peanut or
  vegetable oil

1½ cups soy sauce
2 or 3 cloves garlic, sliced

Place meat in a very large plastic bag. Mix ginger root, oil and soy sauce and add to bag. Squeeze out all air and tie securely. Place in pan in case the bag leaks. Marinate for at least 24 hours, turning often. Before roasting, remove meat from bag, make small gashes in meat and insert slices of garlic and ginger. Roast in 500 degree oven for 35 to 40 minutes. Turn off heat and allow to stand in closed oven 20 minutes. Remove from oven, place on platter and allow to stand for 10 additional minutes before carving.

Emily Preyer

GINGER BEEF

Preparation: 15 minutes   Serves: 4
Cooking: 1$^1/_2$ to 2 hours

2 onions, chopped
1 clove garlic, chopped
1$^1/_2$ teaspoons tumeric
4 teaspoons powdered ginger
1$^1/_2$ teaspoons salt

1$^1/_4$ pounds flank steak or chuck
    roast, cut in strips
$^1/_2$ cup vegetable oil
1 cup canned tomatoes, drained
1 can condensed onion soup

Combine onions, garlic, tumeric, ginger, and salt with beef and let stand for 1 hour. Heat oil in a heavy pan and sauté beef mixture. Add tomatoes and onion soup. Cover and simmer 1$^1/_2$ to 2 hours, adding water if the mixture appears too dry. Serve with hot rice.

Carol Betts

SIRLOIN SESAME STEAK

Preparation: 10 minutes   Serves: 8
Cooking: To taste

$^1/_2$ cup salad oil
$^1/_3$ cup sesame seeds
4 medium onions, thickly sliced
$^1/_2$ cup soy sauce
$^1/_4$ cup lemon juice
1 tablespoon sugar

$^1/_4$ teaspoon cracked pepper
2 garlic cloves, crushed
1 boneless beef top sirloin steak
    cut 1 to 1$^1/_2$ inches thick (about
    2$^1/_2$ to 3 pounds)

In 10 inch skillet, over medium high heat, cook sesame seeds in hot oil until golden. Stir frequently. In 9 × 13 inch baking dish, mix well sesame seed oil mixture, onions, soy sauce, lemon juice, sugar, pepper, and garlic. Push onions aside and add steak. Turn to coat both sides. Cover steak with the onions. Cover with plastic wrap and refrigerate 4 to 5 hours, turning steak occasionally. To cook: Remove steak from marinade sauce and charcoal to desired doneness on grill. Pour marinade and onions into a saucepan and heat until hot. Serve over steak.

Happy Waller

CHINESE STEAK AND BROCCOLI

Preparation: 15 minutes   Serves: 6
Cooking: To taste

2 pound sirloin steak (can use   ³/₄ pound fresh mushroooms
  flank steak)   (thickly sliced)
1 tablespoon cornstarch   3 tablespoons dry sherry
2 tablespoons soy sauce   Chinese oyster sauce (few drops or
3 tablespoons peanut oil   more according to taste)
1 head broccoli (use top 2 inches   1 bunch chopped green onions
  of florets)   including tops

Slice meat on bias into uniform slices. Put into bowl. Mix cornstarch and soy sauce together. Pour over meat and stir to coat well. Marinate, unrefrigerated, at least 5 hours. About 5 minutes before serving, heat oil in wok. Add meat and stir until well coated with oil. Stir in broccoli and mushrooms. Add wine and sauces and stir until heated through. Add extra soy sauce if needed. Sprinkle each serving with chopped green onions.

Irene Mnick

STUFFED BELL PEPPERS

Preparation: 30 minutes   Serves: 6
Cooking: 30 minutes

4 medium to large bell peppers   1 teaspoon tamari (soy sauce)
1 egg   1 cup shredded cheese
¹/₂ pound ground beef   1 cup tomato sauce
2 cups cooked brown rice   3 or 4 tablespoons sunflower seeds
1 teaspoon prepared horseradish

Steam peppers (halved) for 5 minutes, or microwave. Arrange cut side up in a shallow baking dish. Sauté ground beef until cooked through. In large bowl, beat egg slightly and add cooked rice, ground beef, horseradish, tamari and half of the cheese. Mix together lightly and pile into pepper shells. Bake at 350 degrees for 15 minutes. When heated through, remove stuffed peppers from oven, pour tomato sauce over tops, and sprinkle with remaining half of the cheese and the sunflower seeds. Return to oven for 15 minutes more.

Kathryn Lambeth

LONDON BROIL WITH SOUR CREAM MARINADE

Preparation: 15 minutes

1 (8-ounce) carton sour cream	2 tablespoons red wine vinegar
3/4 cup soy sauce	1/4 cup Worcestershire sauce
1/2 teaspoon parsley	1/2 cup mayonnaise and 1/2 cup
1/2 teaspoon garlic	buttermilk mixed together
1 1/2 cup vegetable oil	

Mix all ingredients (except mayonnaise and buttermilk) in blender. Add mayonnaise and buttermilk mixture to thin, as needed. Marinate London broil for two hours. Cook to desired doneness on grill or broil in oven. Heat remaining marinade for sauce.

Donna Thornton

MEATBALLS, STROGANOFF STYLE

Preparation: 30 minutes
Cooking: 15 minutes

Serves: 6

1 1/2 pounds ground beef	2 tablespoons flour
1/4 cup fine dry bread crumbs	1 bouillon cube, dissolved in 1 cup
1/3 cup ice water	boiling water
1 teaspoon grated lemon rind	2 tablespoons catsup
Salt and pepper	1/2 cup dairy sour cream
1/4 cup minced onion	Chopped parsley
1 tablespoon butter or margarine	1 (6-ounce) package yellow rice
1 (3-ounce) can sliced mushrooms, drained (reserve liquid)	

Mix lightly first 4 ingredients. Add 1 1/2 teaspoons salt, 1/4 teaspoon pepper and 2 tablespoons onion. Shape in 18 balls and brown slowly in butter. Remove meatballs and sauté remaining onion and mushrooms in drippings in skillet. Blend in flour. Gradually add mushroom liquid and bouillon. Bring to boil, stirring. Add meatballs, cover and simmer about 15 minutes. Remove meatballs to hot serving dish. Stir catsup and sour cream into liquid in skillet, heat, and correct seasonings. Serve over yellow rice garnished with parsley.

Pat Blythe

SOUTH OF THE BORDER HOT CHILI CON CARNE

Preparation: 30 minutes   Serves: 8
Cooking: 1 hour

2½ pounds ground beef
2 large green peppers, chopped
2 (16-ounce) cans tomatoes
3 cans hot kidney beans
2 teaspoons pepper
3 bay leaves
2 large onions, chopped

1 large red pepper, chopped
2 (8-ounce) cans tomato sauce
3 teaspoons salt
4 tablespoons chili powder
2 teaspoons Worcestershire
1 bag Fritos
2 cups cheddar cheese (grated)

In a large heavy pot, cook meat, onions and peppers, until meat is browned and vegetables are tender. Stir in other ingredients except Fritos and cheese. Cook until all are mixed well and hot. Simmer for one hour, uncovered. Freezes well and gets better each time it is served. Break up Fritos in individual bowls, serve chili and top with cheese.

Charlotte Barney

GROUND BEEF AND NOODLE CASSEROLE

Preparation: 30 minutes   Serves: 6 to 8
Cooking: 20 minutes

1 onion, chopped
1 pound hamburger
3 cups tomato juice
1 teaspoon salt
1½ teaspoons celery salt

2 teaspoons Worcestershire sauce
3 cups uncooked noodles
⅓ cup mushrooms, canned or fresh
1 cup sour cream

In sauce pan, cook chopped onion and hamburger until meat begins to turn brown. Drain excess liquid. Place uncooked noodles over meat. Combine tomato juice, salt, celery salt, Worcestershire sauce and pour over noodles. Bring to boil, cover and simmer over low heat about 20 to 25 minutes. Add mushrooms and sour cream. Heat thoroughly but do not boil.

Barbara Kretzer

CRESCENT LASAGNE

Preparation: 30 minutes
Cooking: 20 to 25 minutes

Serves: 4 to 6

Meat filling:
1/2 pound sausage
1/2 pound ground beef
3/4 cup chopped onion
1/2 clove garlic, minced
1 tablespoon parsley flakes
1 (6-ounce) can tomato paste
1/2 teaspoon basil
1/2 teaspoon leaf oregano
1/2 teaspoon salt
Dash pepper

Cheese filling:
1 cup creamed cottage cheese
1/2 cup grated Parmesan cheese
1 egg

Crust:
2 cans refrigerated crescent rolls
2 slices 7 × 4 inch Mozzarella
  cheese
1 tablespoon milk
1 tablespoon sesame seed

In large skillet, brown meat and drain. Add onion, garlic, parsley, tomato paste and seasonings. Simmer, uncovered for five minutes. Combine cottage cheese, egg and Parmesan cheese. Unroll crescent dough and separate into eight rectangles. Place rectangles of dough together on ungreased cookie sheet, overlapping edges slightly to form a 15 × 13 inch rectangle. Press edges and perforations to seal. Spread half of meat filling lengthwise down center half of dough to within one inch of each 13-inch end. Top meat filling with cheese filling. Spoon remaining meat filling over top, forming 3 layers. Place cheese slices over meat filling. Fold 13-inch ends of dough rectangle over filling one inch. Pull long sides of dough rectangle over filling, being careful to overlap edges only 1/4 inch. Pinch overlapped edges to seal. Brush with milk, sprinkle with sesame seed. Bake at 375 degrees for 20 to 25 minutes or until deep golden brown.

Pat Blythe

PIZZA MEAT LOAVES

Preparation: 15 minutes
Cooking: 40 minutes

Serves: 4

1 pound ground beef
2 cups bread crumbs
1 (8-ounce) can pizza sauce

1 cup (4 ounces) mozzarella,
  shredded
1 (4-ounce) can mushrooms,
  drained and chopped

Combine meat, bread, 1/2 cup sauce, 1/2 cup cheese and mushrooms. Mix lightly. Shape meat mixture into four loaves. Place in shallow baking dish. Bake at 350 degrees for 30 minutes. Brush with remaining sauce, sprinkle with remaining cheese, and bake additional 10 minutes.

Lucy Hilder

MUSHROOM/ALMOND RICE STUFFING

Preparation: 15 minutes
Cooking: 20 to 25 minutes

Yield: 4 cups

6 to 8 fresh mushrooms, sliced
4 tablespoons sliced (or slivered) almonds
4 tablespoons finely chopped onions
2/3 cup uncooked long-grained rice

6 tablespoons butter
2 cups water
2 chicken bouillon cubes
2 teaspoons lemon juice
1 teaspoon salt (optional)

In saucepan, cook mushrooms, almonds, onions, and rice in butter for 5 to 10 minutes, stirring frequently. Add water, bouillon cubes, lemon juice, and salt. Bring mixture to boiling, stirring to dissolve bouillon cubes. Reduce heat, cover and cook slowly about 20 to 25 minutes or until liquid is absorbed and rice is fluffy.

Perfect stuffing for Cornish hen and other fowl.

Susan Huittt

MADEIRA SAUCE

Preparation: 10 minutes
Cooking: 15 minutes

Serves: 4 to 6

7 tablespoons butter
3 tablespoons flour
2 cups beef stock (canned)

1/2 cup Madeira wine
2 cups fresh mushrooms, sliced

Melt 3 tablespoons of butter and mix with flour. Brown and stir until smooth. Add beef stock and wine. Stir until thick. Cook 15 minutes over medium heat. In separate pan, sauté mushrooms in 4 tablespoons butter. Add to sauce. Serve warm over beef tenderloin or steak.

Glenda Johnson

TARTAR SAUCE

Preparation: 10 minutes

Yield: 1 1/4 cups

1 cup mayonnaise
1 1/2 tablespoons sweet pickle cubes
1 teaspoon dill weed

1 1/2 tablespoons capers
1 1/2 tablespoons minced onion
1/8 teaspoon salt

Combine all ingredients, mixing well. Chill several hours before serving.

June Rutherford

MUSHROOM-WINE SAUCE

Preparation: 10 to 15 minutes   Serves: 6 to 8
Cooking: 10 minutes

1/2 pound fresh mushrooms, sliced   1 cup beef broth
1 large onion, chopped   1 tablespoon Dijon mustard
1/4 cup margarine or butter   Pinch thyme and savory
2 tablespoons flour   Salt, pepper to taste
1 cup red wine

Sauté onions and mushrooms in margarine. Sprinkle with flour. Gradually stir in wine, beef broth, mustard and herbs. Stir until thick. Simmer 10 minutes. Season with salt and pepper. This sauce is excellent served over marinated flank or London Broil

Happy Waller

VELOUTE SAUCE

Preparation: 15 minutes   Yield: 1 1/2 cups
Cooking: 1 hour

2 tablespoons butter   1/4 cup mushrooms, minced
2 tablespoons flour   Pinch of nutmeg
2 cups chicken stock   Salt and white pepper to taste

Melt butter in top of double boiler (not aluminum) and stir in flour. When blended, slowly add stock and thicken. Add mushrooms and simmer in double boiler, for about 1 hour. Add nutmeg to taste.

Marian Ferrel

SPICED ORANGE SLICES

Preparation: 20 minutes   Yield: 1 quart
Cooking: 50 minutes

4 seedless oranges cut into 1/2   6 cloves
inch slices   1/2 cup white vinegar
2 cups sugar   1 cinnamon stick
1/4 cup water   3 whole allspice

Discard the stem and blossom ends of each orange. Put orange slices in large heavy pot. Add water to cover. Simmer slices, covered, for one hour. Meanwhile make syrup in fairly large saucepan by combining the sugar, vinegar, water and spices. Boil the syrup for 5 minutes. When orange slices have simmered the hour, transfer them with a slotted spatula to the syrup. Simmer for 45 minutes, basting every 10 minutes. Transfer slices with slotted spoon to 1 quart wide mouth jar. Pour syrup over them. Cover and chill. Serve with poultry, roast pork or ham. Keeps well in refrigerator.

Martha Long

The Southern Railway Station was officially opened on June 9, 1899. It quickly became a source of pride for the city of Greensboro. Train passengers enjoyed the grand experience of the dining car and Greensboro residents purchased the meats, fruits and vegetables of other regions delivered to them by rail. Like the crates of vegetables delivered to the station, our vegetable recipes are endless in variety and combination.

Vegetables

SOUTHERN RAILWAY
STATION

POTATOES SAYONARD

Preparation: 40
Cooking: 55 to 60 minutes

Serves: 8 to 10

2½ pounds potatoes
6 tablespoons butter
2 tablespoons chopped fresh
 parsley

1 teaspoon salt
⅛ teaspoon pepper
1 cup grated Swiss cheese
1¼ cups boiling chicken broth

Peel potatoes and slice thinly. Keep covered in cold water until ready to assemble. Preheat oven to 425 degrees. Grease a shallow 2 quart baking dish with butter. Drain potatoes and dry with paper towels. Put half of potatoes in pan, overlapping. Dot with butter, half the parsley, salt, pepper and half the cheese. Repeat layers. Pour boiling broth over all. Bake 55 to 60 minutes at 425 degrees until potatoes are fork tender, top is browned and broth absorbed.

A good make-ahead recipe!

Emily Pernice

GOURMET POTATOES

Preparation: 25 minutes
Cooking: 25 minutes

Serves: 8

6 medium potatoes
¼ cup butter
3 cups shredded cheddar cheese
1½ cups sour cream

⅓ cup chopped green onions
¼ teaspoon pepper
1 teaspoon salt

Cook potatoes in skins. Cool. Peel and coarsely shred. Combine cheese and butter in pan over low heat, stirring until almost melted. Remove from heat and blend in sour cream, onions, salt and pepper. Fold in potatoes and turn into 8 inch square greased casserole. Bake 25 minutes at 350 degrees.

Donna Tibbals

CREAMY CHEESE POTATOES

Preparation: 15 minutes
Cooking: 30 minutes

Serves: 4 to 6

1¼ cups milk
1 (8-ounce) package cream
  cheese, softened
1 tablespoon snipped chives
½ teaspoon instant minced onion

½ teaspoon salt
4 cups cubed, cooked potatoes (5
  medium potatoes)
Paprika

In medium saucepan, over low heat, blend milk into cream cheese. If necessary, beat until smooth with rotary beater. Stir in chives, onion and salt. Add cubed potatoes. Stir carefully to coat. Turn potato-cheese mixture into 1½ quart casserole. Sprinkle with paprika. Bake in moderate oven at 350 degrees for 30 minutes. (Or, cook in saucepan over low heat until heated through.) Serve immediately.

Joy Morrison

NEW POTATOES WITH SOUR CREAM AND CAVIAR

Preparation: 30 minutes
Cooking: 20 minutes

Serves: 6

12 unpeeled new potatoes, 1 to 1½
  inches in diameter, thoroughly
  scrubbed
Salt
1 to 2 tablespoons finely chopped
  onions or scallions

Freshly ground black pepper
¾ cup sour cream
1 tablespoon black or red caviar,
  to taste
1 tablespoon finely chopped
  parsley

Place potatoes into a 2 quart saucepan of boiling water. Over moderate heat, cook uncovered for 15 to 20 minutes, or until they offer no resistance when pierced with the top of a sharp knife. Drain immediately, and pat potatoes dry with paper towels. Using a melon scoop or teaspoon, neatly scoop out about ⅓ of each potato, and lightly sprinkle the opening with salt. Fill with about ¼ teaspoon of the chopped onions or scallions, a few grindings of black pepper and about 1 tablespoon of sour cream, or a little less than the cavities will hold. Top with about ¼ teaspoon caviar and sprinkle with a little chopped parsley. Serve warm.

Louise Glover

CABBAGE CASSEROLE

Preparation: 35 minutes
Cooking: 30 to 40 minutes

Serves: 6 to 8

1 (10¾-ounce) can cream of celery
  soup
1 cup milk
½ cup mayonnaise
1 stick butter, melted
1 cup crushed cornflakes

4 cups shredded cabbage
Salt and pepper to taste
1 cup sharp grated cheese
½ cup crushed cornflakes
  (topping)

In saucepan, combine and heat soup, milk, mayonnaise and butter. Bring to a boil. Put crushed cornflakes in bottom of 9 × 12 inch pan or 1½ quart casserole dish. Spread shredded cabbage on top of cornflakes. Salt and pepper to taste. Pour hot liquid over cabbage and top with grated cheese and additional ½ cup of crushed cornflakes. Bake at 350 degrees 30 to 40 minutes.

Debbie Bielski

VEGETABLES WITH CURRY

Preparation: 15 minutes
Cooking: 30 minutes

Serves: 8 to 12

1 (10-ounce) package frozen string
  beans
1 (10-ounce) package frozen
  carrots
1 (10-ounce) package frozen
  cauliflower
4 tablespoons flour
4 tablespoons melted butter

2 cups milk
Salt and pepper
Dash of curry
Bacon bits (cooked and drained)
  or crushed Ritz crackers for
  topping, if desired

Cook cauliflower, carrots, and string beans until almost done. Make a medium thick cream sauce with the flour, melted butter and milk. Add dash of curry, salt and pepper to sauce. Pour drained string beans, carrots, cauliflower into creamed curry sauce. Bake at 350 degrees for 30 minutes. Bacon bits or crushed Ritz crackers may be placed on top just before removing from oven.

Bobbie Covington

PARMESAN BRUSSELS SPROUTS

Preparation: 20 minutes
Cooking: 8 to 10 minutes

Serves: 4

2 pints brussels sprouts, washed, trimmed, outer leaves removed
Salted water
3/4 cup diced bacon, blanched
2 tablespoons butter
1 tablespoon oil
3/4 cup diced onion

Salt and freshly ground pepper, to taste
1 tablespoon flour
8 tablespoons cream
4 tablespoons parsley, chopped
4 tablespoons Parmesan cheese, grated

Cut a deep cross in the stem ends of sprouts and cook in boiling salted water to cover, about 8 to 10 minutes or until just tender. Drain. Sauté blanched bacon in butter and oil. When crisp, add onions and sauté until wilted. Season with salt and pepper. Add flour and whisk well. Add cream and parsley and remove from heat. When sprouts are tender, toss in cream sauce. Place in a serving dish and sprinkle with Parmesan cheese.

Trish Green

TOMATO PIE

Preparation: 10 minutes
Cooking: 20 to 25 minutes

Serves: 8

1 9-inch pie shell, baked
3 to 5 peeled, sliced, and drained tomatoes
1/2 cup mayonnaise
2 cups sharp cheddar cheese, grated
1/4 cup chopped onion

1/2 teaspoon basil
Salt and pepper to taste

Topping:
8 Ritz crackers, crumbled
2 teaspoons butter, melted

Arrange tomato slices in bottom of baked pie shell. Sprinkle with salt and pepper. Mix mayonnaise, cheese, basil and onion. Spread over tomatoes. Top with cracker crumbs which have been mixed with butter. Bake at 400 degrees for 35 minutes. Serve immediately. Pie crust may be omitted and tomatoes placed directly in a glass pie plate or baking dish if desired. An excellent variation of this recipe is to substitute 1/2 cup Parmesan cheese for the 2 cups of sharp cheese and omit the onion.

Hughlene Frank

SUMMER SQUASH CASSEROLE

Preparation: 30 minutes
Cooking: 45 minutes

Serves: 8

1 pound yellow squash
1 medium onion
1 teaspoon salt
1½ cups grated sharp cheese
¼ stick butter or margarine

1 egg
¼ cup milk
8 Ritz crackers
2 tablespoons grated sharp cheese

Slice squash, dice onion, and cook until tender in small amount of water. Drain. Place squash in medium to large mixing bowl and mash. While still very hot, add grated cheese and butter. Mash and stir until melted. Slightly beat egg and milk together. Stir into squash mixture, adding pepper to taste. Add crushed crackers. Pour into buttered casserole. Sprinkle with two tablespoons cheese. Cook in 350 degree oven until set and browned, about 45 minutes.

Cissy Hall

FANCY BRUSSELS SPROUTS

Preparation: 15 minutes

Serves: 8

1 (13¾-ounce) can beef broth
1 can water
2 (10-ounce) packages frozen
   Brussels sprouts
2 ounces butter
4 strips bacon, cut in pieces

2 large onions, chopped
2 fresh tomatoes, peeled and
   seeded
1 teaspoon basil
½ teaspoon salt
1 teaspoon lemon pepper

Cook frozen brussels sprouts in broth and water just until tender. Remove from heat and drain. In a separate pan, melt butter. Cook bacon strips in butter just until brown. Add chopped onion and sauté until golden. (Can stop at this point and hold until serving time.) When ready to serve, squeeze juice and seeds out of tomatoes and cut into cubes. Add brussels sprouts, along with the onion mixture and seasonings. Heat and serve.

Lynn Beauchamp

HOLIDAY RELISH

Preparation: 15 minutes

Serves: 6 to 8

1 pound raw cranberries, ground
2 apples, chopped
Juice of 2 oranges

1 (8-ounce) can crushed pineapple
1 cup chopped pecans
2¾ cups sugar

Combine all ingredients and refrigerate. A food processor makes preparing this recipe a breeze!

Barbara Giles

SQUASH CASSEROLE WITH PEANUTS

Preparation: 25 minutes
Cooking: 50 minutes

Serves: 6 to 8

2 pounds squash, cubed and
    cooked
½ teaspoon salt
2 tablespoons butter
Dash of pepper

1 small onion, grated
1 cup whipping cream, unwhipped
¼ cup dry bread crumbs
1 cup salted peanuts, chopped
4 strips bacon, fried and crumbled

Cook squash covered in small amount of salted water until tender, about 15 minutes. Drain well and add salt, butter, dash of pepper, grated onion and whipping cream. Butter sides and bottom of baking dish and dust with the bread crumbs. Pour squash mixture into 8 × 8 inch casserole dish and bake in preheated 350 degree oven for 50 minutes. Fry 4 strips bacon until crisp; then crumble. Mix 1 cup chopped salted peanuts with the crumbled bacon. Top casserole with nut and bacon mixture immediately before serving.

Anne Kirkman

POSH SQUASH

Preparation: 25 minutes
Cooking: 30 minutes

Serves: 6 to 8

2 pounds yellow squash
1 cup mayonnaise
¼ green pepper, chopped
Salt and pepper to taste

2 eggs, well beaten
1 small onion, chopped
¾ cup grated Parmesan cheese
Buttered bread crumbs

Simmer squash till barely tender. Drain. Add all ingredients except crumbs to beaten eggs. Pour into greased baking dish. Top with buttered bread crumbs, if desired. Bake 30 minutes at 350 degrees.

Pat Blythe

PINEAPPLE CASSEROLE

Preparation: 30 minutes
Cooking: 30 minutes

Serves: 8 to 10

2 (16-ounce) cans chunk
   pineapple, drained
6 tablespoons flour
1 cup sugar

2 cups grated sharp cheddar
   cheese
1 stick butter
1 stack (33) Ritz or Towne House
   crackers, crushed

Mix together pineapple, flour, sugar and cheese until flour is moistened. Spread in 9 × 13 inch baking dish. Sprinkle with crushed crackers. Dot with butter. Bake at 350 degrees for 25 to 30 minutes. Serve warm. May be put together the night before and cooked just before serving.

Sylvia Smith

AMBROSIAL APRICOTS

Preparation: 10 minutes
Cooking: 25 to 30 minutes

Serves: 6 to 8

2 (17-ounce) cans apricot halves
   (drain and save liquid)
1 stick margarine, melted

1/2 cup brown sugar
3 to 4 tablespoons apricot juice
Ritz cracker crumbs

Cook margarine, brown sugar and apricot juice on low heat until thick. Arrange apricots in dish and pour thickened sauce over them. Bake 15 to 20 minutes at 375 degrees. Remove from oven. Top with Ritz cracker crumbs. Return to oven to brown, about 5 minutes. Serve hot.

Betty Ellington

ASPARAGUS PUFF

Preparation: 15 minutes
Cooking: 35 to 40 minutes

Serves: 8

1 (14 1/2-ounce) can asparagus,
   drained and chopped
1 cup Ritz crackers, crumbled
1 cup sharp cheese, grated
2 pimentos, chopped (optional)

2 cups milk
3 eggs, beaten
1 teaspoon salt
6 tablespoons butter, melted

Combine crackers, cheese, pimentos, milk, eggs, salt and butter in bowl. Place asparagus in 9 × 13 inch casserole dish. Pour mixture over asparagus. Fold ingredients together lightly. Bake at 350 degrees for 35 to 40 minutes.

Sylvia Smith

HOT CRANBERRY RELISH

Preparation: 15 minutes   Serves: 10 to 12
Cooking: 1 hour

3/4 cup sugar, add more if needed
3 medium unpeeled cooking
    apples, sliced
2 cups cranberries
1/4 teaspoon salt

Topping:
1 stick margarine
1 cup oatmeal
1/3 cup flour
1/2 cup brown sugar
1/4 to 1/2 cup chopped pecans
    (optional)

In a 2 quart greased casserole, layer half of the apples, cranberries, salt and
sugar. Repeat layers. Mix topping ingredients and spread on top. Bake at
350 degrees for 1 hour, or until done.

Nancy Beard

CARROTS AND HORSERADISH

Preparation: 20 minutes   Serves: 6 to 8
Cooking: 20 minutes

6 cooked carrots, cut in lengthwise
    strips
1/4 cup carrot liquid
2 tablespoons grated onions
2 tablespoons prepared
    horseradish
1/2 cup mayonnaise

1/2 teaspoon salt
1/4 teaspoon pepper
1/4 cup fine breadcrumbs
1 tablespoon butter
Dash of paprika
Parsley

Spread cooked carrots, cut in lengthwise strips, in shallow baking dish. Mix
the following ingredients and pour over carrots: carrot liquid, grated onions,
prepared horseradish, mayonnaise, salt and pepper. Top mixture with
breadcrumbs, mixed with butter and paprika. Bake for 20 minutes in 375
degree oven. Garnish with parsley.

Sally Cone

BROWN RICE WITH GRAPES

Preparation: 15 minutes
Cooking: 1 hour

Serves: 8

2 cups brown rice, washed well
4 cups chicken stock
1 tablespoon butter
1/4 teaspoon salt
Freshly ground pepper, to taste

1 bouquet garni: bay leaf, celery,
   thyme, parsley
1 cup halved and seeded red grapes

Place stock, butter, salt, pepper, and bouquet garni in medium sized saucepan. Bring to a boil and add rice, stirring to distribute well. Reduce heat, cover and simmer about 1 hour. At the end of the cooking time, add prepared grapes. Serve from an attractive glass or crystal bowl, garnished with frosted grapes or grape leaves.

Tricia Green

CURRIED OYSTER AND WILD RICE CASSEROLE

Preparation: 20 minutes
Cooking: 45 minutes

Serves: 10 to 12

1 pint oysters, drained
3/4 cup cooked Uncle Ben's Wild
   Rice Mix
1 teaspoon curry powder
1/4 cup hot water
Dash Tabasco
Salt and pepper to taste

1/2 cup butter
3/4 can cream of chicken soup,
   heated
3/4 cup Half-and-Half
3/4 tablespoon onion powder
1/2 teaspoon thyme

Dissolve curry powder in 1/4 cup hot water. Spread 1/2 cup rice on bottom of casserole. Layer drained oysters, salt and pepper, and a little Tabasco. Top with remaining rice. Combine butter, curry water, chicken soup, half and half, onion powder and thyme. Pour over rice. Bake 300 degrees for 45 minutes. Serve immediately.

Delicious served with country ham.

Sally Cone

150

BAKED SPINACH RICE

Preparation: 20 minutes
Cooking: 45 minutes

Serves: 6 to 8

3 cups cooked rice
2 (10-ounce) packages frozen,
   chopped spinach (cooked and
   drained well)
1/4 cup butter
1 tablespoon grated onion
1/2 teaspoon marjoram

1 cup milk
1/2 cup grated sharp cheddar
   cheese
1/3 cup minced parsley
1 1/4 teaspoon salt
1/2 teaspoon thyme

Carefully stir above ingredients into the cooked rice. Pour into 2 quart casserole. Bake uncovered at 325 degrees for 45 minutes.

Barbara Thompson

WILD RICE WITH SNOW PEAS

Preparation: 20 minutes
Cooking: 15 to 20 minutes

Serves: 8

2 (6-ounce) boxes Uncle Ben's
   long-grain and wild rice
1/2 cup chopped onion
1/3 cup chopped celery
1/4 cup chopped parsley
1/4 cup chopped green pepper
2 tablespoons vegetable oil

1/2 pound fresh mushrooms, sliced
2 tablespoons butter
1 (8-ounce) can water chestnuts,
   sliced
1 (7-ounce) package frozen Chinese
   pea pods, thawed
1/2 cup slivered almonds, toasted

Cook rice according to package directions. Sauté onion, celery, parsley and green pepper in oil until tender. Sauté mushrooms in butter for 5 minutes. Combine the cooked rice, vegetables, mushrooms, water chestnuts and pea pods and toss gently. Spoon into a buttered 2 quart casserole. Dish may be prepared ahead of time to this point. When ready to serve, heat covered in a 350 degree oven for 15 to 20 minutes. Sprinkle with almonds for last 5 minutes of cooking.

Pat Blythe

RICE SURPRISE

Preparation: 15 minutes
Cooking: 25 to 30 minutes

Serves: 12

1 cup Minute Rice
1 pound Monterey Jack cheese
1 cup sour cream
1/2 cup creamy Italian dressing

1 cup sliced water chestnuts
1 Jalepeno pepper, chopped
 (remove seeds)
1 teaspoon pepper juice

Prepare Minute Rice according to package directions. Grate cheese. Mix together and set aside sour cream, salad dressing, water chestnuts, pepper, and pepper juice. Add rice to sour cream mixture. In 3 quart casserole, make two layers of rice mixture with cheese (ending with cheese). Bake at 400 degrees for 25 to 30 minutes.

Susan Franklin

BROCCOLI-PEA CASSEROLE

Preparation: 45 minutes
Cooking: 45 minutes

Serves: 12

3 (10-ounce) packages frozen
 chopped broccoli, cooked and
 drained
1 can LeSeur peas, drained well
1 (10 3/4-ounce) can Cream of
 Mushroom soup
1 cup mayonnaise
1 teaspoon salt
1/2 teaspoon pepper
1/2 teaspoon Worcestershire sauce

2 eggs, beaten
1 medium onion, chopped,
 sauteed, and drained (or 2
 tablespoons minced onion)
1 cup grated sharp cheese

Topping:
1 stick margarine
1 1/4 cup canned bread crumbs

Cook broccoli in boiling water 3 to 4 minutes and drain well. In a bowl, mix soup, mayonnaise, salt, pepper, Worcestershire sauce and egg. Stir vigorously. Add onion and cheese and mix well. Grease a shallow 2-quart baking dish. Spoon a layer of broccoli into the dish and cover with a layer of peas. Top with generous layer of soup mixture. Repeat layers, ending with soup layer.
Topping: In a skillet, melt margarine over low heat. Stir in bread crumbs and brown lightly. Pour desired amount of crumbs over broccoli-soup mixture. Do not put topping on until ready to bake. Bake, uncovered, for 45 minutes at 350 degrees.

Jane Gibson

MUSHROOM CASSEROLE

Preparation: 10 minutes
Cooking: 20 minutes

Serves: 4

1 pound cleaned mushrooms
½ cup melted butter
1 tablespoon marjoram
1 teaspoon minced chives

Salt and pepper
½ cup chicken bouillon
¼ cup dry white wine

Place mushrooms in casserole dish. Mix remaining ingredients and pour over mushrooms. Cover and bake at 350 degrees for 20 minutes.

Hazel Blackwelder

POLYNESIAN CELERY

Preparation: 20 minutes
Cooking: 35 minutes

Serves: 8

4 cups sliced celery
1 can sliced water chestnuts
¼ cup sliced pimentos
1 (10¾-ounce) can cream of
   chicken soup, undiluted

½ cup dry bread crumbs
¼ cup toasted almond slivers
2 tablespoons melted butter

Cook sliced celery in small amount of boiling salted water until crisp tender. Drain. Add water chestnuts, pimento, and soup. Mix and place in a 1 quart casserole. Top with mixture of dry bread crumbs, toasted almond slivers and melted butter. Bake at 350 degrees for 35 minutes.

Terry Lashley

CHARLESTON RICE

Preparation: 5 minutes
Cooking: 1 hour

Serves: 10

1 (7-ounce) package yellow rice
   mix
1 (8-ounce) can sliced water
   chestnuts, drained
1 (2-ounce) jar chopped pimentos,
   drained

1 (8-ounce) can chopped
   mushrooms, drained
1 (10½-ounce) can consomme
1 (10½-ounce) can French onion
   soup
1 stick margarine

Combine all ingredients except margarine in 2-quart casserole dish. Dot with margarine. Bake 350 degrees for 1 hour or until liquid is absorbed.

Nancy Beard
Carol Aplington

SWEET POTATOES IN ORANGE CUPS

Preparation: 1 hour
Cooking: 20 minutes

Serves: 6

3 oranges
2½ cups cooked, mashed sweet
   potatoes
½ cup cream

½ teaspoon salt
1 tablespoon brown sugar
Marshmallows

Preheat oven to 350 degrees. Cut oranges in half and remove pulp. Cut pulp into small pieces. Beat cream with sweet potatoes. Add salt, brown sugar and pulp. Spoon into orange halves. Bake at 350 degrees for 20 minutes. Add marshmallows during last few minutes and bake until golden brown. To ensure upright position of orange cups, slice tip off bottom of each orange half.

Joyce Kiser

AMBROSIA SWEET POTATOES

Preparation: 30 minutes
Cooking: 30 minutes

Serves: 16

7 to 8 medium sized sweet
   potatoes
2 oranges, seeds removed
2 lemons, seeds removed
1 (16-ounce) can crushed
   pineapple

½ cup brown sugar
½ cup melted butter
Shredded coconut
1 (8-ounce) can slice pineapple
Maraschino cherries

Boil sweet potatoes. Cool and slice into ¼ inch slices. Slice lemons and oranges ⅛ inch thick. Alternate potatoes and fruit in layers in 9 × 13 × 2 inch buttered pyrex dish. Combine crushed pineapple, brown sugar and melted butter. Pour over all. Sprinkle with shredded coconut. Decorate with pineapple slices and maraschino cherries. Can be made ahead to this point. Cover with foil and bake at 350 degrees for 30 minutes.

Lucy Major

154

SOPHIA'S EGGPLANT

Preparation: 1 hour
Cooking: 15 minutes

Serves: 8

2 medium eggplants
Olive oil
1 (1-pound) can Italian tomatoes
1 clove garlic, chopped

½ pound Parmesan cheese
1 package sliced Mozzarella
   cheese
1 pound sliced salami

Peel eggplants and slice ¼ inch thick. Cover with lightly salted water. Soak for 30 minutes. Dry. Sauté in oil to a light golden color. In separate pan, simmer tomatoes and garlic in one tablespoon oil until sauce consistency. Layer eggplant, tomato sauce, cheeses and salami in greased casserole. Sprinkle with Parmesan cheese. Bake at 350 degrees for 15 minutes. Serve hot or cold.

Elissa Fuchs

HOT BROCCOLI MOLD

Preparation: 10 minutes
Cooking: 45 to 60 minutes

Serves: 8

1 (10-ounce) package frozen,
   chopped broccoli
3 eggs
1 cup sour cream
1 cup mayonnaise
1 cup sharp cheese, grated

1 teaspoon flour
Salt to taste
4 tablespoons wine vinegar
Pimento slices

Cook broccoli according to package directions. Drain. Beat eggs and add to broccoli. Combine remaining ingredients except pimento, and add broccoli mixture. Line ring mold with waxed paper or spray with vegetable spray. Arrange pimento slices on the bottom. Pour mixture into mold. Place mold in a pan of water and bake at 350 degrees about 45 minutes, or until knife blade is clean when inserted. Unmold and serve.

Judy Murray

155

CHINESE PEA POD CASSEROLE

Preparation: 30 minutes
Cooking: 45 minutes

Serves: 12

1 (10-ounce) package frozen peas
2 cups chopped celery
1 onion, thinly sliced
1 green pepper, thinly sliced
1 cup sliced water chestnuts
1 cup sliced mushrooms, fresh or
   canned

1 (10-ounce) package frozen pea
   pods, slightly thawed
1 (10½-ounce) can mushroom
   soup
1 can Chinese noodles

In a 2 quart casserole dish, layer first seven ingredients in order. Top with soup and noodles. Cook 45 minutes at 350 degrees.

Quick and easy!

Pat Austin

PEA PODS WITH ALMONDS

Preparation: 15 minutes
Cooking: 15 minutes

Serves: 4 to 6

¼ cup chopped green onions with
   tops
2 tablespoons butter
½ pound fresh Chinese pea pods,
   or 16-ounce package frozen pea
   pods
1 cup sliced fresh mushrooms
2 teaspoons cornstarch

⅔ cup cold water
1 teaspoon instant chicken
   bouillon granules
2 teaspoons soy sauce
2 tablespoons slivered almonds,
   toasted

Cook onion in butter until tender. Add pea pods and mushrooms. Toss and cook over high heat 1 minute. Remove from heat. Combine cornstarch and cold water. Stir cornstarch mixture, bouillon granules and soy sauce into pea pods and mushrooms. Cook and stir until vegetable mixture thickens and bubbles. Toss with toasted almonds.

Serve immediately to retain crunchy texture!

Beverly Stocks

GOURMET PEAS

Preparation: 15 minutes

Serves: 4 to 6

1 (16-ounce) package frozen green
  peas
1/2 stick margarine
1 heaping tablespoon chopped
  onion
1/2 cup chopped celery

1/2 cup sliced fresh mushrooms
1 (2-ounce) jar pimentos
1/2 (4-ounce) can water chestnuts,
  sliced

Cook peas according to package instructions. Drain. (Do not overcook. Peas should be bright green.) Melt margarine. Add chopped onion and celery. Cook slightly. (Celery should be crunchy.) Add mushrooms, pimento and chestnuts and heat thouroughly. Pour into drained peas. Mix and serve.

Marge Monroe

PERSON COUNTY CORN PUDDING

Preparation: 15 minutes
Cooking: 20 to 30 minutes

Serves: 8

3 well beaten eggs
5 tablespoons sugar
3 tablespoons butter
1 cup milk

1 (17-ounce) can white cream-style
  corn
Black pepper

Mix all ingredients except pepper. Pour into ungreased 9 × 9 inch casserole. Sift black pepper lightly on top. Cook 20 to 30 minutes in 400 degree preheated oven. Best if removed from oven 30 minutes prior to serving.

Janie Reece

SWEET POTATO PUDDING

Preparation: 45 minutes
Cooking: 50 to 60 minutes

Serves: 12

4 or 5 medium sized sweet
  potatoes (shredded or coarsely
  grated), or 1 (29-ounce) can of
  sweet potatoes mashed
  thoroughly with small mixer
4 eggs

1/4 cup flour
1 cup coconut
2 teaspoons vanilla
2 cups sugar
2 cups milk
1/4 pound melted butter

Beat eggs. Add sugar and beat until stiff. Add other ingredients except potatoes. Mix well and add potatoes. Cook in two well greased 6 × 9 inch baking dishes or one 9 × 13 inch pan, 50 to 60 minutes at 350 degrees.

Doris Robinson

SQUASH PROVENCALE

Preparation: 40 minutes   **Serves: 6 to 8**

1 pound yellow squash
1 medium onion, chopped fine
2 cloves garlic, chopped fine
2 tablespoons olive oil
2 tablespoons butter
1/2 pound fresh tomatoes, skinned
  and diced
1/4 teaspoon thyme

1/2 teaspoon basil
1 teaspoon sugar
1 teaspoon chopped parsley
1 cup Gruyère cheese, grated
1/2 cup Parmesan cheese
Salt and pepper to taste

Sauté onion and garlic in the oil and butter. Add tomato, thyme, basil, sugar, parsley, salt and pepper. Simmer to thicken sauce. Cut squash into rectangular pieces and cook in boiling water until tender but firm. Drain well. Mix tomato sauce and squash. Place in casserole and top with Gruyère cheese and Parmesan. Place under broiler until cheese melts and is bubbly hot. Serve immediately.

Recipe courtesy of Chef Bill Veraldi of T. K. Tripps restaurant.

Judy Mincher

TOMATO-ARTICHOKE CASSEROLE

Preparation: 30 minutes   **Serves: 10**

1/4 cup salad oil
2 cups sliced onion (2 large)
2 cloves garlic, minced
3 green peppers, cut in strips
4 ripe tomatoes, quartered

2 cans artichoke hearts, drained
  and quartered
1/4 teaspoon thyme
Salt and pepper to taste
1 tablespoon parsley

Sauté onion in oil until yellow. Add remaining ingredients, except parsley, and sauté until just tender. Put in serving dish and sprinkle with parsley. Serve immediately.

This dish can also be chilled and served as a cold salad.

Dawn Long

ZUCCHINI ROUNDS

Preparation: 10 minutes   **Serves: 8 to 10**

1/3 cup packaged biscuit mix
1/4 cup grated Parmesan cheese
1/4 teaspoon salt
1/4 teaspoon pepper

1 1/2 teaspoons grated onion
2 slightly beaten eggs
2 tablespoons margarine
2 cup shredded, unpared zucchini

Stir together biscuit mix, cheese, pepper, salt and onion. Stir in eggs until mixture is moistened. Fold in zucchini. Melt margarine in 10-inch skillet over medium heat. Use one tablespoon mixture for each patty. Cook four patties at a time for 3 to 5 minutes on each side or until brown.

Betsy Schweizer

CREAMED SPINACH RING

Preparation: 45 minutes
Cooking: 30 to 35 minutes

Serves: 6 to 8

2 (10-ounce) packages frozen,
   chopped spinach
4 tablespoons butter
1 cup light cream
$^1/_2$ teaspoon sugar
Dash nutmeg
$^1/_2$ cup dry breadcrumbs

Grated Parmesan cheese
$^1/_2$ cup chopped onion
1 teaspoon salt
Dash fresh ground pepper
4 eggs
$^1/_3$ cup grated Swiss cheese

Cook spinach until just defrosted. Put in colander and press out liquid. In large fry pan, cook onions in butter until tender. (Stir to keep from getting too brown.) Add spinach, salt, sugar, nutmeg, pepper and cream. Heat just to boiling point. Remove from heat. In large bowl, beat eggs slightly. Add bread crumbs and Swiss cheese. Gradually stir in spinach mixture. Let mixture remain in bowl until baking time the following day. Also on the day before, heavily grease a 6-cup ring mold with butter. Make liner of wax paper for bottom of pan. Again spread butter over wax paper. Dust sides and bottom of pan with Parmesan cheese. (Press on sides with fingers.) Cover with plastic wrap and put in refrigerator until next day. Turn spinach in to mold. Set mold in pan of hot water in oven. Cover mold with wax paper. Bake at 350 degrees for 30 to 35 minutes, until inserted knife blade comes out clean and mold is firm. Loosen and unmold onto platter. Peel off wax paper. If recipe is doubled, use 7 eggs instead of 8.

Evelyn Sturm

SPINACH ARTICHOKE CASSEROLE

Preparation: 40 minutes
Cooking: 25 minutes

Serves: 8 to 10

2 (10-ounce) packages frozen
   spinach
1 (10-ounce) package artichoke
   hearts

1 bunch green onions, diced
1 stick butter
$^1/_2$ pint sour cream
$^1/_2$ cup Parmesan cheese

Cook spinach and artichokes according to package directions. Drain. Sauté onions in butter. Combine with spinach and artichokes. Add sour cream and cheese. Bake 25 minutes at 350 degrees.

Pat Carter

VEGETABLE STRUDEL

Preparation: 1 hour and 45 minutes
Cooking: 20 to 30 minutes

Serves: 10 to 12

3 cups chopped fresh broccoli
3 cups chopped fresh cauliflower
2½ cups chopped carrots
2 tablespoons butter
1 large onion, coarsely chopped
2 garlic cloves, finely chopped
3 eggs
2 teaspoons minced fresh parsley
1½ teaspoons dried basil, crumbled

1 teaspoon minced fresh tarragon
  or ½ teaspoon dried, crumbled
1 teaspoon salt
Freshly ground pepper
1 pound Swiss or cheddar cheese, shredded
14 phyllo pastry sheets
6 tablespoons butter, melted
Sesame seeds (optional)
Hollandaise sauce

Combine broccoli, cauliflower and carrots in steamer. Place over boiling water and steam until crisp-tender. Let cool slightly. Melt butter in medium skillet over medium heat. Add onion and garlic. Cover and cook, stirring occasionally until golden, about 10 minutes. Let cool slightly. Combine eggs, parsley and seasoning in large bowl and beat well. Add steamed vegetables, onion mixture and shredded cheese. Mix gently but thoroughly. Preheat oven to 375 degrees. Oil a large baking sheet and set aside. Place 1 phyllo sheet on work surface (cover remaining phyllo with plastic wrap to prevent drying). Brush with melted butter. Stack remaining phyllo sheets on top, brushing all but last sheet with butter. Spread vegetable mixture onto dough, leaving 3 inch border on all sides. Fold in short ends of dough; then fold in long sides, overlapping at center. Brush with butter to seal. Carefully transfer strudel to prepared baking sheet. Brush top with butter. Sprinkle with sesame seed, if desired. Bake until golden brown, about 20 to 30 minutes. Transfer to heated platter and serve immediately with hollandaise sauce.

Nan Fogle

SPINACH CASSEROLE

Preparation: 20 minutes
Cooking: 20 to 30 minutes

Serves: 6

2 (10-ounce) packages frozen, chopped spinach
1 (3-ounce) package cream cheese
1 stick butter, halved

1 cup Pepperidge Farm herb dressing
Salt and pepper to taste

Cook spinach according to package directions. Drain. Add cream cheese, half stick of butter and seasonings. Melt remaining half stick of butter and combine with herb dressing. Sprinkle on top of spinach mixture and bake at 350 degrees for 20 to 30 minutes.

Jackie Adams

STUFFED ACORN SQUASH

Preparation: 1 hour   Serves: 6
Cooking: 1 hour

3 acorn squash, unpeeled
1 cup water
1 (15$\frac{1}{4}$-ounce) can crushed
  pineapple, drained
1$\frac{1}{2}$ cups diced apple, unpeeled
1 cup chopped celery

$\frac{1}{2}$ cup butter (not margarine),
  melted
$\frac{1}{2}$ cup brown sugar
$\frac{1}{2}$ teaspoon cinnamon
$\frac{1}{4}$ teaspoon salt
$\frac{1}{2}$ cup walnuts (or pecans)

Cut squash in half and remove seeds. Place (cut side down) in baking dish with 1 cup of water. Bake 45 minutes at 350 degrees. Mix all other ingredients and spoon into baked squash halves. Return to oven and bake an additional 15 to 20 minutes.

Ann Rives

SUMMER GREEN BEANS

Preparation: 30 minutes   Serves: 8
Cooking: 1 hour

1$\frac{1}{2}$ pounds fresh green beans
5 medium tomatoes
1 small onion

1 teaspoon salt
5 slices cooked bacon, crumbled
$\frac{1}{2}$ teaspoon garlic salt

Combine all ingredients except bacon. Bring to a boil, lower heat and cook on low heat for 1 hour. Garnish with cooked bacon bits before serving.

Gail Huggins

CONNOISSEUR'S CASSEROLE

Preparation: 15 minutes   Serves: 8 to 10
Cooking: 45 minutes

1 (12-ounce) can white shoepeg
  corn, drained
1 (16-ounce) can French cut green
  beans, drained
$\frac{1}{2}$ cup celery, chopped
$\frac{1}{2}$ cup onion, chopped
1 (2-ounce) jar pimentos, chopped
$\frac{1}{2}$ cup sour cream
$\frac{1}{2}$ cup sharp cheddar cheese,
  grated

1 (10$\frac{3}{4}$-ounce) can cream of celery
  soup
$\frac{1}{2}$ teaspoon salt
$\frac{1}{2}$ teaspoon pepper

Topping:
1 cup Ritz crackers, crumbled
$\frac{1}{2}$ stick melted butter
$\frac{1}{2}$ cup slivered almonds, optional

Mix all ingredients except topping. Place in 1$\frac{1}{2}$ quart casserole. Combine ingredients for topping and sprinkle over casserole. Bake at 350 degrees for 45 minutes.

Julie Blalock

The film "Painting the Town" was the featured movie at the 1927 opening of the Carolina Theatre. A showplace with its rococo decor and outstanding film presentations, the theatre was truly a "movie palace." Today, meticulous renovation and restoration have restored the charm and elegance of this entertainment center. For those who attend evening events, the "after theatre" supper is often a part of a night out on the town. The salads included here could easily appeal to the most discriminating late night palate.

Salads and Dressings

THE CAROLINA THEATRE

7-UP PARTY SALAD

Preparation: 25 minutes

Serves: 8

1 cup 7-Up
¼ pound marshmallows
1 (3-ounce) package lime gelatin
2 (3-ounce) packages cream
   cheese
1 (20-ounce) can crushed
   pineapple, undrained

¾ cup walnuts or pecans, chopped
1 (8-ounce) carton heavy cream,
   whipped
⅔ cup mayonnaise, as optional
   dressing

Combine 7-Up and marshmallows in saucepan. Cook over medium heat until melted. Add gelatin, stirring until dissolved. Have cream cheese room temperature. Add hot mixture slowly to cream cheese and beat until smooth. Add pineapple and nuts. Chill until partially set. Fold in whipped cream and mix until smooth. Put in ring mold and refrigerate until firm.

Patsy Adams

ORANGE SHERBET SALAD

Preparation: 20 minutes

Serves: 12

2 (3-ounce) packages orange jello
1 cup boiling water
1 pint orange sherbet

1 (8-ounce) carton Cool Whip
1 (11-ounce) can Mandarin orange
   slices, drained

Pour boiling water over jello. Stir until dissolved. Add orange sherbet. Stir until melted. Fold in Cool Whip. Add orange slices. Pour into 9 x 9 inch or 8 x 8 inch pan and refrigerate.

Jeanne Rives

CRANBERRY SALAD

Preparation: 30 minutes

Serves: 12

3 cups cranberries
2 cups water
2½ cups sugar
2 (3-ounce) packages lemon jello

1 cup red grapes, seedless
1 cup chopped walnuts
1 cup crushed pineapple,
   undrained

Cook cranberries, water, sugar until cranberries pop. Dissolve lemon jello in hot cranberries. Add grapes, walnuts, pineapple. Pour into 13 x 9 inch glass pyrex dish. Takes 2 days to set firm.

Mary Elam

CHERRY SALAD

Preparation: 30 minutes   Serves: 12

1 (16-ounce) can tart red pie
   cherries
1 cup sugar
1 (3-ounce) package cherry jello
½ cup cold water
1 envelope plain gelatin

2 oranges (juice and pulp of both
   and grated rind of one)
1 (8-ounce) can crushed pineapple,
   undrained
½ cup chopped pecans

Bring cherries and sugar to boiling point. Add jello to hot mixture. Dissolve gelatin in cold water. Pour hot jello mixture over gelatin and cool. Then add juice and pulp of two oranges and grated rind of one. Add crushed pineapple and broken pecans. Pour into molds and refrigerate until set.

Nancy Beard

BLUEBERRY JELLO MOLD

Preparation: 5 minutes   Serve: 10

1 (6-ounce) package raspberry
   jello
2 cups hot water
1 cup cold water

1 (15-ounce) can blueberries
1 cup sour cream

Dissolve jello in 2 cups hot water. Stir and add one cup of cold water. Put blueberries with syrup and sour cream in blender and blend thoroughly. Mix all ingredients together and place in 2 quart mold, greased with mayonnaise. Refrigerate until time to serve.

Elaine Abrams

APRICOT NECTAR SALAD

Preparation: 10 minutes   Serves: 6

1 (12-ounce) can apricot nectar
Juice of 1 lemon
1 (3-ounce) package lemon jello
Water to add to apricot nectar

1 (16-ounce) can orange and
   grapefruit sections, drained (or
   Mandarin oranges or white
   grapes)

Combine apricot nectar and water to make 2 cups. Heat to boiling and pour over jello. Stir to dissolve. Add lemon juice and fruit. Pour into 5 individual molds or a 2½ cup mold. Chill well until set before serving on lettuce leaf.

Lib Boone

FRUIT SALAD ICE

Preparation: 15 minutes   Serves: 24

1 (20-ounce) can apricots
1 (20-ounce) can crushed
   pineapple
½ cup sugar
3 (10-ounce) packages frozen
   strawberries, thawed

1 (6-ounce) can frozen orange
   juice, thawed
2 tablespoons lemon juice
3 bananas, diced

Drain apricots and crushed pineapple, reserving juice. Add enough water to the juice to make 1 cup of liquid. Heat liquid and sugar until sugar is dissolved. Chop apricots into small pieces. Combine all ingredients. Pour mixture into muffin tins with or without muffin papers. Freeze. Serve frozen on lettuce. May remove from muffin tins and freeze in plastic bags for later use.

Jane Peterson

CHICKEN N' TOMATO ASPIC

Preparation: 15 minutes   Serves: 8 to 10

1 (6-ounce) package lemon jello
1 cup boiling water
1 (24-ounce) can V8 juice
1½ tablespoons creamy-style
   horseradish sauce
2 tablespoons vinegar
1 teaspoon Worcestershire sauce

½ teaspoon salt
2 (5-ounce) cans chunk white
   chicken, chopped
½ cup green pepper, chopped fine
½ cup celery, chopped fine
¼ cup stuffed green olives, sliced
   (optional)

Topping:
½ cup mayonnaise
1 teaspoon curry powder

1 tablespoon creamy-style
   horseradish sauce
Paprika for color, if desired

Dissolve jello in boiling water. Mix together V8 juice and horseradish sauce until smooth. Slowly add jello mixture, blending well. Stir in vinegar, Worcestershire sauce and salt. Pour into a 9 x 9 inch dish and chill mixture until slightly thickened. Carefully fold in chicken, green pepper, celery and olives. Chill until set. Cut into squares and serve on a bed of lettuce. If desired, garnish with a spoonful of topping, blended well, and sprinkled with paprika.

Jane Gibson

RUBY PEARS

Preparation: 30 minutes   Serves: 12

1 (6-ounce) package   6 inches stick cinnamon
  strawberry-flavored gelatin   6 whole cloves
1½ cups boiling water   6 pears, halved, pared and cored
1 cup cranberry juice cocktail

In deep two-quart casserole, combine gelatin and boiling water. Stir in cranberry juice, cinnamon and cloves. Add pears. Bake in 350 degree oven for 45 to 50 minutes, basting pears often wth syrup. Serve warm or cool.

Betty Jo Meadows

SALAD BOWL PUFF

Preparation: 1½ hours   Serves: 8 to 10

Crust:
⅔ cup water   1 cup Bisquick
¼ cup butter   4 eggs

Ham Salad Filling:
2 cups cooked ham, cut in chunks   ¾ cup Easy Gourmet Cooked
1 cup cheddar cheese, shredded   Salad Dressing (see index) or
2 tablespoons finely chopped onion   commercial salad dressing plus
1 (16-ounce) package frozen green   1½ teaspoons prepared mustard
  peas

Crust:
Heat water and butter to boiling in 2 quart pan. Add Bisquick all at once. Stir vigorously over low heat until mix forms a ball (about 1½ minutes). Remove from heat. Beat in eggs, 1 at a time. Continue beating until smooth. Spread in bottom of greased pie plate (do not spread up side). Bake at 400 degrees until puffed and dry in center (35 to 40 minutes). Cool. Puff will fall as it cools. Just before serving, fill with ham salad filling. Cut in wedges.
Filling:
Rinse frozen peas under cold water to separate, drain. Add remaining ingredients. Mix well. Cover and refrigerate 2 hours.

Mary Fran Schickedantz

GAZPACHO GELATIN SALAD

Preparation: 30 minutes   Serves: 8 to 10

1 envelope unflavored gelatin
1½ cup vegetable juice
½ cup Hellman's mayonnaise
¼ cup red wine vinegar
2 tablespoons vegetable oil
¼ teaspoon hot pepper sauce

1 clove garlic, crushed
1 cup diced cucumber
½ cup diced green pepper
½ cup diced onion

Sprinkle gelatin over juice. Heat, stirring constantly until gelatin is dissolved. Chill until slightly thickened. Add remaining ingredients and pour into 4 cup mold. Chill until firm.

Nancy Smith

TERRIFIC TOMATO ASPIC

Preparation: 30 minutes   Serves: 6 to 8

2 (16-ounce) cans stewed tomatoes
1 tablespoon vinegar
1 teaspoon salt
1 teaspoon sugar

2 (3-ounce) packages lemon jello
¼ cup chopped green onion tops
¼ cup chopped celery
¼ cup chopped green pepper

Put stewed tomatoes, vinegar, salt, sugar in blender. Blend thoroughly. Heat contents until hot. Dissolve jello in tomato mixture. Remove from heat and add chopped onion tops, celery and green pepper. Pour in jello molds and chill until set, 4 to 5 hours or overnight.

Carolin Powell

BEET SALAD JULIENNE

Preparation: 40 minutes   Serves: 8 to 10

1 (3-ounce) package raspberry
    gelatin
1 package unflavored gelatin
1 can julienne beets (20 ounce),
    drain, reserving juice
1 can crushed pineapple (20
    ounce), drained, reserving juice

¼ cup water
¼ cup white vinegar
3 tablespoons lemon juice
1 tablespoon sugar
1 cup water

Add ¼ cup water to reserved juices. Heat to boiling and use to dissolve gelatin. Add vinegar, lemon juice, sugar and 1 cup water. Mix well and chill until partially set. Mix in beets and pineapple and chill in individual molds or 2 quart mold.

Marilyn Robinson

PORTABLE PICNIC TABBOULEH

Preparation: 1 hour

Serves: 10 to 12

1 cup uncooked bulghur (cracked
   wheat or wheat pilaf)
1/2 cup olive oil
1/3 to 1/2 cup fresh lemon juice
1 cup green onions, finely chopped
   (including green tops)
1 cup celery, chopped
1 cup parsley, chopped (or half
   parsley and half watercress)

1 cup fresh mint, chopped
3 tomatoes, finely chopped
3 green peppers, finely chopped
2 large cucumbers, peeled and
   chopped
2 teaspoons salt
Fresh ground black pepper, to
   taste
Lettuce leaves

Use a glass jar or container (1 1/2 to 2 quarts) with a screw-on top if possible. Place the bulghur in bottom of container. In a small bowl, mix oil and lemon juice and pour over bulghur. Add vegetables in layers, as listed above. Sprinkle last layer with salt and pepper. Cover and refrigerate for at least 24 hours, or until bulghur has expanded and is light tan in color. Just before serving, shake jar well, or toss salad to blend ingredients completely.

Sallie Nolan

MOTHER'S POTATO SALAD

Preparation: 45 minutes

Serves: 12

10 medium red potatoes, boiled
1 medium onion, diced
2 tablespoons green pepper, diced
2 stalks of celery, hearts and
   leaves, chopped
4 slices "Bread and Butter"
   pickles, diced
1/2 teaspoon pepper
1 teaspoon salt

1 teaspoon whole mustard seed
3/4 teaspoon celery seed
3 slices of bacon, cut up
2 teaspoons sugar
1 teaspoon mustard
1/2 cup juice from jar of pickles
3 tablespoons mayonnaise
2 hard boiled eggs, diced

Slice boiled potatoes, after cooling and peeling, into thin pieces. Add onion, green pepper, celery, pickles, pepper, salt, mustard seed and celery seed. Fry bacon until crisp, drain. In same pan add sugar, mustard, and pickle juice. Pour this warm mixture over the potatoes, after cooking and stirring for 1 minute. Add the mayonnaise and hard-cooked eggs. Toss gently. Flavor improves when made a few hours before serving time.

Elaine Wright

ARTICHOKE-RICE SALAD

Preparation: 30 minutes

Serves: 8

1 (8-ounce) package Rice-A-Roni, chicken flavored
4 scallions, sliced thin
⅛ green pepper, sliced thin
10 pimento-stuffed olives, sliced thin

2 (6-ounce) jars marinated artichoke hearts
¾ teaspoon curry powder
⅓ cup mayonnaise
Lettuce leaves

Cook Rice-A-Roni as directed on package. Drain if needed, and cool in large bowl. Add onions, pepper and olives to cooled rice. Drain artichoke hearts well and cut to bite size, reserving marinade. Combine desired amount of artichoke marinade with curry powder and mayonnaise to form dressing. Mix well. Add artichoke hearts to rice and gradually toss with dressing. Chill in covered dish several hours and serve on lettuce.

*Use only ½ to ⅔ of the artichoke marinade. Some jars contain more marinade than others.

Carolyn Maddux

MEXICAN SALAD

Preparation: 30 minutes

Serves: 8 to 10

1 head lettuce
4 large ripe tomatoes
1 large onion
½ pound ground round
6 ounces shredded medium cheddar cheese
1 (16-ounce) can dark red kidney beans
¾ bottle (8 ounce) Kraft French Dressing

1 tablespoon El Paso Jalapeno Relish or to taste
½ (8-ounce) package Tostitos (traditional flavor)
1 teaspoon garlic powder
Salt and freshly ground pepper to taste

Wash and dry lettuce. Shred coarsely and put in salad bowl. Add tomatoes (cut in eighths) and coarsely chopped onion to lettuce. Brown ground round in skillet. Salt and pepper to taste, and add to lettuce. Finally, add cheese and drained kidney beans to salad. (Can be made ahead to this point.) When ready to serve, toss well with remaining ingredients. Add more jalapeno relish if desired.

Irene Snowberger

MOLDED SPINACH SALAD

Preparation: 1 hour   Serves: 10 to 12

2 envelopes unflavored gelatin
1 (10-ounce) can Swanson's beef
   broth
¼ cup water
½ teaspoon salt
2 tablespoons lemon juice
1 cup mayonnaise

1 (10-ounce) package chopped
   spinach, thawed
½ cup green onions, chopped
4 hard boiled eggs, chopped
½ pound bacon, cooked and
   crumbled

Soften gelatin in beef broth over low heat in medium saucepan. Add water, salt and lemon juice. Add mayonnaise. Chill until slightly thickened. Add remaining ingredients. Pour into 6 cup mold. Refrigerate until set.

A unique spinach salad!

Jane Peterson

BROCCOLI AND GREEN PEA SALAD

Preparation: 30 minutes   Serves: 8

4 cups fresh broccoli
1 can (16-ounce) LeSeur green
   peas

1 (3-ounce) jar stuffed green olives
4 green onions
4 tablespoons mayonnaise

Wash broccoli and, using top 4 to 5 inches, slice into ¼ inch pieces. Drain peas and add to broccoli. Slice olives and green onions Add to broccoli. Add mayonnaise and mix. Cover with plastic wrap and refrigerate for 3 to 4 hours. Keeps well in refrigerator for several days.

Alice Pearce

LETTUCE WITH STRAWBERRIES

Preparation: 10 minutes   Serves: 6 to 8

1 head leaf lettuce, thoroughly
   dried and torn into pieces
1 cup green grapes

1 cup sliced strawberries
½ cup sliced almonds, toasted

Mix ingredients with Poppy Seed Dressing (see Index) immediately before serving.

Marian Ferrel

LETTUCE WITH ORANGES AND GRAPES

Preparation: 30 minutes

Serves: 8 to 10

1 head lettuce (leaf is nice)
1 cup halved green grapes
1 (11-ounce) can mandarin
   oranges, drained
½ cup chopped green onions
½ cup sliced toasted almonds,
   divided
1 avocado, sliced
⅔ cup salad oil

⅓ cup orange juice
¼ cup sugar
3 tablespoons vinegar
Salt to taste
Dash of dry mustard
1 teaspoon celery seeds
2 tablespoons parsley, chopped

Wash lettuce and tear into bite size pieces. Combine lettuce, orange sections, grapes, onions, avocado and half of almonds in a large salad bowl. Combine remaining ingredients except parsley in a covered container. Shake well. Pour over salad and toss well. Sprinkle with parsley and remaining almonds.

Beverly Stocks

MARINATED VEGETABLE MEDLEY

Preparation: 10 minutes

Serves: 4

1 (10-ounce) package frozen mixed
   vegetables
¼ cup vinegar
¼ cup vegetable oil
2 tablespoons sugar
¼ teaspoon salt

¼ teaspoon pepper
½ teaspoon dried basil
⅓ medium onion, sliced thinly
1 (3-ounce) can sliced mushrooms,
   drained
Florets of fresh broccoli, if desired

Cook vegetables according to directions, but do not overcook (al dente). Drain and set aside. In a jar with a tight-fitting lid, shake vigorously the vinegar, oil, sugar, salt, pepper and basil. In a bowl, gently mix onions, mushrooms and broccoli with vegetables. Pour marinade over all and chill for a few hours or overnight, stirring occasionally. Drain and serve. (Save the marinade, if desired, and pour over a salad.)

Peggy Tager

SALADE NICOISE

Preparation: 20 minutes   Serves: 6 to 8

1 (14-ounce) can whole string
   beans, drained
3 cups cooked new potatoes, sliced
2 (4½-ounce) cans tuna, drained
⅓ cup olive oil
⅓ cup wine vinegar
1 teaspoon salt
¼ teaspoon white pepper

2 teaspoons Dijon mustard
Romaine leaves
Black olives, sliced
2 tomatoes, sliced
Capers
Fresh tarragon (optional)

Place string beans, potatoes, and tuna in a bowl. Combine tuna liquid, oil, vinegar, salt, pepper and mustard. Pour over salad in bowl. Toss lightly. Chill. Arrange romaine in a circle on a round platter. Mound salad in center. Top with olives and capers. Arrange halved tomato slices around base of salad. Garnish with tarragon.

Caroline Lee

CAESAR SALAD

Preparation: 20 minutes   Serves: 8 to 10

1 clove garlic, crushed
¾ cup salad oil
¼ cup olive oil
2 cups ½ inch bread cubes
1½ teaspoons salt
½ teaspoon dry mustard
½ teaspoon freshly ground black
   pepper
1 tablespoon Worcestershire sauce

12 anchovy fillets, drained and
   chopped
½ clove garlic
2 medium heads romaine, washed
   and chilled
½ cup grated parmesan cheese
¼ cup crumbled blue cheese
2 raw eggs
¼ cup lemon juice

In jar with tight fitting lid, combine crushed clove garlic with salad oil and olive oil. Refrigerate 1 hour. In medium skillet, sauté bread crumbs in ¼ cup garlic and oil mixture or butter until brown on all sides. Set aside. To remaining garlic-oil mixture in jar add salt, mustard, pepper, Worcestershire sauce and anchovies. Shake dressing vigorously. Refrigerate until needed. Rub inside of wooden salad bowl with cut clove of garlic. Tear greens in bite size pieces into salad bowl. (Greens should measure about 4 quarts). Shake dressing. Pour over greens. Sprinkle with Parmesan cheese and blue cheese. Toss to coat evenly. Break eggs over middle of salad. Pour lemon juice directly over eggs. Toss well. Add bread cubes, toss again, if desired. Serve at once.

Lucy Hilder

24-HOUR SALAD

Preparation: 30 minutes

Serves: 10 to 12

1 large head lettuce
¼ cup chopped onions
¼ cup chopped celery
1 (6-ounce) can water chestnuts
   (optional)

½ (10-ounce) package frozen small
   peas (not thawed or cooked)
2 cups Hellman's mayonnaise
2 teaspoons sugar
Parmesan cheese as desired

Shred lettuce in 9 x 12 inch pyrex dish. Sprinkle onions, celery and chestnuts on top of lettuce. Break and separate peas. Sprinkle on top. Spread mayonnaise on top like frosting. Sprinkle with sugar and parmesan cheese. Refrigerate overnight. Top with bacon chips, tomato wedges and/or egg slices and/or parsley.

Iris Haislip

MUSHROOM-BACON SALAD

Preparation: 1 hour

Serves: 8

1 pound fresh mushrooms
3 green onions, (about ¼ cup),
   thinly sliced (including part of
   green tops)
⅔ cup olive or vegetable oil
4 tablespoons lemon juice

1 teaspoon Worcestershire sauce
½ teaspoon salt
⅛ teaspoon pepper
½ teaspoon dry mustard
12 thin slices bacon
Lettuce

Slice cleaned mushrooms about ⅛ inch thick and put into a bowl. In a small bowl or jar combine onions, oil, lemon juice, Worcesterhsire sauce, salt, pepper and mustard. Shake or stir until well blended. Pour over mushrooms. Mix gently. Cover and refrigerate for at least 4 hours or overnight. Uncover and stir several times. Shortly before serving, cook bacon very slowly until crisp. Drain well. To serve, spoon mushroom mixture over lettuce. Crumble bacon and sprinkle over top. Drizzle with any remaining marinade.

Jean Finley

ASPARAGUS VINAIGRETTE

Preparation: 20 minutes   Serves: 10 to 12

3 tablespoons sweet pickle relish
2 tablespoons parsley, chopped
¾ teaspoon sugar
6 tablespoons vinegar
1 teaspoon salt
¾ cup light salad oil
6 cans asparagus strips,
  well-drained

Combine first 6 ingredients and purée in blender. Place asparagus in dish. Pour sauce over all 2 hours before serving. Refrigerate. For color, garnish with strips of pimento.

Janelle Snider

HEALTHY SPROUTS

Preparation: 5 minutes   Serves: 6

1 (10-ounce) package frozen
  Brussels sprouts
½ cup low-calorie Italian dressing
1 small white onion, chopped
¼ teaspoon instant minced garlic
1 tablespoon dried parsley flakes
  (or fresh)
1 teaspoon prepared mustard
¼ teaspoon herbed or seasoned
  pepper

In small saucepan, cook sprouts, following package instructions. Drain. Cut large sprouts in half or thirds. Mix dressing, onion, garlic, parsley, mustard, and pepper. Pour over warm sprouts in glass utility dish. Toss gently to coat sprouts. Cover with plastic wrap. Refrigerate overnight.

Joyce Somers

TANGY CHILLED ASPARAGUS

Preparation: 10 minutes   Serves: 6

2 cans fancy asparagus tips
  (chilled and well drained)
½ cup Hellman's mayonnaise
1 tablespoon creamy style
  horseradish sauce
1 tablespoon honey
Paprika to garnish
1 tablespoon Dijon mustard
¼ teaspoon salt
1 tablespoon vinegar

In a small bowl, mix together mayonnaise, mustard, horseradish, honey, vinegar and salt. Stir well and refrigerate until time to serve. After asparagus has been well drained, cover tightly and store in refrigerator. To serve, place asparagus in shallow dish and pour desired amount of sauce over asparagus. Sprinkle lightly with paprika.

Jane Gibson

SPINACH AND BLUE CHEESE SALAD

Preparation: 15 minutes   Serves: 10 to 12

2 pounds washed and broken
   spinach
3 or 4 squares blue cheese (Kraft)
Small onion, chopped
3 hard boiled eggs, chopped
1 pound fresh mushrooms, sliced

Dressing:
1 cup oil
1 fresh garlic
¼ teaspoon paprika
⅓ cup tarragon vinegar
½ tablespoon dry mustard
Pepper
½ small jar pimento, chopped

Mix and let all dressing ingredients set up in refrigerator at least 2 hours.
Just before serving, toss dressing with salad ingredients.

Glenda Johnson

SAD LETTUCE SALAD AND DRESSING

Preparation: 30 minutes   Serves: 8

Salad:
1 head lettuce (or combination of
   lettuces)
4 green onions, chopped

Dressing:
¼ cup sugar
Salt and pepper to taste
¼ teaspoon dry mustard
1 egg, beaten
3 tablespoons water
3 to 4 talbespoons vinegar
2 to 3 slices bacon, diced and
   cooked

Combine lettuce and onions. Set aside. Cook bacon, do not drain. Set aside.
Combine in a bowl the sugar, salt and pepper, dry mustard, egg, water, and
vinegar. Add this mixture to bacon in pan and stir over low heat until thick.
Pour over lettuce and onions to make a wilted salad and serve immediately.

*Dressing may be cooled first and then tossed with the greens
for a delicious cold salad.*

Duilla Harkins

PAPAYA SALAD

Preparation: 20 minutes   Serves: 8

Salad: Dressing:
Papaya, peeled, cubed or sliced   1 cup sugar
Romaine lettuce, torn in pieces   1 tablespoon salt
Red onion, sliced, and separated   1 cup tarragon wine vinegar
   into rings   1 cup salad oil
Avocado, peeled and cubed   1 small onion, chopped
                                          3 tablespoons fresh papaya seeds

Dressing:
Place dry ingredients and vinegar in blender. Blend and add oil and onion. Then add seeds and blend until seeds are size of coarse pepper. (Seeds in dressing keep papaya from turning dark.) Refrigerate. Pour dressing on salad when ready to serve.

Jane Henning

RUSSIAN SHRIMP SALAD

Preparation: 2 hours   Serves: 4

1 pound shrimp, cooked and diced   Hollandaise sauce (may use
1 avocado, diced   ready-prepared), see Index
Mayonnaise, (enough to hold   4 hard-boiled eggs, chopped
   ingredients together)   coarsely
Salt and pepper to taste   Lettuce leaves

Mix and chill first five ingredients. Serve on lettuce leaf. Sprinkle with chopped eggs and pour Hollandaise sauce over all.

Pat Neill

DIJON DRESSING

Preparation: 5 minutes   Yield: 1½ cups

1 cup vegetable oil   2 teaspoons salt
¼ cup vinegar   ¼ teaspoon pepper
2 tablespoons dry sherry   2 tablespoons Dijon-style mustard

Combine all ingredients and whisk or shake well. (This can be made ahead and stored in the refrigerator.) Whisk or shake well before serving.

Darlene Young

CHEDDAR CHEESE DRESSING

Preparation: 30 minutes   Serves: 12

2 eggs
2 teaspoons brown sugar
1½ teaspoons salt
1 teaspoon dry mustard
1 teaspoon Worcestershire sauce
1 teaspoon prepared horseradish

2 cups salad oil
¼ cup vinegar
¼ cup fresh lemon juice
¼ pound cheddar cheese, grated
3 green onions, finely chopped

Combine eggs, sugar, salt, mustard and Worcestershire sauce in mixing bowl and beat with electric mixer 2 to 3 minutes. Blend in horseradish. Very slowly, pour in ½ cup oil, beating constantly. Mix in vinegar and lemon juice alternately with remaining oil and beat 2 to 3 minutes. Transfer to blender and mix until creamy, 10 to 15 seconds. Do not allow consistency to be as thick as mayonnaise. Combine cheese and onion in medium bowl. Pour first mixture over and blend well. Refrigerate until ready to serve. Serve with green salad.

Trish Green

DIP (OR TOPPING) FOR FRUIT

Preparation: 35 minutes   Serves: 8

¼ cup sugar
1 tablespoon unflavored gelatin
1 cup sour cream

2 teaspoons Grand Marnier, or
    other liqueur
1 cup whipping cream, whipped
Bite size pieces of fruit

In top of double boiler over hot water, mix first 3 ingredients until sugar melts and gelatin dissolves. Stir in liqueur. Cool. Fold in whipped cream. Refrigerate. Serve as an appetizer dip for fruit or serve on top of lettuce-lined bowl of fruit for a salad.

Gale Owens

EASY GOURMET COOKED SALAD DRESSING

4 tablespoons melted butter or
    margarine
1 teaspoon salt
1 teaspoon Coleman's Dry Mustard
1 rounded tablespoon flour

2 scant tablespoons sugar
2 egg yolks
¾ cup milk
3 tablespoons vinegar

In a saucepan, blend butter or margarine, salt, mustard, flour and sugar. Add egg yolks to mixture and stir until well mixed. Add milk. Cook until it comes to a boil, stirring constantly. Remove from heat and stir in vinegar. Cool quickly by placing pan in cold water and stirring until heat is out. (This keeps film from forming on top.) Place in covered refrigerator dish and store in refrigerator. Use as a delightful substitute for commercial mayonnaise. Especially good in Waldorf salad, deviled eggs, chicken or tuna salad, and in salad bowl puff (see Index).

Mary Fran Schickedantz

SWEET AND SOUR DRESSING

Preparation: 5 minutes   Serves: 8 to 10

1 cup corn oil
½ cup catsup
½ cup malt vinegar
½ cup fruit sugar
1 teaspoon salt

¼ teaspoon powdered cloves
1 teaspoon grated onion
1 teaspoon Worcestershire sauce
1 clove garlic, crushed

Combine ingredients in a glass jar with lid. Shake well. Refrigerate until serving.

Allison Callicott

ITALIAN DRESSING

Preparation: 5 minutes   Serves: 10 to 12

2 large cloves garlic
2 teaspoons salt
3 tablespoons sugar
¼ cup vinegar

1 teaspoon basil (2 fresh)
1 teaspoon oregano
1 cup oil

Combine first 6 ingredients in food processor or blender. Process 30 to 60 seconds. Continue to process and add oil. Process until blended. Serve over any salad. Also great marinade for artichoke hearts, etc.

Lynda Middlemas

POPPY SEED DRESSING

Preparation: 10 minutes   Yield: two cups

½ cup sugar
1 teaspoon dry mustard
1 teaspoon salt
1 cup vegetable oil

⅓ cup vinegar
1 teaspoon grated green onion
1½ teaspoons poppy seeds

Mix sugar, salt, mustard. Add vinegar. Slowly beat in salad oil. Add grated onion then poppy seeds.

Delicious with "Lettuce and Strawberry Salad" (see index).

Marian Ferrel

179

Dolley Payne Todd Madison, one of our nation's most famous first ladies, was born in Greensboro in 1768. Madison memorabilia is a highlight of the Greensboro Historical Museum exhibitions. A celebrated hostess, it seemed fitting that she should introduce our dessert section.

Desserts

DOLLEY MADISON

CREMA CARAMELLA

Preparation: 1 hour　　　　　　　　　　　　　　Serves: 10
Cooking: 1 hour

1 ½ cups sugar
1 quart milk, scalded
6 to 8 eggs, slightly beaten (8
　small, 6 large)

Dash of salt
Rind (grated) of ½ lemon or 2
　teaspoons vanilla flavor

To caramelize sugar: Place 1 cup sugar in a heavy shallow pan. Cook over low heat, without stirring, until sugar is melted, and begins to form a light brown syrup. Agitate pan for sugar to brown evenly. Pour into 1 ½ quart mold or 12 individual custard cups, turning and rotating molds until bottom and sides are coated. Prepare custard: Beat eggs slightly, add ½ cup sugar, salt and flavoring. Slowly add warm milk, stirring to blend. Pour into prepared mold. Place mold in pan of warm water. Bake in 350 degree oven, 1 hour for 1 ½ quart mold or 30 minutes for small molds, or until firm when tested with knife. Cool. Refrigerate overnite. To serve: Run knife around edge of custard to loosen. Invert on serving dish with raised rim to retain caramel sauce.

A classic, traditional flan!

Titsa Dermatas

STRAWBERRY MOUSSE

Preparation: 20 minutes　　　　　　　　　　　Serves: 8 to 10

1 quart strawberries
½ cup sugar
4 envelopes unflavored gelatin
½ cup cold water

1 cup boiling water
2 cups (1 pint) whipping cream
½ cup sifted confectioners sugar
Whole and sliced strawberries for
　garnish

Purée strawberries in processor or blender. Add ½ sugar and process until blended. Soften gelatin in ½ cup cold water in a large bowl. Add boiling water, stirring until gelatin completely dissolves. Cool. Stir strawberry mixture into gelatin. Chill until the consistency of unbeaten egg whites. Beat whipping cream until foamy. Gradually add confectioners sugar, beating until soft peaks form. Fold cream into strawberry mixture. Spoon into lightly oiled 2 quart mold. Refrigerate until set. Unmold on serving plate and garnish with strawberries and extra cream, if desired.

Trish Green

WHITE CHOCOLATE MOUSSE

Preparation: 25 minutes   Serves: 8 to 10

½ pound white chocolate
4 tablespoons sweet butter
3 tablespoons light rum

3 eggs, separated
½ cup heavy cream, beaten

Oil an 8-inch springform pan. Melt chocolate in bowl with butter and rum (in a very low oven with door ajar or in microwave). Beat yolks in mixer bowl until thick. Transfer yolks to bowl placed over hot water and continue to beat to thicken. Put back in mixer bowl. When chocolate is melted, slowly beat into yolks. Beat cream and fold in. Beat egg whites and fold in. Place in oiled pan. Freeze overnight. To serve: Unmold and cut mousse into wedges. Place wedge on chilled plate. Drizzle chocolate sauce from your favorite recipe over top.

Elizabeth West

CHOCOLATE MOUSSE

Preparation: 20 minutes   Serves: 8

6 ounces semi-sweet chocolate
2 tablespoons Kahlua
1 tablespoon orange juice
2 egg yolks

2 eggs
1 teaspoon vanilla extract
¼ cup sugar
1 cup whipping cream

Melt the chocolate in the Kahlua and orange juice over very low heat. Set aside. Put egg yolks, eggs, vanilla, and sugar in blender container. Blend for 2 minutes at medium high speed. Add the whipping cream and blend for another 30 seconds. Add the melted chocolate mixture and blend until smooth. Pour into a bowl or small individual demi-tasse cups. Refrigerate.

Kitty Robison

COFFEE SOUFFLÉ

Preparation: 15 minutes   Serves: 8

1½ cups hot coffee, strong
36 large marshmallows

½ pint heavy cream
½ pint of heavy cream, for garnish

Melt marshmallows in hot coffee, stirring until they dissolve. Let cool, stirring occasionally. After mixture has set, whip cream stiff. Whip mixture into the cream until perfectly smooth. Refrigerate for at least 3 hours. Serve in stemmed goblet garnished with additional whipped cream and a dusting of cocoa if desired.

Joan Rowan

ADULT BANANA SPLIT

Preparation: ½ hour   Serves: 8

1 cup butter
1 cup plus 2 tablespoons brown
  sugar, firmly packed
4 medium bananas, peeled and
  sliced into rounds
Juice of 1 medium orange,
  strained (4+ tablespoons)
Juice of 1 medium lemon, strained
  (3+ tablespoons)

1 tablespoon Grand Marnier
1 tablespoon orange liqueur
1 tablespoon banana liqueur
1 quart vanilla ice cream
Unsweetened whipped cream
Chopped macadamia nuts

Melt butter in a medium saucepan or skillet. Add brown sugar and stir until smooth. Add bananas and stir to coat. Stir in juices and liqueurs and bring to a simmer. Let simmer 2 minutes. Divide ice cream among eight dishes. Spoon hot sauce over. Top with whipped cream and nuts. Similar to Bananas Foster, but better!

Darlene Young

FROZEN CHOCOLATE VELVET

Preparation: 30 minutes   Serves: 8 to 10

Crust:
1 box Nabisco chocolate wafers,
  ground

1 tablespoon sugar
⅓ cup butter or margarine, melted

Filling:
1 (8-ounce) package cream cheese
½ cup sugar
1 teaspoon vanilla
2 egg yolks

1 (6-ounce) package semi-sweet
  chocolate pieces
2 egg whites
1 cup heavy cream, whipped
¾ cup pecans, chopped (optional)

Crust: Combine all ingredients and press into 9-inch springform pan or pie plate. Bake 10 minutes at 325 degrees.
Filling: Combine semi-sweet chocolate pieces with 1 tablespoon water over very low heat till melted. Add vanilla and cool. Combine cream cheese with ¼ cup sugar, beating thoroughly. Continue beating. Add egg yolks and chocolate mixture. In separate bowl, beat egg whites and remaining ¼ cup sugar. Fold into chocolate mixture along with the whipped cream. Pour mixture over chocolate wafer crust and freeze. If desired decorate with pastry tube filled with whipped cream flavored with 1 tablespoon sugar and 2 tablespoons Kahlua or Grand Marnier.

Peggy Brame

DAFFODIL LEMON SPONGE

Preparation: 20 minutes
Cooking: 40 to 45 minutes

Serves: 4 to 6

2 tablespoons melted butter
1 cup sugar
2 tablespoons light brown sugar
⅓ cup lemon juice
Grated rind of one lemon

3 eggs, separated
1¼ cups milk
¼ cup flour
⅛ teaspon salt
⅛ teaspoon ginger

Cream butter and sugars. Add lemon juice and lemon rind. Blend in egg yolks and add milk. Add sifted dry mixture of flour, salt, and ginger and mix well. Fold in stiffly beaten egg whites. Pour into greased casserole dish and set in pan of hot water. Bake at 350 degrees for 40 to 45 minutes until top is light brown and knife comes out clean.

Merle Frazier

LUSCIOUS LEMON SOUFFLÉ

Preparation: 45 minutes

Serves: 10 to 12

5 large eggs, separated
1½ cups sugar
3½ large lemons (juice)
2 cups whipping cream
1 tablespoon lemon peel

6 teaspoons (2 packages) plain
    gelatin soaked in ½ cup cold
    water
Cream of tartar, pinch

Beat together egg yolks, sugar, grated lemon rind. Add strained lemon juice from the 3 lemons. Beat until thick and mousse-like. Add whipping cream (half-whipped) on low speed of mixer. Melt gelatin in water over gentle heat and add to mixture. Fold in egg whites (whipped until stiff, not dry). Add a pinch of cream of tartar. Turn immediately into prepared soufflé pan and put into refrigerator to set. When firm, add garnish if desired.

Sandra Snider

GRANDMOTHER'S DATE NUT PUDDING

Preparation: 10 minutes
Cooking: 35 to 45 minutes

Serves: 6 to 8

2 cups chopped pitted dates
2 cups chopped pecans
1 cup sugar

3 eggs, beaten
1 teaspoon baking powder
2 tablespoons flour

Mix all ingredients together. Pour in buttered casserole dish. Bake in preheated 300 degree oven for 35 to 45 minutes. Serve warm with whipped cream.

Cookie McAdoo

CHERRIES JUBILEE

Preparation: 1 hour   Serves: 8 to 10
Cooking: 1 hour

Peel of 1 lemon   1 cup port wine
Peel of 1 orange   3 tablespoons cornstarch
½ cup water   ¼ cup toasted almonds
½ cup sugar   Juice of 1 lemon
2 (1-pound) cans dark, sweet,   ½ cup of brandy
   pitted cherries   1 quart vanilla ice cream

Cut peels into thin slivers. Add water and sugar and simmer for 10 minutes or until peel is translucent. Combine liquid from cherries with enough wine to make 2 cups. Reserve cherries. Stir mixture slowly into cornstarch. Add orange and lemon peel in syrup, then almonds and lemon juice. Cook, stirring until sauce bubbles and thickens. Add cherries and pour into serving dish or chafing dish. (Sauce with cherries can be made ahead and reheated.) Warm brandy to lukewarm and pour over sauce. Set aflame and spoon, flaming, over servings of vanilla ice cream.

Gloria Stanfield

BAILEY'S IRISH CREAM CHEESECAKE

Preparation: 25 minutes   Serves: 16
Cooking; approximately 1½ hours

Batter:
2 pounds cream cheese, room   4 eggs
   temperature   2 ⅔ cup sugar
⅓ cup heavy whipping cream   ½ cup Bailey's Irish Cream
⅓ cup sour cream

Add each ingredient, one at a time, whipping for 5 minutes after each is added. After last ingredient is added, whip until creamy smooth.

Crust:
6 ounces graham cracker crumbs   1 tablespoon ground nutmeg
¾ cup almonds (sliced, blanched)   5 ounces melted sweet butter
1 tablespoon ground cinnamon   3 ounces grated white chocolate

Mix first four ingredients, then add butter and mix well. Pack crust mixture evenly in bottom of spring form pan. Bake for 5 minutes in 350 degree oven. Sprinkle grated chocolate over crust while still hot. Add batter and bake in a water bath at 350 degrees for approximately 1½ hours or until golden brown. Cool in oven.

This recipe was shared by Chef Jeffery Rouse of London's restaurant.

KAY'S CHEESE CAKE

Preparation: 30 minutes   Serves: 10
Cooking: 35 minutes

Graham Cracker Crust:

1¾ cup fine graham cracker   ½ teaspoon cinnamon
   crumbs   ½ cup of melted butter

Preheat oven to 375 degrees for 10 minutes. Combine all ingredients. Reserve 3 tablespoons of mixture. Press remainder on bottom and 2½ inches up sides of 9-inch springform pan.

Filling:

3 eggs, well beaten   ¼ teaspoon salt
2 (8-ounce) packages softened   2 teaspoons vanilla
   cream cheese   ½ teaspoon almond extract
1 cup sugar   3 cups dairy sour cream

Combine all ingredients except sour cream. Beat until smooth. (Make sure all lumps are out) Blend in sour cream. Pour into crust. Trim with reserved crumbs. Bake 375 degrees for 35 minutes. Should be "just set." Cool. Chill well at least 3 to 4 hours.

Pat Austin

ORANGE CHEESECAKE

Preparation: 1 hour   Serves: 8
Cooking: 8 to 10 minutes

Crust:

1 cup sifted flour   ½ cup butter
¼ cup sugar   1 egg yolk
1 tablespoon grated orange rind   ½ teaspoon vanilla

Orange Cheese Filling:

5 (8-ounce) packages soft cream   ¼ teaspoon vanilla
   cheese   5 eggs
1¾ cups sugar   2 egg yolks
1 tablespoon grated orange rind   ⅛ cup frozen orange juice
¼ teaspoon salt   concentrate, undiluted
3 tablespoons flour

Crust: Combine flour, sugar, rind. Cut in butter until mixture resembles coarse meal. Add egg yolk and vanilla. Blend well. Pat ½ cup dough onto bottom of 9-inch springform pan. Bake 5 minutes at 400 degrees. Cool. Pat remaining dough evenly around sides to ½ inch from top. Fill with orange cheese filling below.

Orange cheese filling: Combine first 6 ingredients in large mixer bowl. Beat at low speed. Add eggs and yolks one at a time, beating well after each, stir in orange concentrate. Pour into prepared pan. Put foil under pan on oven rack. Bake at 400 degrees for 8 to 10 minutes. Reduce temperature to 225 degrees and bake about 1⅓ hours. Cool slowly. Refrigerate or freeze.

Shirley Smith

ALMONDRADA DEVINE

Preparation: 30 minutes   Serves: 8 to 10

Meringue:
1 envelope gelatin
⅓ cup cold water
6 egg whites, room temperature

1 cup sugar
1 teaspoon almond extract

Sauce:
1 large (4¾-ounce) package Jello
   vanilla pudding mix
½ teaspoon almond extract
1 cup heavy cream, whipped

Bourbon to taste
½ cup toasted almonds for garnish

Meringue: Soak 1 envelope gelatin in ⅓ cup cold water for 5 minutes. Dissolve gelatin over hot water. Beat 6 egg whites until stiff. Beat in sugar gradually. Add gelatin and almond extract on slow speed. (Has consistency of 7 minute frosting.) Pour into 2 quart bowl or mold. Run a knife blade through mixture to alleviate air pockets. Cover with saran and refrigerate overnight. (This mixture may be divided and tinted for red and green layers if desired.)

Sauce: Make pudding mix according to package directions. Cool. Add ½ teaspoon almond extract, whipped cream and bourbon. Stir.

To serve: Spoon egg white mixture in large rounded spoonfuls into sherbet glasses (or unmold and slice if molded). Spoon approximately ½ cup of sauce over meringue and sprinkle generously with toasted almonds.

A delightful and easy almond version of Floating Island!

Patsy Adams

CHOCOLATE MINT FRANGOS

Preparation: 30 minutes   Serves: 18

1 cup butter
2 cups sifted powdered sugar
4 squares unsweetened chocolate,
   melted
4 eggs
2 teaspoons vanilla

1 teaspoon peppermint extract
1 cup heavy cream, whipped
Maraschino cherries
18 vanilla wafers
Chopped nuts, toasted
18 cupcake papers

Cream butter and sugar. Blend in melted chocolate. Add eggs and beat well, then blend in flavorings. Put a vanilla wafer into cupcake papers. Fill with chocolate mixutre, ¾ full. Place a dollop of whipped cream on top, sprinkle with nuts and top with half a cherry. Freeze in muffin tins to keep shape. Store in plastic bags after frozen.

Sue Gillison, Carolin Powell, Beverly Stocks

CHOCOLATE PEANUT DESSERT

Preparation: 1 hour   Yield: 24
Cooking: 20 minutes

½ cup butter or margarine,
   softened
1 cup all purpose flour
1 cup finely chopped dry roasted
   peanuts (hand chop; processor
   is too fine)
1 (8-ounce) package cream
   cheese, softened
⅓ cup creamy peanut butter
1 cup powdered sugar

1 (12-ounce) carton frozen
   whipped topping, thawed
1 (3¾-ounce) package vanilla
   instant pudding
1 (4½-ounce) package chocolate
   instant pudding
2¾ cups milk
1 (1.2-ounce) milk chocolate candy
   bar, shaved

Cut butter into flour until mixture resembles coarse meal. Stir ⅔ cup peanuts into the flour mixture. Press mixture into a 13 × 9 × 2 inch baking pan. Bake at 350 degrees for 20 minutes. Cool completely. Combine cream cheese, peanut butter and powdered sugar. Beat until fluffy. Stir 1 cup whipped topping into cream cheese mixture. Spread over crust. Chill. Combine pudding mixes and milk. Beat 2 minutes at medium speed of electric mixer. Spread pudding over cream cheese layer. Spread remaining whipped topping over pudding layer. Sprinkle top with shaved chocolate (use a potato peeler) and ⅓ cup chopped peanuts. Store in the refrigerator.

Judy Jolly

TRIXIE'S CHERRY TORTE

Preparation: 50 minutes   Serves: 12
Cooking: 1 hour and 15 minutes

1½ cups flour
7½ tablespoons powdered sugar
1½ sticks butter or margarine
3 eggs, beaten
2¼ cups sugar
·¾ teaspoon salt

1½ teaspoons baking powder
⅓ & ⅙ cup flour
1½ teaspoons vanilla
1 cup chopped pecans
2 (16-ounce) cans sour cherries,
   water packed

Blend first 3 ingredients and press in bottom of greased 11 × 13 inch pan. Bake 15 minutes at 350 degrees. Combine all remaining ingredients except cherries and pour over crust. Spoon cherries on top. Bake 1 hour at 325 degrees.

Kay Arthur

CHOCOLATE CREAM CAKE

Preparation: 30 minutes
Cooking: 1 hour

Serves: 12

1 (12-ounce) package semi-sweet
  chocolate chips
½ cup (1 stick) unsalted butter
6 eggs, separated, room
  temperature
1 cup sugar
½ cup finely chopped pecans

1 tablespoon Irish cream liqueur
½ teaspoon vanilla
Pinch of cream of tartar
2 cups whipping cream
¼ cup powdered sugar
2 tablespoons Irish cream liqueur
2 ounces chocolate curls (optional)

Preheat oven to 350 degrees. Grease and flour 10-inch springform pan. Melt chocolate chips and butter in top of double boiler over hot, but not boiling, water. Beat yolks in large bowl of electric mixer until very thick, about 5 minutes. Beat in ½ cup sugar 1 tablespoon at a time. Stir in melted chocolate, pecans, liqueur and vanilla. Beat whites with cream of tartar in another large bowl until soft peaks form. Gradually add remaining ½ cup sugar and beat until stiff but not dry. Gently fold ¼ of whites into chocolate mixture, then fold chocolate mixture back into remaining whites. Pour into prepared pan. Bake 30 minutes. Reduce oven temperature to 275 degrees and continue baking 30 minutes. Turn off oven. Let cake stand in oven for 30 minutes with door ajar. Remove cake from oven. Dampen paper towel and place on top of cake for 5 minutes. Remove towel (top of cake will crack and fall). Cool cake in pan. Remove springform. Transfer cake to platter. Beat whiping cream in large bowl of electric mixer until soft peaks form. Beat in powdered sugar and liqueur. Spoon whipped cream onto top of cake and smooth evenly. Sprinkle with chocolate curls if desired. Refrigerate 6 hours. Let stand at room temperature 30 mintues before serving.

Marian Ferrel

COFFEE TOFFEE ICE CREAM CAKE

Preparation: 10 minutes

Serves: 25

28 Oreo cookies
6 large Heath candy bars
  (coffee-toffee bars)

½ gallon coffee ice cream
½ gallon chocolate ice cream
8 ounces Hershey chocolate syrup

Put 14 Oreo cookies in one plastic bag and 14 Oreo cookies in another plastic bag. Crush with a rolling pin or mallet. Do not use food processor. Place 6 Heath candy bars in a plastic bag and crush. Lightly oil a 10 inch springform pan. Sprinkle bottom of pan with one bag of cookies. Add ½ gallon softened chocolate ice cream. Drizzle 4 ounces of Hershey syrup over ice cream. Sprinkle second bag of cookies over syrup. Add ½ gallon softened coffee ice cream. Drizzle with 4 ounces of Hershey syrup. Sprinkle top with bag of crushed Heath bars. Cover with foil. Freeze until hard.

Irene Mnick

GINGER AND CREAM

Preparation: 35 minutes   Serves: 10
Cooking: 12 to 15 minutes

Cake:
3 eggs
½ cup sugar
¼ teaspoon salt
⅔ cup cake flour
2 teaspoons baking powder

1 teaspoon cinnamon
1 teaspoon ginger
1 teaspoon allspice
¼ cup molasses
Sugar for sprinkling

Chantilly Cream:
1 cup whipping cream, chilled
½ teaspoon vanilla

2 tablespoons powdered sugar

Brandied Walnut Sauce:
1 cup brown sugar
4 tablespoons butter
¼ cup cream

2 tablespoons light corn syrup
¼ cup brandy
½ cup toasted chopped walnuts

Prepare a 10½ × 14½ inch jelly roll pan by oiling well, lining with waxed paper, allowing a 1-inch overhang, and oiling waxed paper well. Cake: In the bowl of an electric mixer, combine eggs, sugar and salt. Whip until fluffy and mixture "forms a ribbon." Sift together flour, baking powder, cinnamon, ginger and allspice. Fold flour mixture into egg/sugar mixture gently but thoroughly. Fold in molasses. Spread into the prepared jelly roll pan. Place in a 375 degree oven and bake 12 to 14 minutes, until cake tests done. Remove from oven. Dust with granulated sugar and turn upside down onto a piece of sugared, waxed paper. Remove paper from cake. Roll up width-wise and chill. When well-chilled, unroll and spread with chantilly cream. Re-roll and chill until serving time.
Chantilly cream: In the bowl of an electric mixer, combine whipping cream, vanilla and powdered sugar. Whip until firm peaks form.
Brandied Walnut Sauce: In a small saucepan, combine brown sugar, butter, cream, and corn syrup. Bring mixture to a boil, stirring constantly. Reduce heat and let cook 5 minutes. Remove pan from heat. Add brandy and toasted walnuts. Return pan to heat and simmer 1 minute. Arrange cake on a serving platter and spoon warm sauce over gingeroll. Serve remainder of warm sauce with individual servings.

Trish Green

YUMMY YOGURT SPICE CAKE

Preparation: 45 minutes   Serves: 20
Cooking: 1 hour

Cake:
1 cup butter   2 cups flour
2 cups sugar   1 teaspoon cinnamon
6 eggs, well beaten   1 teaspoon clove
1 cup almonds, chopped fine   2 teaspoons baking soda
1 cup yogurt   1 jigger whiskey

Syrup:
3 cups sugar   Juice of ½ orange
2 cups water   Juice of ½ lemon

Cake: Beat butter and sugar together for 10 minutes. Add well-beaten eggs.
Beat 5 minutes more. Add yogurt, almonds, flour and spices and blend.
Dissolve baking soda in whiskey, and add to mixture, blending thoroughly.
Pour into greased 9 × 13 inch pan. Bake in 350 degrees oven for 1 hour.
Allow to cool slightly. Cut into squares. Pour warm syrup slowly over cake.
Let stand to cool. Syrup: Mix ingredients and cook together for a light
syrup, about 15 minutes.

Titsa Dermatas

STRAWBERRY ALMOND ROLL

Preparation: 2 hours   Serves: 8 to 10
Cooking: 12 to 15 minutes

1 cup sifted cake flour   3 tablespoons chopped almonds
1 teaspoon baking powder   Confectioners sugar
¼ teaspoon salt   1 cup whipping cream (whipped)
4 eggs   1 quart strawberries
1 cup sugar   Additional whipped cream for
¼ cup water   garnish
1 teaspoon vanilla

Grease a jelly roll pan, line with waxed paper and grease again. Preheat
oven to 375 degrees. Beat eggs at high speed until very thick and light in
color. Add sugar gradually and continue to beat until very thick. Add water
and vanilla. At low speed, add dry ingredients. Do not over mix. Pour into
pan and sprinkle almonds on top. Bake 12 to 15 minutes until springy to the
touch. Spread out a clean cup towel and sprinkle heavily with powdered
sugar. Wash and cut up strawberries, reserving a few nice ones for garnish.
When cake is done, turn out onto cup towel. Roll cake up in the towel and let
cool. Before serving, unroll cake. Spread with whipping cream and strawberries and re-roll. Serve on a silver platter garnished with whole berries
and extra whipped cream!

Louann Harlow

GERMAN MOCHA TORTE

Preparation: 35 minutes
Cooking: 45 to 50 minutes

Serves: 10 to 12

Batter:
1 cup cake flour, sifted
1 cup sugar
1 teaspoon baking powder
6 eggs, separated
¼ cup boiling water with 2
   teaspoons instant coffee
1 teaspoon vanilla

Frosting:
1½ pints heavy whipping cream
1 teaspoon vanilla
2 to 3 tablespoons confectioners
   sugar
2 tablespoons instant coffee (if
   using freeze dry, put through
   fine strainer)
1 (5.5-ounce) can Hershey's Syrup
   (or ½ cup)

Preheat oven 325 to 350 degrees. Line bottom of 9 or 10 inch spring-form pan with wax paper. Beat egg yolks and sugar for 5 minutes. Add hot coffee mix and beat 5 more minutes. Beat egg whites until stiff, but not dry. Resift flour with baking powder and add by spoonfuls into yolk mixture. Fold egg white mixture into yolk mixture, making sure there are no lumps. Add vanilla and mix. Pour into pan and bake 45 to 50 minutes, until it springs back. Cool and slice into 3 layers.

Frosting: Beat cream until almost stiff, slowly add sugar, coffee, and vanilla. Add chocolate syrup, beating slowly. Be careful not to overbeat. If not sweet enough, add 1 to 2 tablespoons more confectioners sugar. Put frosting on first layer, add second layer and repeat. Add last layer and frost top and sides. May be frozen and covered loosely with foil. Unfrosted, uncut cake may also be frozen.

Evelyn Sturm

RAW APPLE CAKE

Preparation: ½ hour
Cooking: 1 hour

Serves: 20

3 cups flour
2 cups sugar
2 eggs
1 cup mayonnaise
⅓ cup milk
½ teaspoon salt
Icing:
1½ sticks margarine
1 cup light brown sugar

2 teaspoons baking soda
1 teaspoon cinnamon
3 cups chopped or diced apples
¾ cup chopped pecans
¾ cup raisins
1 teaspoon vanilla

¼ cup canned evaporated milk
1 teaspoon vanilla

Combine flour, sugar, salt, baking soda, cinnamon, eggs, mayonnaise, and milk. Mix together remaining ingredients and stir into batter. Pour into greased, floured tube pan. Bake at 350 degrees for one hour or more. Cool before icing. To prepare icing: Melt margarine in saucepan. Add sugar and milk. Cook for 3 minutes. Let cool and beat thoroughly. Icing will be thin.

Peggy Johnson

CREAM CHEESE POUND CAKE

Preparation: 20 minutes

Cooking: 1½ hours

Serves: 10 to 16

1 (8-ounce) package cream cheese, room temperature

3 sticks margarine, room temperature

3 cups sugar

Dash of salt

1 teaspoon almond flavoring

1 teaspoon vanilla flavoring

6 large eggs, room temperature

3 cups sifted cake flour

Preheat oven to 325 degrees. Cream margarine, cream cheese and sugar until light. Add salt and flavorings. Beat well. Add eggs one at a time, beating well after each one. Stir in flour gradually, beating well. Spoon mixture into greased and floured tube pan. Bake at 325 degrees for 1½ hours. Let cool 10 minutes before removing from pan.

Dot Spence

MARY ELIZABETH'S HOT MILK COCONUT CAKE

Preparation: 30 minutes

Cooking: 30 minutes

Serves: 24

Cake:

4 eggs

2 cups sugar

2 cups plain flour

1 rounded teaspoon baking powder

Pinch of salt

1 cup milk

4 tablespoons butter

Icing:

1½ cups sugar

1 cup milk

2 (8-ounce) packages fresh, frozen coconut

Cake: Beat eggs well. Add sugar, flour, baking powder and salt. In a saucepan, bring milk and butter to a boil. Pour into flour mixture. Mix 2 more minutes. Pour into 13 × 9 inch pan. Bake 30 minutes at 350 degrees. Icing: About 5 minutes before cake is done, bring sugar and milk to a boil in a saucepan. Remove from stove and add frozen coconut. Mix well and spoon over warm cake. (It is a lot of liquid but cake will absorb it.)

Tastes even better after being frozen!

Glenda Johnson

MOTHER'S LEMON POUND CAKE

Preparation: 30 minutes   Yield: 18 slices
Cooking: 1½ hours

2 sticks butter   1 teaspoon baking powder
½ cup Crisco   1 cup milk
2½ cups sugar   2 teaspoons lemon juice
5 eggs   2 teaspoons vanilla
3 cups flour

Glaze:
Juice of 1 lemon (or more)   ½ box confectioners sugar,
Grated rind of lemon   approximately
½ stick butter

In mixer bowl, beat butter and Crisco, then add sugar slowly. Add eggs one at a time. Add flour and baking powder alternately with milk. Add lemon juice and vanilla last. Pour mixture into greased and floured tube pan. Bake at 300 degrees for 1½ hours. Mix glaze ingredients and pour over cake while hot.

                        Joan Sherrill

COCONUT POUND CAKE

Preparation: 1 hour   Serves: 16 to 20
Cooking: 1½ hours

3 cups sugar   1 cup milk
2 sticks butter   5 eggs (6 small)
⅔ cup Crisco   1½ teaspoon vanilla
3 cups flour   1 (7-ounce) can Angel Flake
½ teaspoon salt   Coconut
1 teaspoon baking powder

Cream butter, shortening and sugar until fluffy. Add eggs, one at a time, beating well after each egg. Combine flour, salt, and baking powder. Add flour mixture and milk (to which vanilla has been added) alternately, beginning and ending with flour. Fold in coconut. Bake in large greased tube pan 325 degrees for 1½ hours. Can be frozen.

                        Nancy Beard

MOTHER'S WHITE FRUIT CAKE

Preparation: 40 minutes
Cooking: 3 hours

Serves: 15 to 20

12 ounces glazed red cherries
8 ounces glazed yellow pineapple
8 ounces glazed green pineapple
4 cups pecans
¼ cup flour
1¾ cups sifted flour
½ teaspoon baking powder
1 cup sugar

¼ pound butter
5 large eggs
1 tablespoon vanilla extract
1½ teaspoons lemon extract
1½ teaspoons orange extract
½ cup light corn syrup
¼ cup water

Chop fruit and nuts, and using ¼ cup flour, toss to coat completely. Sift 1¾ cups flour and baking powder together. Set aside. Measure sugar. Set aside. Cream butter and add sugar gradually, creaming well until fluffy. Add eggs which have been beaten well with rotary beater, and blend into creamed mixture. Fold flour into egg and butter mixture. Add lemon and orange extracts. Mix well and fold in fruits and nuts. Pour into 10 inch tube pan which has been greased. Place in cold oven. Bake at 250 degrees for 3 hours or until golden brown. Glaze with a mixture of ½ cup light corn syrup and ¼ cup water which have been boiled for 2 minutes. Decorate with fruits and nuts. Cool and store in foil or freeze.

Rachel Hull

TURTLE CAKE

Preparation: 30 minutes
Cooking: 45 minutes

Serves: 15 to 20

1 box devil's food cake mix
¾ cup butter
2 cups chopped pecans
1 (6-ounce) bag chocolate chips

1 (14-ounce) package Kraft
   caramels
½ cup evaporated milk

Grease and flour a 9 × 13 inch pan. Prepare cake mix as directed. Pour half the batter in pan and bake 15 minutes in preheated 350 degree oven. In a pan over low heat, melt caramels and butter and mix in milk. (Stir constantly until caramels and butter are melted.) Pour this mixture over the cake, sprinkle morsels and nuts over caramel layer, pour remaining half of cake mixture over this. Return to oven and bake 25 to 30 minutes more at 350 degrees. Test until toothpick is clean. Let cool completely before cutting. Better the next day.

Delores Wellmaker

COFFEE ANGEL PIE

Preparation: 30 minutes   Serves: 6 to 8
Cooking: 1 hour

Meringue: Sauce:
2 egg whites   3 tablespoons butter
1/2 teaspoon vanilla   1 cup brown sugar
1/4 teaspoon salt   1/3 cup evaporated milk
1/4 teaspoon cream of tartar   1 teaspoon vanilla
1/2 cup sugar   1/2 cup of chopped pecans (or 1/2
1/2 cup finely chopped pecans   cup raisins may be substituted)
1 quart coffee ice cream

Beat together egg whites, vanilla, salt, and cream of tartar until soft peaks form. Gradually beat in sugar until very stiff peaks form and sugar is dissolved. Fold in nuts. Spread in well-buttered 9-inch pie plate, building up sides to form a shell. Bake in a very slow oven (275 degrees) for 1 hour. Turn off heat and let dry in oven (door closed) for 1 hour. Cool. Pile scoops of ice cream in shell. Freeze. Remove from freezer 15 minutes before serving. Serve with warm sauce. Sauce: In small pan, melt butter, stir in brown sugar and evaporated milk. Cook and stir over medium heat just till mixture boils. Remove from heat. Add vanilla and nuts. Cool down until sauce is warm and spoon over ice cream pie.

Delores Wellmaker

PEANUT BUTTER CHIFFON PIE

Preparation: 1 hour   Serves: 6 to 8

Pie Shell:
3/4 cup crushed pretzel crumbs   6 tablespoons melted butter
3 tablespoons sugar

Filling:
1 packet unflavored gelatin   1/2 cup peanut butter
1/4 cup sugar   2 egg whites
1/4 teaspoon salt   1/4 cup sugar
1 cup milk   2 cups (1 4-ounce container) Cool
2 egg yolks, slightly beaten   Whip, thawed

Combine ingredients for pie shell. Bake at 350 degrees for 8 minutes. Cool pie shell. Mix gelatin, 1/4 cup sugar and salt in a saucepan. Add milk and yolks. Cook and stir over medium heat until boiling. Remove from heat. Add peanut butter, stirring until blended. Chill. Beat whites until foamy. Adding 1/4 cup sugar, beat until stiff. Fold into cooled mixture with Cool Whip. Spoon into crust. Chill until firm, about 2 hours. Garnish with grated chocolate, if desired.

Judy Murray

FAMOUS COFFEE-TOFFEE PIE

Preparation: 1½ hours
Cooking: 1 hour

Serves: 8

Pastry Shell:
½ (10-ounce) package piecrust mix
¼ cup brown sugar, firmly packed
¾ cup finely chopped walnuts

1 square unsweetened chocolate, grated
1 teaspoon vanilla extract

Filling:
½ cup soft butter or margarine
¾ cup granulated sugar
1 square unsweetened chocolate, melted and cooled

2 teaspoons instant coffee
2 eggs

Coffee Topping:
2 cups heavy cream
2 tablespoons instant coffee granules

½ cup confectioners sugar
Chocolate curls (1 square unsweetened chocolate)

Preheat oven to 375 degrees. Make pastry shell: In medium bowl, combine piecrust mix with brown sugar, walnuts, and grated chocolate. Add 1 tablespoon water and the vanilla. Using fork, mix until well-blended. Turn into 9-inch well-greased pie pan. Press firmly against bottom and side of pie pan. Bake for 10 to 15 minutes or until light brown (do not overbake). Cool on wire rack. Meanwhile, make filling: In small bowl with electric mixer at medium speed, beat butter until creamy. Gradually add granulated sugar, beating until light. Blend in melted chocolate and 2 teaspoons instant coffee. Add 1 egg. Beat 5 minutes. Add remaining egg. Beat 5 minutes longer. Turn filling into baked, cooled pie shell. Refrigerate, covered, overnight. Next day, make Coffee Topping: In large bowl, combine cream with 2 tablespoons instant coffee and the confectioners sugar. Refrigerate, covered, 1 hour. With electric mixer, beat cream mixture until stiff. Decorate pie with topping and chocolate shavings.

Irene Mnick

LEMON CURD FILLING

Preparation: 30 minutes
Cooking: approximately 15 minutes

Serves: 8

Grated rind of 2 lemons
½ cup lemon juice
2 cups sugar

1 cup butter
4 beaten eggs

Mix lemon rind, lemon juice, sugar, and butter in double boiler until butter is melted. Add eggs. Stir, cooking until thickened (about 15 minutes). Pour in baked tart shells or store in jar with tight fitting lid in refrigerator and use as jam. (When using as tart filling, never recook the curd!)

Claire Kelleher

BETTER THAN MOM'S APPLE PIE

Preparation: 30 minutes   Serves: 8
Cooking: 50 minutes

Crust: Filling:
2 cups sifted flour   1½ pounds peeled and diced
½ teaspoon sugar   apples (4 to 5 cups — Wine Sap
¼ teaspoon salt   or Rome)
¾ cup butter or shortening   8 ounces light brown sugar
5 tablespoons water   ¾ teaspoon cinnamon
1 egg, beaten   ½ teaspoon nutmeg
                                    5 tablespoons flour
                                    Grated rind of ½ lemon
                                    ¼ teaspoon vanilla

Crust: Mix flour, sugar, and salt. Cut in butter with pastry blender. Add cold water gradually and stir just until dough is moistened. Cover and refrigerate 1 to 2 hours. Place half of dough on floured pastry cloth. Roll to ¼ inch thickness. Cut 11 inch diameter circle, place in 9-inch pie tin. Prick surface lightly and bake 5 minutes in 400 degree oven. Brush with a little beaten egg and bake 1 minute longer. Filling: Combine filling ingredients. Place apple mixture in crust. Roll top crust as above and place on top of pie. Trim excess dough and crimp edges to seal. Cut 3 to 4 vents in top crust, then brush with beaten egg and sprinkle with sugar. Bake 50 minutes to 1 hour at 400 degrees or until golden brown.

Lorraine Valitutto

VALLECITO LAKE LODGE PEPPERMINT ICE CREAM PIE

Preparation: 1 hour   Serves: 12

2 baked pie shells   Syrup:
½ gallon vanilla ice cream   1 stick margarine
1 large stick of peppermint candy   4 squares chocolate
4 drops red food coloring   1½ cups sugar
                                    ½ cup cocoa
                                    1 (13-ounce) can evaporated milk

Put peppermint stick candy in cloth bag and crush with a hammer (or use food processor). Put ice cream in large bowl. As ice cream becomes soft, stir in crushed candy and add food coloring. Turn mixture into pie shells and place in freezer. Take pie from freezer and slice a few minutes before serving. Garnish with a spoonful of chocolate syrup.
Syrup: Melt margarine and chocolate in double boiler. Mix sugar and cocoa and add to chocolate mixture. Slowly add milk and cook until thick.

Dene Mead

APPLE ALMOND SWISS PIE

Preparation: 30 minutes   Serves: 8
Cooking: 40 minutes

1 8-inch pie shell
1 (3-ounce) package slivered
   almonds
4 medium apples
Sugar to sprinkle on apples

Custard:
1/2 cup sugar
1 egg
1/2 cup light cream
1 teaspoon vanilla
1 tablespoon cornstarch
Sugar and cinnamon to sprinkle
   on top

Place crushed almonds in pie shell. Add sliced apples and sprinkle with sugar. Bake 10 minutes at 425 degrees. Custard: Beat sugar, egg, cream, vanilla, and cornstarch and pour over apples. Bake at 375 degrees for 30 minutes or until custard is set. While hot, sprinkle with cinnamon and sugar mixed together.

Judy Breece

OATMEAL PIE

Preparation: 15 minutes   Serves: 8
Cooking: 1 hour

2 eggs, beaten
2/3 cup sugar
2/3 cup uncooked oatmeal (regular
   or quick cooking)
1/4 teaspoon salt

1 teaspoon vanilla extract
1 unbaked 8-inch pie shell
2/3 cup melted margarine
2/3 cup white corn syrup

Mix all ingredients together and pour into uncooked pie shell. Bake at 350 degrees about one hour.

Mary Elizabeth Irvin

PEACH CUSTARD PIE

Preparation: 10 minutes   Serves: 6 to 8
Cooking: 40 to 50 minutes

1 stick butter
1 cup sugar
2 tablespoons flour

1 heaping cup sliced canned
   peaches, drained
3 eggs
1 9-inch pie shell

Cream butter, sugar and flour together. Add 3 egg yolks (reserve whites for meringue). Mix well with peaches. Pour into unbaked 9-inch pie shell. Cook at 350 degrees for 40 to 50 minutes until done. Beat egg whites with 3 tablespoons sugar, top pie and brown.

Grace Lowdermilk

MIXED FRUIT CRISP

Preparation: 45 minutes
Cooking: 1 hour

Serves: 12

6 graham crackers
12 dried apricots
⅓ cup sugar
2 tablespoons all purpose flour
½ cup golden raisins
1½ pounds Granny Smith apples, peeled, halved lengthwise and cored
1½ pounds firm ripe Bosc pears, peeled, halved lengthwise and cored

1 cup unbleached all purpose flour
½ cup firmly packed dark brown sugar
½ cup (1 stick) unsalted butter, cut into 8 pieces, well chilled
2 teaspoons vanilla
Pinch of salt
1 cup sour cream

Position rack in center of oven and then preheat to 350 degrees. Steel Knife (food processor): Finely chop 4 graham crackers. Add apricots, ⅓ cup sugar and 2 tablespoons flour. Finely chop apricots, using 8 on/off turns. Add raisins and mix 2 seconds. Leave mixture in work bowl. Carefully remove steel knife and insert medium slicer.

Medium Slicer: Stand apples upright in feed tube and slice, using firm pressure. (If using processor with small work bowl, transfer mixture to large bowl.) Repeat with pears. Spoon all fruit into 9-inch square baking dish. Mix gently. Do not clean work bowl.

Steel Knife: Take out medium slicer of processor and insert steel knife. Finely chop remaining 2 graham crackers. Add 1 cup flour, brown sugar, butter, vanilla and salt and mix until blended but granular, about 15 seconds. Spoon evenly over fruit mixture. Bake at 350 degrees until top is crisp, about 1 hour. Serve hot, warm or at room temperature with sour cream, Dream Whip or whipped cream.

Nancy Balderacchi

PEACH COBBLER

Preparation: 5 minutes
Cooking: 24 minutes

Serves: 10

1 stick margarine
1 cup sugar
1 cup plain flour

1 cup milk
3 teaspoons baking powder
1 can peach pie mix

Preheat oven to 350 degrees. Melt margarine in 2 quart dish in oven. Mix together sugar, flour, milk, baking powder. Pour this mixture into dish with melted margarine. Add peach pie mix, do not stir. Bake at 350 degrees for 24 minutes or until lightly browned. Serve hot. Top with vanilla ice cream.

Anne Davis

PUMPKIN PECAN PIE

Preparation: 10 minutes
Cooking: 40 minutes

Serves: 6 to 8

4 slightly beaten eggs
2 cups canned or mashed cooked
   pumpkin
1 cup sugar
1/2 cup dark corn syrup

1 teaspoon vanilla
1/2 teaspoon cinnamon
1/4 teaspoon salt
1 unbaked 9-inch pie shell
1 cup chopped pecans

Combine ingredients except pecans. Pour into pie shell. Top with pecans. Bake at 350 degrees for 40 minutes, or until set.

Nancy Reagan

Nancy Reagan

APRICOT DELIGHT

Preparation: 30 minutes

Serves: 10 to 12

1/2 pound vanilla wafers
1 cup butter (no substitute)
1 1/2 cups powdered sugar
3 medium eggs

1 (16-ounce) can apricots, drained
   and chopped
1 cup chopped pecans
1 pint heavy cream, whipped

Crush vanilla wafers fine and save 1/2 cup to sprinkle on top. Cream butter, add sugar and beat thoroughly. Add eggs one at a time, beating very well after each addition. Put torte together as follows: Pat vanilla wafer crumbs in bottom of spring form pan. Spread on butter-cream mixture, spread apricots, sprinkle nuts, top with whipped cream, and sprinkle reserved crumbs on top. Cover with plastic wrap and chill 24 hours. To serve, remove sides of pan and cut in wedges.

Laura Stroupe

EXTRA SPECIAL APPLE CRISP

Preparation: 20 minutes
Cooking: 40 minutes

Serves: 6 to 8

6 cups sliced apples
1 cup white granulated sugar
1 cup water
2 tablespoons cornstarch
2 teaspoons cinnamon

1 cup flour
3/4 cup quick oatmeal
1 cup brown sugar
1/2 cup melted butter

Spread apples in a 9-inch square greased baking pan. Cook white sugar, water and cornstarch until clear and thickened. Pour over apples. Sprinkle with cinnamon. Mix the flour, oatmeal, brown sugar and butter until crumbly and sprinkle over apples. Bake at 350 degrees for about 40 minutes, until apples are tender.

Laurie Southworth

CHOCOLATE CHIP PECAN PIE

Preparation: 10 minutes   Serves: 12 to 16
Cooking: 40 minutes

½ cup butter	1 cup pecans
1 cup sugar	1 teaspoon vanilla
1 cup white Karo syrup	Pinch of salt
4 eggs	3 ounces chocolate chips

Melt butter in saucepan. Mix with sugar and white Karo syrup. Beat eggs and add to mixture. Stir in pecans, vanilla, salt, and chocolate chips. Pour into two unbaked 8-inch pie shells. Bake at 350 degrees for 40 minutes.

Omit the chocolate chips and you have a great pecan pie!

Glenda Johnson

FRENCH SILK CHOCOLATE PIE

Preparation: ½ hour   Serves: 6

¼ pound butter	1 teaspoon vanilla
¾ cup sugar	2 chilled eggs
1 square melted bitter chocolate	Toasted almond slivers
	Whipped cream

Using an electric beater, cream the butter with the sugar. Add chocolate and vanilla. Add chilled eggs one at a time, beating 2 minutes after each. Pour into a baked pie shell. Chill for 1 hour. Top with whipped cream. Sprinkle with black walnuts or toasted almond slivers.

Connie Wortham

CAROLINE'S CHOCOLATE PIE

Preparation: 5 minutes   Serves: 6
Cooking: 40 minutes

1 9-inch unbaked pie crust	2 eggs
1½ cups sugar	1 teaspoon vanilla
3½ tablespoons cocoa	½ stick butter
1 small (5⅓-ounce) can evaporated milk	

Beat eggs well. Set aside. Sift together sugar and cocoa. Add cocoa-sugar mixture to eggs. Add milk, melted butter, and vanilla. Pour in unbaked 9-inch prepared pie shell. Cook 40 minutes at 350 degrees.

Caroline Lee

BASIC BUTTERMILK PIE

Preparation: 15 minutes   Serves: 6 to 8
Cooking: 30 to 45 minutes

1 stick butter or margarine, melted
2 cups sugar
1 tablespoon flour, heaping
3 eggs

1 cup buttermilk, scant
2 teaspoons vanilla
Pinch of nutmeg, optional
2 (8-inch) frozen pie shells, thawed

In mixer, combine melted butter with sugar and flour. Add eggs, one at a time. Add buttermilk, vanilla, and nutmeg. Pour into pie crust shells. Bake at 350 degrees for 35 to 45 minutes. Freezes beautifully.

Helen Lineberry

FUDGE PIE

Preparation: 20 minutes   Serves: 8

1 can Eagle brand sweetened
   condensed milk
Pinch of salt
2 squares (ounces) of bittersweet
   chocolate

$1/4$ cup water
$1/2$ teaspoon vanilla
1 baked 9-inch pie shell

Put milk in double boiler with salt and chocolate. Stir until chocolate is melted and thickened. Pour in $1/4$ cup water and stir until it thickens again. Add $1/2$ teaspoon of vanilla and pour in cooked pie shell. Refrigerate for 3 hours and serve with whipped cream.

Nan Brittsen

HELEN'S BREAD PUDDING

Preparation: 20 minutes   Serves: 12
Cooking: 40 to 45 minutes

1 stick butter
1 cup sugar, scant
4 eggs
2 cups milk, warmed

Pinch salt
½ teaspoon vanilla
2 slices bread

Cream butter and sugar. Beat eggs, one at a time and add to creamed mixture. Add warm milk, pinch of salt and vanilla. Toast bread on one side. Cut into one-inch cubes. Stir into mixture. Place in greased 1½ quart casserole. Place casserole in pan of hot water and bake at 350 degrees for 40 to 45 minutes. Best when served warm.

Many years ago one of Greensboro's finest cooks, the late Helen Mulvey, shared this "secret" recipe.

Nancy Beard

RUM PUMPKIN PIE

Preparation: 30 minutes   Serves: 8

¾ cup brown sugar
1 envelope unflavored gelatin
1 teaspoon cinnamon
½ teaspoon nutmeg
½ teaspoon salt
¼ teaspoon ginger

3 eggs, separated
¾ cup milk
1¼ cups cooked pumpkin (or
   14-ounce can)
⅓ cup light rum
⅓ cup sugar
1 9-inch pie shell, baked

In saucepan, mix together brown sugar, gelatin, cinnamon, nutmeg, salt and ginger. In bowl, beat 3 egg yolks with milk and stir into sugar mixture. Bring mixture to a boil and simmer one minute, stirring constantly. Remove from heat and stir in pumpkin and rum until well blended. Chill until thickens slightly. Fold in 3 egg whites beaten with sugar until they hold definite peaks. Spoon pumpkin mixture into baked pie shell and chill until firm. Serve with sweetened whipped cream.

Ginny Leone

STRAWBERRIES CARDINAL

Preparation: 10 minutes   Serves: 6

1½ quarts fresh strawberries
¼ to ½ cup sugar
1 (10-ounce) package frozen
   raspberries, thawed

2 tablespoons sugar
1 tablespoon orange liqueur
1 teaspoon fresh lemon juice
Fresh mint springs, if available

Empty strawberries into a colander and wash well under cold water. Remove hulls, Gently pat berries dry on paper towels. If small, leave whole. If large, halve. Place in bowl and sprinkle with ¼ to ½ cup sugar. Stir lightly with rubber spatula to distribute sugar. Cover and chill for several hours. In electric blender or food processor, blend thawed raspberries in their syrup and 2 tablespoons sugar at high speed until thoroughly pureed and slightly frothy. Strain to remove seeds. Stir in orange liqueur and lemon juice. Cover and chill. Just before serving, transfer strawberries to a serving bowl and ladle sauce over them, using just enough to coat them lightly. Garnish with mint springs.

Elizabeth Little

MILE-HIGH MERINGUE

Preparation: 15 to 20 minutes   Serves: 8 to 10

2 egg whites   ½ cup boiling water
½ cup sugar   ½ teaspoon vanilla
½ teaspoon cream of tartar

Combine egg whites, sugar and cream of tartar in a large bowl. Add boiling water and beat at once. Continue beating until very thick and fluffy. Add vanilla. Bake as you would any meringue just until browned.

Lousie Glover

BAKLAVA

Preparation: 2 hours   Serves: 48 to 60
Cooking: 2 hours

1 pound phyllo dough   1 pound pecans, finely chopped
1 pound clarified butter, melted   Syrup (recipe follows)
   (recipe follows)

Clarified Butter (1 pound):
Cook 3 pounds of butter over low heat in a heavy pot until foam on top turns light brown, and sediment goes to bottom and turns light brown. Strain through cheese cloth. May store on shelf or keep for months in refrigerator.
Syrup:
1 lemon
5 cups sugar
2½ cups water
Using candy thermometer, let water and sugar cook to 224 degrees, then add lemon juice and cook to 226 degrees. Cool.
Pastry:
Thaw frozen dough 3 to 4 hours before using. Spread dough flat and cover with damp cloth to prevent drying. Layer 4 sheets of dough, buttering each one. Sprinkle ½ cup nuts over entire sheet. Roll jelly roll fashion from narrow end. Butter roll lightly and set aside. Repeat until all dough is used. Cut each roll into 8 to 10 slices. Use remaining butter on top. Place in buttered pan the way they were cut (prevents nuts from falling out). Bake in 250 degree oven for 2 hours or until golden brown. While pastry is cooking, make syrup. Pour cold syrup over cookies as soon as they are removed from oven. Cover lightly and let "season" until next day. Keeps well in cookie tins for several weeks!

Cindy Joseph

PRALINE BROWNIES

Preparation: 25 minutes
Cooking: 30 minutes

Yield: 24 squares

2 sticks of butter
4 squares baking chocolate
4 eggs
2 cups sugar
1½ cups flour
1 teaspoon vanilla
Pinch of salt

Topping:
3 tablespoons melted butter
¾ cup light brown sugar
¾ cup chopped pecans

Melt together the butter and chocolate. Mix lightly beaten eggs with sugar, flour, vanilla, and salt. Add melted butter and chocolate. Spread in 13 × 9 × 2 inch pan. Combine 3 tablespoons melted butter, brown sugar and pecans. Sprinkle evenly over batter. Bake 25 to 30 minutes at 350 degrees. Do not overcook. Brownies should be creamy in the center.

Sandra Burns

KAHLUA FUDGE BROWNIES

Preparation: 15 minutes
Cooking: 30 minutes

Yield: 2 dozen

1½ cups sifted flour
½ teaspoon baking powder
½ teaspoon salt
⅔ cup butter or margarine
3 ounces unsweetened chocolate
3 large eggs

2 cups sugar
¼ cup Kahlua
¾ cup chopped walnuts
1 tablespoon Kahlua for tops of
   bars

Preheat oven to 350 degrees. Sift flour with baking powder and salt. Melt butter with chocolate over very low heat or over hot water. Beat eggs with sugar until light. Stir in chocolate mixture and ¼ cup Kahlua. Add flour mixture and mix well. Stir in walnuts. Turn into greased 9 inch square pan lined in bottom with greased foil (or use Pam). Bake in center of 350 degree oven for 30 minutes, until top springs back when touched lightly in the center and edges begin to pull away from pan. Be careful not to overbake. Remove from oven and cool in pan. When cold, brush top with 1 tablespoon Kahlua. Let stand until thoroughly cold before cutting. Use sharp knife for cutting into bars. (Wet knife in hot water for easy cutting). Do not use homemade Kahlua. Brownies remain soft, moist and fudgy in the center — with a thin, crisp, top and bottom crust.

Caroline Lee

BOURBON BROWNIES

Preparation: 30 minutes

Cooking: 30 minutes

Yield: 3 dozen

Brownies:
1 cup sugar
⅔ cup shortening
¼ cup water
12 ounces semi-sweet chocolate
    chips
2 teaspoons vanilla
4 eggs
1½ cups flour
½ teaspoon soda
½ teaspoon salt
2 cups nuts, chopped
½ cup bourbon

White Frosting:
1 cup butter, softened
1 pound box confectioners sugar
2 teaspoons rum extract

Chocolate Glaze:
12 ounces semi-sweet chocolate
    chips
2 tablespoons shortening (will not
    work with butter or margarine)

Combine sugar, shortening and water in a saucepan and bring to a boil. Remove from heat and stir in chocolate chips and vanilla. Beat in eggs, then flour, soda and salt. Add nuts. Spread in greased 13 × 9 × 2 inch pan. Bake at 325 degrees for 30 minutes or until done. Remove from oven and sprinkle with bourbon. Let cool. Beat frosting ingredients together until smooth. Spread over cooled brownie and chill. Melt chocolate glaze ingredients over low heat. Spread over frosting. Chill again. Cut into squares. Store in refrigerator, but for best flavor let come to room temperature before serving.

Darlene Young

MONODNOCK BARS

Preparation: 15 minutes

Cooking: 20 minutes

Yield: 2 dozen

¼ cup butter or margarine
½ cup light brown sugar minus 1
    tablespoon (sugar should be
    packed)
½ cup granulated sugar minus 1
    tablespoon
1 egg

1 teaspoon vanilla
½ cup plain flour
¼ teaspoon baking powder
¼ teaspoon salt
½ cup Nestles semi-sweet
    chocolate morsels
½ cup chopped pecans

Cream butter and sugars. Add egg and vanilla. Blend until fluffy. Add sifted flour, baking powder and salt to creamed mixture. Mix well. Spread batter in greased 8 x 8 inch pan. Sprinkle chocolate bits and chopped pecans evenly over the batter. Bake at 350 degrees for 20 minutes. Do not overcook.

Ruth Davis

THREE LAYER BROWNIES

Preparation: 30 minutes   Yield: 24
Cooking: 20 minutes

Layer 1:

2 squares semi-sweet baking   1 cup sugar
   chocolate   2 eggs, beaten
1 stick butter or margarine   1/2 cup flour

Melt chocolate and butter together. Add sugar and cook about 2 minutes or until dissolved well. Add beaten eggs and blend well. Add flour and pour into a 9 × 9 inch greased metal pan. Bake at 350 degrees for 15 to 20 minutes. Do not overcook! Cool.

Layer 2:

1/2 stick butter or margarine   2 tablespoons evaporated milk
2 cups confectioner's sugar   1 tablespoon vanilla

Mix ingredients together, adding additional milk if needed for spreading consistency. Spread over cooled first layer and smooth out. Refrigerate for one hour.

Layer 3:

2 squares semi-sweet baking cho-   2 tablespoons butter or margarine
   colate

Melt chocolate and butter together. Drizzle over second layer. Put in refrigerator and chill. Let stand out for about ten minutes to cut into small squares. Can be frozen. Can be doubled and baked in a jelly roll pan.

Nancy Jones

BUTTERSCOTCH SQUARES

Preparation: 20 minutes   Yield: 48 squares
Cooking: 25 to 30 minutes

1 (12-ounce) butterscotch morsels   1 (14-ounce) sweetened condensed
1/2 cup butter   milk
2 cups graham cracker crumbs   1 egg
1 cup chopped nuts   1 teaspoon vanilla
1 (8-ounce) cream cheese, softened

Melt butterscotch and butter together over low heat. Stir in graham cracker crumbs and nuts. Press 1/2 of the mixture in the bottom of a 9 × 13 inch pyrex dish. Beat the cream cheese, add the condensed milk, egg, and vanilla. Pour into the dish over crumbs. Top with the remainder of crumbs. Bake 25 to 30 minutes at 350 degrees. Cool to room temperature. Chill well and cut into 48 squares. Store in refrigerator.

Darlene Young

COCONUT LEMON SQUARES

Preparation: 20 minutes
Cooking: 50 minutes

Yield: 24

²/₃ cup butter or margarine
1½ cups all-purpose flour,
   measured before sifting
4 eggs
2 cups firmly packed brown sugar
1½ cups shredded coconut

¼ teaspoon baking powder
1 teaspoon vanilla extract
1⅓ cups powdered sugar
2 tablespoons grated lemon rind
3 tablespoons freshly squeezed
   lemon juice

Cut butter into flour until mixture holds together. Pat out evenly into an ungreased 12×8×2 inch pan. Bake at 350 degrees for 20 minutes. Meanwhile, beat eggs. Add brown sugar, coconut, baking powder, and vanilla extract. Spread over baked base, return to oven and bake for 25 to 30 minutes longer. Blend together powdered sugar, lemon rind, and lemon juice. Frost cookies while they are very hot, immediately after removing from oven. Leave uncovered, at least overnight, before cutting into 2-inch squares. Store in airtight container.

Sylvia Smith

PUMPKIN BARS

Preparation: 25 minutes
Cooking: 30 minutes

Yield: 20 bars

4 eggs
1⅔ cups sugar
1 cup oil
1 (16-ounce) can pumpkin

2 cups all purpose flour
2 teaspoons baking powder
2 teaspoons cinnamon
1 teaspoon salt

Beat eggs and then add remaining ingredients. (Can do by hand.) Pour batter into greased 13 x 9 x 2 inch pan and bake at 350 degrees for 25 to 30 minutes. Do not overcook! Ice while still in pan. Cut into wedges. Store in refrigerator. Can be frozen.

Frosting:
3 ounces softened cream cheese
½ cup butter

1 teaspoon vanilla
2 cups powdered sugar

Beat together and spread on cooled cake.

Madelyn Phillips

SEMI-SWEET GRAHAM LOAF

Preparation: 30 minutes   Serves: 12

1 (6-ounce) package semi-sweet
  chocolate bits
1/2 cup light corn syrup
2 tablespoons water

1 cup heavy cream, whipped
1 teaspoon vanilla
20 graham crackers

Melt chocolate bits over hot (not boiling) water. Remove from water and stir in syrup and water until smooth. Reserve 1/4 cup of this mixture for use as glaze. Fold whipped cream and vanilla into remainder. Place 5 graham crackers, broken into large pieces, in bottom of wax paper lined pan, 10 × 5 × 3 inches. Pour 1/3 of filling over crackers. Repeat to get 4 cracker layers and 3 filling layers. Drizzle glaze over top. Freeze until glaze is firm. Wrap and freeze. Serve frozen. Slice lengthwise in half, then crosswise in 2-inch slices.

Barbara Thompson

JEAN'S DATE NUT SQUARES

Preparation: 45 minutes   Yield: 16 squares
Cooking: 30 minutes

2 eggs
1/2 cup sugar
1/2 teaspoon vanilla flavoring
1/2 cup sifted flour

1/2 teaspoon baking powder
1/2 teaspoon salt
1 cup chopped walnuts
2 cups finely chopped dates

Beat eggs until foamy. Add sugar and vanilla flavoring. Sift together flour, baking powder, and salt. Stir into mixture. Add walnuts and dates. Spread into well greased 8-inch square pan. Bake at 325 degrees for 25 to 30 minutes, or until top has a dull crust. Cut into squares while warm. Cool. Remove from pan. Dip in powdered sugar.

Jean Herrmann

CHRISTMAS FRUIT BARS

Preparation: 1/2 hour   Yield: 30 squares
Cooking: 1 hour

1 cup chopped pecans
1/2 stick margarine
1/2 stick butter
1/2 box brown sugar
1 teaspoon vanilla

2 eggs
1 cup self-rising flour
1 pound candied fruit, cut-up
  (pineapple and cherries)

Preheat oven to 300 degrees. Grease and flour 9 × 13 inch pan. Cover bottom with chopped pecans. Cream margarine and butter with brown sugar. Add vanilla, eggs, and flour. Stir in fruit. Spread batter over pecans. Bake 300 degrees for one hour. Cut while hot.

Mary Henrie French

211

SOUR CREAM CHEESECAKES

Preparation: 15 minutes

Yield: 24

Cooking: 35 minutes

3 (8-ounce) packages cream
  cheese, room temperature
5 eggs
1½ teaspoons almond extract
1 cup sugar

Topping:
16 ounces sour cream
½ cup sugar
1 teaspoon vanilla

Beat cream cheese, eggs, almond extract and sugar together for 5 minutes. Fill foil muffin cups ¾ full. Place on cookie sheet. Bake at 300 degrees for 20 to 25 minutes. Remove from oven and cool for 10 minutes.
Topping: Mix together sour cream, sugar, and vanilla. Top each cheesecake with mixture. Bake for 10 minutes longer. Chill. Can be topped with strawberries or favorite fruit pie filling. Freeze beautifully!

Donna Moore

DAINTY TEA CAKES

Preparation: 20 minutes

Serves: 6 to 8

Cooking: 8 to 10 minutes

½ cup Crisco
¾ cup sugar
1 egg
¾ teaspoon vanilla
1½ cups flour

½ teaspoon baking powder
¼ teaspoon salt
1 tablespoon milk (maybe a bit
  more)
Strawberry, apple, or grape jelly

Cream Crisco and sugar well. Blend in slightly beaten egg and vanilla. Sift flour, baking powder and salt twice and add alternately with the milk. Mix well. Chill thoroughly in the refrigerator, even overnight. Roll in small balls. Place on cookie sheets and then make a dent with the end of your finger in center of each ball of dough. Place a bit of jelly in the indenture and bake at 400 degrees for 8 to 10 minutes.

Ellen Adams

CHOCOLATE TURTLE COOKIES

Preparation: 20 minutes
Cooking: 18 to 22 minutes

Yield: 3 to 4 dozen

Crust:
2 cups all purpose flour
1 cup firmly packed brown sugar
1/2 cup butter, softened
1 cup whole pecans

Caramel layer:
2/3 cup butter
1/2 cup firmly packed brown sugar
1 cup milk chocolate chips

Crust:
Preheat oven to 350 degrees. In large mixer bowl, combine flour, brown sugar, and butter. Mix at medium speed 2 to 3 minutes or until well mixed and particles are fine. Pat firmly into ungreased 13 × 9 × 2 inch pan. Sprinkle pecans evenly over unbaked crust.
Caramel layer:
In a heavy saucepan, combine butter and brown sugar. Cook over medium heat, stirring constantly until surface of mixture begins to boil. Boil one minute, stirring constantly. Pour caramel layer evenly over pecans and unbaked crust. Bake near center of 350 degree oven for 18 to 22 minutes or until entire layer is bubbly and crust is light golden. Remove from oven and immediately sprinkle with milk chocolate chips. Allow chips to begin to melt. Slightly swirl chips as they melt, saving some whole for marbled effect. Cool completely before cutting into squares.

Margaret Albright, Vivien Bauman

CHOCOLATE-FILLED SNOWBALLS

Preparation: 45 minutes
Cooking: 12 minutes

Yields: 5 dozen

1 cup soft butter
1/2 cup sugar
1 teaspoon vanilla
2 cups sifted flour

1 cup finely chopped pecans
1 (5 3/4-ounce) package chocolate
   kisses
Confectioner's sugar

Cream butter, sugar and vanilla until very ight and fluffy. Add sifted flour and nuts, blending well. Cover bowl with plastic wrap and chill dough about 1 hour. Remove foil wrappers from kisses. Preheat oven to 375 degrees. Shape dough around kisses, using about 1 tablespoon of dough for each roll to make a ball. Cover completely. Bake 12 minutes until set, not brown. Remove from cookie sheet onto absorbent paper and cool slightly. While still warm, roll in confectioners sugar. Cool completely before storing. Roll in confectioners sugar again if desired.

Sue Nelson

MAMIE'S SUGAR COOKIES

Preparation: 30 minutes
Cooking: 10 to 12 minutes

Yield: 3 dozen

1½ cups flour
1 teaspoon baking powder
½ teaspoon salt
½ cup butter
1 cup sugar

2 egg yolks, well beaten
½ teaspoon vanilla
1 teaspoon cream
1 egg white
Granulated sugar to sprinkle

Mix and sift flour, baking powder, and salt. Set aside. Cream butter. Add sugar slowly and cream until fluffy. Stir in well beaten egg yolks and vanilla. Add dry ingredients and cream. Mix well and chill one hour. Roll and cut in any desired shape. Brush with egg white and sprinkle with granulated sugar. Bake on an ungreased cookie sheet at 350 to 375 degrees for 10 to 12 minutes.

Millie Ronemus

EASY TART COOKIES

Preparation: 5 minutes
Cooking: 13 minutes

Yield: 36

1 roll refrigerated Slice and Bake Chocolate Chip Cookies

36 Reese's Peanut Butter cups (miniature)

Cut cookie roll according to directions into 36 pieces. Put each piece into a greased and floured muffin tin. Bake at 350 degrees for approximately 7 minutes. Remove from oven. Place 1 miniature Reese's cup on top of each cookie. Press gently. Return to oven and cook approximately 5 minutes. Remove carefully from muffin cups. Cookies should be crisp.

Martha Neill

EVELYN'S OATMEAL COOKIES

Preparation: 30 minutes
Cooking: 10 minutes

Yield: 6 dozen

1 cup shortening
1 cup brown sugar
1 cup white sugar
2 beaten eggs
1 teaspoon vanilla

1½ cups plain flour
1 teaspoon salt
1 teaspoon soda
3 cups quick cooking oatmeal
1 cup chopped nuts

Cream shortening and sugars. Add eggs and vanilla. Beat well. Add sifted dry ingredients, oats, and nuts. Mix. Shape into rolls, wrap in wax paper and chill thoroughly. Slice into ¼ inch pieces. Bake on ungreased cookie sheet in 350 degree oven for ten minutes.

Margaret Albright

NUT SNACKERS

Preparation: 30 minutes
Cooking: 30 to 35 minutes

Serves: 12

1½ cups walnut halves
½ teaspoon salt
1 cup blanched almonds
½ cup butter

3 egg whites, stiffly beaten
1 cup sugar
¾ cup all purpose flour

Toast walnut halves, salt, and almonds in $15 \times 10 \times 1$ inch pan in 325 degree oven until light brown. Remove from oven. Melt butter in pan. Combine egg whites with sugar and flour. Fold in toasted nuts and spread in pan containing butter. Bake at 325 degrees for 30 to 35 minutes, stirring occasionally to break apart, until brown. Serve as cookies or candy. Makes a lovely gift from the kitchen!

Nancy Durham

SESAME SEED COOKIES

Cooking: 30 minutes

Yield: 13 dozen

2 cups butter, softened
  (no substitutes)
1½ cups sugar
3 cups all-purpose flour

1 cup sesame seeds
2 cups shredded coconut
½ cup finely chopped almonds
1 teaspoon almond flavoring,
  optional

Cream butter. Gradually add sugar. Beat until fluffy. Add flour and mix. Stir in sesame seeds, coconut and almonds. Divide dough into three 2-inch rolls. Wrap in wax paper. Refrigerate until firm. Cut into ¼ inch slices. Bake at 300 degrees for 30 minutes on ungreased cookie sheet. These crisp cookies freeze well.

Marilyn Robinson

CRUNCHY JUMBLE COOKIES

Preparation: 20 minutes
Cooking: 10 to 12 minutes

Yield: 4 to 5 dozen

1¼ cups all purpose flour
½ teaspoon baking soda
¼ teaspoon salt
½ cup margarine, softened
1 cup sugar

1 teaspoon vanilla
1 egg
2 cups Rice Krispies
1 (6-ounce) package Butterscotch
  Morsels

Sift together flour, soda, salt. Set aside. Measure margarine and sugar into large mixing bowl. Beat until well blended and smooth. Add egg and vanilla. Beat well. Add sifted ingredients and mix until combined. Stir in Rice Krispies and butterscotch morsels. Drop by teaspoons full onto lightly greased baking sheet. Bake at 350 degrees for 10 to 12 minutes until golden brown. Let cool 2 to 3 minutes before removing from cookie sheet.

Janelle Snider

BUTTERSCOTCH CHOCOLATE CHEWIES

Preparation: 15 minutes
Cooking: 35 minutes

Yield: 2 dozen

1 (18½-ounce) package yellow
  cake mix
1 cup brown sugar
2 tablespoons melted margarine
2 tablespoons honey

2 tablespoons water
2 eggs
1 (6-ounce) package chocolate
  morsels
1 cup chopped nuts

Combine cake mix, brown sugar, margarine, honey, water and eggs. Mix well. Add chocolate morsels and nuts. Stir until well blended. Spread in a greased and floured 13 × 9 × 2 inch pan. Bake at 350 degrees for about 35 minutes or until done. Cool and cut into squares.

Rachel Hull

VANILLA CRESCENTS

Preparation: 1 hour
Cooking: 30 minutes

Yield: 3 dozen

3 cups sifted flour
½ cup sugar
1 cup butter

2 egg yolks, ice cold
1 cup ground almonds
½ cup powdered sugar

Combine flour and granulated sugar. Cut in butter. Add egg yolks and almonds. Work together with hands. To shape crescent: firmly roll together a piece of dough about 3 inches long and ¾ inches thick. On lightly floured board curve dough into a crescent. Bake on lightly buttered cookie sheet in preheated 325 degree oven for 30 minutes (or until dry but not brown). Gently roll hot crescents in powdered sugar. Cool on flat surface.

Mary Ann Fuchs

KENTUCKY BOURBON CANDY

Preparation: 1 hour

Yield: 3 pounds

1 cup chopped nuts soaked in ½
  cup bourbon
½ cup Eagle Brand milk
½ cup bourbon

⅓ stick butter
2½ pounds confectioners sugar
⅓ block paraffin
6 ounces semi-sweet chocolate

Mix together milk, bourbon, and butter and add confectioners sugar, a little at a time, until you use 2½ pounds. Work up until stiff. Add cup of soaked nuts and refrigerate until stiff. Pinch off in pieces and roll into balls. Place in refrigerator. Dip in paraffin and chocolate melted together. Refrigerate. Reheat chocolate mixture if necessary.

George Anna McKenzie

ROCKY ROAD TOADS

Preparation: 5 minutes   Yield: 2 dozen

2 bars (6½ ounces each) plain   1 cup seedless raisins
   milk chocolate (or 6 ounces   1 cup miniature marshmallows
   semi-sweet chocolate)   ½ cup chopped walnuts

Break chocolate in small pieces into top of double boiler. Put over warm water. Water must never get really hot or the chocolate will have white streaks in it when it sets. Set double boiler over very low heat. Stir chocolate frequently and when it is completely melted, stir in raisins, marshmallows and walnuts. Cover a baking sheet with waxed paper. Dip a teaspoonful of the candy and push onto waxed paper with another spoon. Refrigerate.

Wanda Poole

AUNT MAULINE'S PEANUT BRITTLE

Preparation: 20 minutes   Serves: 16 to 20
Cooking: 4 minutes

1½ cups sugar   2 cups Planter's cocktail peanuts
½ cup boiling water   2 tablespoons butter or margarine
½ cup white Karo syrup   1½ teaspoons soda

Using iron skillet and wooden spoon, mix sugar, syrup, and boiling water. Boil until spins thread or forms ball in cool water. Add peanuts. Cook until golden brown. Remove from heat. Add butter and soda. Beat with wooden spoon one minute. Pour on buttered cookie sheet. When cool, break into pieces. Do not make on a humid day.

Janice Hicks

IRISH COFFEE

Preparation: 5 minutes   Serves: 1

1½ ounces Irish whiskey (bourbon   2 tablespoons sugar, may add
   may be substituted)   more but not less
½ cup freshly brewed coffee or   1½ tablespoons whipping cream,
   Sanka   lightly whipped

Heat Irish Coffee glasses with hot water or in the dishwasher. Pour in whiskey, add sugar and stir vigorously. Add coffee or Sanka. Top with cream that has been whipped (but not stiff). It is best to drop the cream onto the coffee from a cold spoon. Serve immediately!

Recipe given by a young bartender in Waterford, Ireland.

Holly Lucas

The statue of American Revolutionary War hero, Nathanael Greene is a familiar landmark to Greensboro residents. Located in the heart of Guilford Courthouse National Military Park, the statue commemorates the efforts of Greene and the American army in the South to bring about the end of the war. A favorite picnic site for city residents, the park is a tranquil setting for outings — a perfect introduction to our picnic section.

Picnic
and
Tailgating

NATHANAEL GREENE APPOINTED
NAAL GENERAL GREENE IN
COMMAND OF THE SOUTHERN
OCTOBER 14TH 1776 BORN
IN RHODE ISLAND AUGUST OF
DIED IN GEORGIA JUNE 19,178

GENERAL
NATHANAEL GREENE

FOOTBALL TAILGATE

Blender Senegalese Soup
Oven Fried Chicken
Dilly Brussels Sprouts
Gazpacho Salad, Stuffed Eggs
Pimento Cheese Sandwiches
Marcile's Fudge Cake

BLENDER SENEGALESE SOUP

Preparation: 5 minutes

Serves: 8

1 can cream of chicken soup
1 (12-ounce) carton sour cream
1 (13¾-ounce) can chicken broth
Pinch curry powder

2 shredded cucumbers
Drop Tabasco
Celery salt

Combine all ingredients in blender and serve chilled.

Chick Bolton

OVEN FRIED CHICKEN

Preparation: 15 minutes
Cooking: 45 minutes

Serves: 6 to 8

1 cup crushed herb-seasoned
   stuffing
⅔ cup grated Parmesan cheese
¼ cup snipped parsley

½ cup butter or margarine melted
2½ to 3 pounds fryer chicken
   pieces

Combine crushed stuffing, cheese, and parsley. Dip chicken pieces in melted butter, then roll in stuffing mixture. Arrange skin side up in large shallow baking pan (do not crowd). Sprinkle with remaining butter and crumbs. Bake in moderate oven (375 degrees) 45 minutes or until tender. (Turning is unnecessary.)

Alice Pearce

DILLY BRUSSELS SPROUTS

Preparation: 15 minutes   Serves: 8 to 10
Cooking: 10 minutes

2 (10-ounce) packages frozen   1 cup Italian dressing
   Brussels sprouts   1 teaspoon dillweed
Dash of salt   2 tablespoons chives

Cook Brussels sprouts in seasoned water according to package directions. Do not overcook. Drain and place in a plastic container. Add remaining ingredients and chill at least overnight before serving. Lift from dressing into serving dish. Supply toothpicks.

Anne Rendleman

GAZPACHO SALAD

Preparation: 15 minutes   Serves: 6 to 8

2 cucumbers, peeled and finely   2 garlic cloves
   diced   Salt
4 tomatoes, peeled, seeded, and   ¼ teaspoon ground cumin seed (or
   finely diced   more to taste)
2 green peppers, seeded and diced   ¼ cup vinegar
1 red onion, finely chopped   ½ cup olive oil
Salt and pepper to taste   1 tablespoon parsley, finely
12 black olives   chopped

In a glass jar or deep bowl, arrange alternate layers of cucumbers, tomatoes, green peppers and onions. Sprinkle the layers lightly with salt and pepper. Intersperse vegetables with black olives, placing some so that they show on the outside of the bowl. In a wooden mixing bowl, mash garlic cloves to a paste with a little salt and cumin seed. Beat in vinegar and olive oil. Stir in parsley. Pour dressing over salad. Chill for 2 or 3 hours. Toss to serve.

This colorful Spanish salad recipe was shared by Anne Byrd, former Greensboro resident and past president of the International Association of Cooking Schools.

STUFFED EGGS

Preparation: 20 minutes   Yield: 10 to 12 halves

5 to 6 eggs, hard boiled   Sugar, to taste
1 to 2 tablespoons oil   Garnish: pimento, parsley, chives,
Vinegar, to taste   bacon bits, or cherry tomatoes
Salt and pepper, to taste

Hard boil eggs for approximately 15 minutes and cool in cold water. Shell and cut in half lengthwise. Remove and mash yolks, reserving whites. Add remaining ingredients (except garnish). Stuff whites and garnish as desired.

A favorite of our maestro and his mother!

Mary Ann Fuchs

WORLD'S BEST PIMENTO CHEESE

Preparation: 15 minutes

2 pounds medium sharp cheddar
cheese
2 pounds New York sharp cheddar
cheese
3 ounces Parmesan cheese
2 tablespoons cracked black
pepper
1/4 teaspoon Tabasco

1 tablespoon Worcestershire sauce
1 tablespoon Lawry's Seasoned
Salt
3/4 quart jar Hellman's mayonnaise
1 (13-ounce) can Pet evaporated
milk
2 (7-ounce) jars chopped pimentos
and juice

Coarsely grate cheese. Mix remaining ingredients in another bowl and add to cheese. Food processor may be used.

Ginny White

MARCILE'S FUDGE CAKE

Preparation: 15 minutes   Serves: 8
Cooking: 40 minutes

1/2 pound butter (no substitutes)
4 squares unsweetened chocolate
1/4 cup sugar
2 cups sugar
1 1/2 cups plain flour

4 eggs, unbeaten
1/4 teaspoon salt
2 teaspoons vanilla
1 1/2 cups whole pecans

Preheat oven to 275 degrees. In top of double boiler, dissolve butter, chocolate and 1/4 cup sugar. Let cool slightly and add 2 cups sugar. Add flour alternately with eggs. Add salt, vanilla, and pecans. Pour batter in 9-inch aluminum pan, and place in oven. Raise heat to 300 degrees. Bake for approximately 40 minutes or until cake feels firm when touched by hand. Do not let it bake dry! Frost finished cake with 7 minute frosting if desired.

Kay Edwards

POLYNESIAN PICNiC

Pineapple Cheese Ball with Crackers
Ribs with Plum Sauce
Hawaiian Wings
Island Rice
Oriental Spinach Salad
Banana Bread
Hula Hula Pie
Planter's Punch or Fruit Punch

PINEAPPLE CHEESE BALL

Preparation: 15 minutes   Serves: 20

2 (8-ounce) packages cream
 cheese, softened
1 small can crushed pineapple,
 completely drained
2 tablespoons onion, chopped fine

¼ cup chopped green pepper
1 teaspoon seasoning salt
1 cup chopped nuts (reserve ⅔ for
 top)

Mix all ingredients and put in the refrigerator overnight. Next day, divide
and form in two balls, rolling them in finely chopped nuts. Then put in saran
wrap and back in refrigerator until ready to use. Put out 15 to 30 minutes
ahead of time.

Brenda Frost

RIBS WITH PLUM SAUCE

Preparation: 15 minutes   Serves: 6
Cooking Time: 1 hour

3 pounds country style pork ribs
1 envelop (¾-ounce) au jus gravy
 mix
¼ cup soy sauce
2 tablespoons vinegar
2 tablespoons honey
¼ teaspoon minced garlic

Plum Sauce:
½ cup plum preserves
1 tablespoon soy sauce
1 tablespoon vinegar

Place ribs in broiler pan. Combine ingredients and brush ribs on both sides.
Let stand one hour. Roast at 375 degrees for 45 minutes or until tender. Heat
ingredients for plum sauce and serve with ribs.

Judy Murray

HAWAIIAN WINGS

Preparation: 15 minutes   Yield: 48 pieces
Cooking: 1 hour

4 dozen chicken wings
1/2 cup honey
1/2 cup Kikkoman's soy sauce (no
   substitution)
1/2 cup cooking oil

1/2 cup sherry
2 cubes chicken bouillon
Salt and pepper to taste
   (remember soy sauce is salty)

Put all of the above ingredients in a sealed plastic container and marinate overnight. Turn in marinade occasionally. Bake in a foil lined 9 × 13-inch pan 20 minutes, then turn wings over. Bake another 20 minutes, again turning the chicken wings. Bake a final 20 minutes, watching carefully to see that wings do not burn. Take from oven when rich golden brown. May be used as an entree with larger chicken pieces!

Beverly Rogers

ISLAND RICE

Preparation: 10 minutes   Serves: 6
Cooking: 50 minutes

1 cup uncooked rice
3 tablespoons butter or margarine,
   melted

1 can (10³/₄-ounce) chicken broth,
   undiluted
5 ounces water

Preheat oven to 350 degrees. Combine all ingredients in a 1¹/₂ quart casserole. Bake uncovered at 350 degrees for 50 minutes. Garnish with parsley before serving if desired.

Judy Johnson

ORIENTAL SPINACH SALAD

Preparation: 35 minutes   Serve: 8 to 10

2 pounds fresh spinach: washed,
   dried, and cut up
1 cup croutons
4 to 6 hard cooked eggs, sliced
3/4 pound bacon, cut in bite size
   pieces
1/2 can bean sprouts, drained

Dressing:
1 cup vegetable oil
1/3 cup catsup
1 teaspoon chopped onion
1/4 cup vinegar
1/2 cup sugar
1 teaspoon Worcestershire sauce
1 teaspoon salt

Fry pieces of bacon and drain off 3/4 of grease. Add croutons and set aside. Add eggs, bacon and croutons to spinach. Let stand in refrigerator until ready to serve. At last minute, add dressing.

Pat Bennett

BANANA BREAD
(see page 65)

HULA HULA PIE

Preparation: 30 minutes   Serves: 6

1 9-inch pie shell, baked
1 cup crushed pineapple
1/2 cup sugar
2 tablespoons flour

1/4 cup chopped nuts
2 bananas
Whipped topping

Mix sugar, flour and pineapple. Cook over low heat to thicken. Cool. Slice 2 bananas and line pie shell. Sprinkle nuts over bananas, pour pineapple mixture over nuts. Top with whipped topping. Refrigerate about 1 hour before serving.

Nita Karnes

PLANTER'S PUNCH

Preparation: 5 minutes   Serves: 8

1 1/2 cups pineapple juice
1 1/2 cups orange juice (not
   concentrate)
1 (6-ounce) can frozen limeade

1 (6-ounce) can white rum (or 6
   ounces white rum)
2 to 4 tablespoons grenadine
   (depending on eye appeal)

Mix all ingredients and serve over ice. This punch can be made ahead and kept in refrigerator. Add the rum just before you serve. If you prefer tamer version, eliminate the rum.

Pat Austin

FRUIT PUNCH

Preparation: 15 minutes   Serves: 50

6 cups water
4 cups sugar (boil 3 minutes and
   cool)
1/2 cup lemon juice
1 1/2 cups orange juice

7 to 12 bananas liquified in
   blender
1 large can pineapple juice
4 quarts Sprite

Boil water and sugar for 3 minutes. Cool. Add remaining ingredients. Freeze all the above in container or containers. Place in punch bowl slightly thawed and add 4 quarts Sprite.

Mary Henrie French

NORTH CAROLINA PIG PICKING

Buck's Eastern Carolina Brunswick Stew
Barbecued Pig
Bourbon Baked Beans
Slaw
Spoonbread
Picnic Cake
Iced Tea Concentrate and Beer

BUCK'S EASTERN CAROLINA BRUNSWICK STEW

Preparation: 4 to 5 hours   Yield: 45 pints

15 pounds potatoes, pared and cubed

4 chickens, 4 to 5 pounds each, cooked, deboned, cubed

Stock from 4 chickens

10 (16-ounce) cans of midget-size butterbeans (or limas)

16 (16-ounce) cans of tomatoes

6 (16-ounce) cans of white shoe peg corn (not yellow)

1/2 pound smoked pork, cubed

1 pound salt pork, cubed

1 or 2 red pepper pods (to taste)

The day before, cook chickens until tender. Reserve stock. Debone chicken and refrigerate until next morning. Early on an autumn Saturday morning, build a fire outdoors, using hickory wood so that it *surrounds* the pot and is not directly under the pot. Pour the chicken stock into the pot. When the stock begins to get hot, add the chicken, tomatoes, beans, potatoes, smoked pork, salt pork, and red pepper pods. Simmer slowly for about 4 to 5 hours, stirring occasionally to prevent vegetables from scorching. When stew thickens, allow fire to die down. Add white shoe peg corn, stirring occasionally. Cover and let settle about 30 minutes. To add to the festivity, invite the neighbors over to assist in the stirring. You'll have plenty for company . . . and enough for the freezer, too. If pouring stew into freezer cartons, allow to cool overnight before storing in freezer.

This Brunswick Stew recipe has been handed down in the
Hoffler Family (Enfield, N.C., Halifax County) for so
long that no one remembers who stirred the first pot!

Mary Hoffler

BARBECUED PIG

Preparation: 1 hour   Serves: 40
Cooking: 10 to 12 hours

1 (80 pound) pig or pig half,   Barbecue Sauce:
   dressed by butcher   1 gallon vinegar less 1 quart
1 portable cooker or pit dug with   1 (14-ounce) bottle catsup
   screen wire over top   1/2 bottle (11/2 ounces) Texas Pete
30 pounds charcoal   1/2 box salt (61/2 ounces)
Hickory or other hard wood pieces   3/4 small can black pepper (3/4
                                             ounce)

Prepare sauce: After pouring off one quart of the vinegar, put all other ingredients into gallon jar with vinegar and shake well. Sauce will last indefinitely, and can be used on chicken, ribs, or anything you wish to barbecue. Needs no refrigeration.

To cook pig: Start heating coals in metal trash can or grill one hour before placing pig on wire rack. Place pig skin side down for the first hour. Turn skin side up for next 7 hours, continually placing hot coals in bottom of pit. Turn pig skin side down for the next 3 hours. (Skin acts as a pan to hold the sauce.) Baste often. Pig is ready when meat can easily be pulled from bones, hence the name "pig picking."

North Carolina is famous for barbecued pig prepared in this manner!

Nan Price

BOURBON BAKED BEANS

Preparation: 10 minutes   Serves: 12 to 16
Cooking: 1 hour, 20 minutes

4 cans B&M baked beans   1/2 cup bourbon
1 teaspoon dry mustard   1/2 cup coffee
1/2 cup chili (canned or   Brown sugar, to taste
   homemade)   8 pineapple slices
1 tablespoon molasses

Mix all ingredients except brown sugar and pineapple. Let stand at room temperature overnight. Cook, covered, in 375 degree oven for 40 minutes. Remove, sprinkle with brown sugar and pineapple slices. Bake, uncovered, 40 minutes longer.

Louise Glover

GOOD OLD SOUTHERN SPOON BREAD

Preparation: 20 minutes   Serves: 12
Cooking: 50 minutes

1 cup cornmeal   3 eggs, yolks and whites beaten
2 cups milk   separately
1 teaspoon salt   3 tablespoons butter

Cook corn meal, milk and salt to "mush" consistency over direct heat. Drop
in butter. Fold in egg yolks and egg whites. Pour into greased 1½-2 quart
casserole. Bake 325 degrees for 50 minutes.

Mary Hoffler

PICNIC CAKE

Preparation: 15 minutes   Serves: 20
Cooking: 35 to 45 minutes

1 cup dates, cut up   ½ cup granulated sugar
1 teaspoon soda   ½ cup brown sugar
1½ cups boiling water   ¾ cup margarine
½ cup chocolate chips   2 eggs
½ cup chopped walnuts   2 cups flour
1 teaspoon margarine   ¾ teaspoon salt
½ teaspoon water   ¾ teaspoon soda

Mix and let stand: dates, soda, boiling water. Mix together in small bowl:
chocolate chips, nuts, margarine and water. Cream together: sugars,
margarine, and eggs. Sift together: flour, salt, soda. Add date and flour
mixtures alternately to the creamed sugars, margarine, and eggs. Pour into
a greased and floured 9 × 13 inch pan. Sprinkle nuts and chocolate mixture
evenly over top. Bake at 350 degrees for 35 to 45 minutes until deep golden
brown.

Beverly Rogers

ICED TEA CONCENTRATE

Preparation: 10 minutes   Yield: ½ gallon

2 cups water   1 cup sugar
7 small tea bags   ½ cup fresh lemon juice

Bring water to boil. Add tea bags and simmer for 5 minutes. Remove from
heat, add sugar and lemon juice, and mix well. Let sit for 25 to 30 minutes.
This can be stored in refrigerator in concentrate form. When ready to serve,
add enough cold water to make ½ gallon.

Barbara Cone

BACKYARD BEACHCOMBER BUFFET

Clam Fritters
Broiled Scampi
Creamed Crab Superb
Carrots au Sucre
Stuffed Tomatoes
Artichoke Salad
Daiquiri Pie
Lime Cooler

TOPSAIL CLAM FRITTERS

Preparation: 30 minutes   Serves: 12

1 (8-ounce) package cream
  cheese, softened
2 egg yolks and 4 whole eggs
1 small can minced clams, drained
2 teaspoons lemon juice

1 teaspoon salt
Scant pepper
1 tablespoon chopped onion
1 cup flour
2 teaspoons baking powder

Blend cheese and eggs together. Add clams, lemon juice, salt, pepper and onion. Add flour which has been mixed with baking powder. Allow this to sit for ½ hour before dropping by spoonfuls into hot fat. Drain on paper before serving.

Mary Gay Brady

CREAMED CRAB SUPERB

Preparation: 15 minutes   Serves: 4
Cooking: 10 minutes

1 pound backfin crabmeat
2 tablespoons butter
2 tablespoons flour
1 cup cream (half and half)
1 teaspoon salt
¾ teaspoon dry mustard

Dash of white pepper
Dash of red pepper
1 teaspoon Worcestershire
½ teaspoon lemon juice
¾ tablespoon onion juice

Pick crabmeat to remove any shells. Put aside. In medium size saucepan, melt butter. Add flour, and mix well. Add cream and stir with wooden spoon until slightly thickened. Add other ingredients. Add crab. Spoon into shells. Cook 5 to 10 minutes in 350 degree oven until warmed.

Bernie Cole

BROILED SCAMPI

Preparation: 10 minutes
Cooking: 5 minutes

Serves: 6

4 dozen large shrimp
4 green onions, chopped
2 sticks butter, melted
4 cloves garlic, crushed

3 tablespoons A-1 Sauce
2 tablespoons lemon juice
2 teaspoons salt
1 teaspoon coarse black pepper

Peel shrimp, split, and leave tails on. Place in oiled baking dish. At serving time broil 4 inches from flame for 5 minutes. Mix all other ingredients for sauce and heat. Pour the heated sauce over the cooked shrimp.

Carolyn Maddux

STUFFED TOMATOES

Preparation: 20 minutes
Cooking: 20 minutes

Serves: 8

8 medium tomatoes
1 (10-ounce) package frozen, chopped spinach
1 cup Pepperidge Farm herb stuffing
3 eggs beaten

1/2 cup margarine, melted
1/4 cup Parmesan cheese
1/2 teaspoon garlic salt
1/2 teaspoon "Accent"
1/2 teaspoon pepper (plain or lemon)

Top the tomatoes, scoop out, and drain. Mix cooked spinach with stuffing. Add eggs, margarine, Parmesan cheese, garlic salt, "Accent", and pepper. Stuff the tomatoes with this mixture and bake for 20 minutes at 350 degrees.

Ruth Davis

CARROTS AU SUCRE

Preparation: 10 minutes
Cooking: 30 to 40 minutes

Serves: 8

2 pounds carrots
1/4 cup butter

1 cup sugar
1 teaspoon salt

Scrape carrots, cut into thin strips or rounds. Put all in a heavy covered skillet. Cover and cook very slowly, shaking pan frequently, 30 to 40 minutes or until tender. Uncover pan as little as possible so steam will not escape.

Donna Tibbals

ARTICHOKE SALAD

Preparation: 20 minutes   Serves: 4

2 cups chicken broth
1 cup uncooked rice
1/4 cup chopped green onions
1/4 cup chopped green pepper
1/4 cup sliced stuffed olives

1 (6-ounce) jar marinated
   artichoke hearts, drained and
   chopped
1/2 teaspoon dried dill weed
1/2 cup mayonnaise

Cook rice in broth until tender. Add other ingredients and mix. May be served chilled or at room temperature. Serve in lettuce-lined bowl, garnished with sliced olives.

Judy Stuart

DAIQUIRI PIE

Preparation: 45 minutes   Serves: 8

4 eggs, separated
Sugar (3/4 cup and 1/2 cup)
Pinch of salt
3 tablespoons lime or lemon juice
   (fresh only)

1 tablespoon unflavored gelatine (1
   envelope)
3 tablespoons rum
1 (8 or 9 inch) graham cracker
   crust, baked

In top of double boiler, combine 4 egg yolks, 3/4 cup of sugar, pinch of salt. Stir until smooth. Over low heat in small sauce pan dissolve 3 tablespoons of lime or lemon juice and gelatin. Add this to yolk mixture and stir for 3 minutes. Remove from heat and stir in rum. Beat 4 egg whites and as they thicken gradually add 1/2 cup of sugar. Fold yolk mixture into egg whites. Pour into crust. Put in freezer. To serve: Thaw, but serve cold. Decorate with whipped cream.

Joan Dilworth

LIME COOLER

Preparation: 5 minutes   Serves: 10

2 (6-ounce) cans frozen limeade,
   partially thawed
4 cups water
1/2 cup lemon juice

1 quart chilled ginger ale
1 1/2 cups vodka (optional)
Pineapple slices or mint sprigs

Place limeade and water in blender and blend at medium speed until frothy. Stir in lemon juice. Transfer into container and chill at least 1 hour. When ready to serve, add soda and vodka and shake. Garnish each glass with a mint sprig or a twisted pineapple ring.

Julie Blalock

FOURTH OF JULY COOKOUT

Chilled Cherry Soup
Grilled Shoulder Roast
Hash Brown Potato Casserole
Sweet and Sour Green Beans
Fresh Blueberry Muffins
Fruit Pizza
Bees Knees

CHILLED CHERRY SOUP

Preparation: 15 minutes

Serves: 8 to 10

3 pints fresh red tart cherries or 3 cans (16 ounces each) pitted red tart cherries, drained, reserving juice
1/2 teaspoon cinnamon

1/4 teaspoon cloves
Water to make 1 quart when added to cherry juice
1/2 cup sugar
3/4 cup dairy sour cream

Combine cherries, cinnamon, and cloves with water and cherry juice in large saucepan. Bring to boiling. Reduce heat and simmer 15 minutes. Puree fruit by pressing through a sieve, or use an electric blender. Add sugar and stir until it dissolves. Cool thoroughly. Beat in sour cream or serve by spoonfuls on top of soup. May be served in mugs or bowls as a refreshing first course.

Joni Bowie

MARINATED SHOULDER ROAST FOR THE GRILL

Preparation: 10 minutes
Cooking: 45 minutes

Serves: 6 to 8

Shoulder roast, 1 1/2-inch thick

Unseasoned meat tenderizer

Sauce:
One (5-ounce) bottle soy sauce
1/4 cup brown sugar
1 tablespoon lemon juice

1 teaspooon Worcestershire sauce
1 1/2 cups water
1/4 cup sherry (optional)

Pour sauce over meat. Cover pan and leave in refrigerator 12 to 24 hours. Cook on charcoal grill about 45 minutes for 4 pound roast and 30 minutes for 3 pounds. Allow 1/2 pound per serving.

Janet Sheffield

SWEET AND SOUR GREEN BEANS

Preparation: 10 minutes   Serves: 6

4 cups cooked French style frozen
   green beans or canned beans
1 large onion, sliced thin
2 cloves of garlic, minced
1/2 cup vinegar
1/4 cup water

1/2 cup sugar
2 tablespoons salad oil
Salt and pepper to taste
1/2 teaspoon MSG (Accent)
   (optional)

Combine beans and garlic in a bowl. Heat in a pan the vinegar, water and sugar until mixture boils. Stir to dissolve sugar. Remove from heat. Add salad oil. Pour over beans, onion, and garlic. Season with salt, pepper, and MSG. Toss gently until well blended. Serve hot or cover and chill several hours or overnight before serving.

Madelyn Phillips

HASH BROWN POTATO CASSEROLE

Preparation: 20 minutes   Serves: 8
Cooking: 40 minutes

2 pound bag frozen hash-brown
   potatoes
1/4 pound margarine, melted
2 cups shredded sharp cheese
1 pint sour cream

1 (10 3/4-ounce) can cream of
   chicken soup
1/2 cup chopped onion
1 teaspoon salt
1/2 teaspoon pepper

Partially thaw potatoes and mix all ingredients together. Put into a greased 9 × 13 inch casserole dish. Bake at 350 degrees for 40 minutes. Can be frozen. For a crispy topping, sprinkle with crushed cornflakes combined with melted butter.

Becky Brown

BEES KNEES

Preparation: 15 minutes   Serves: 1

1 ounce lemon juice
1 ounce honey
1 jigger gin

1 teaspoon cherry juice
Gingerale
Crushed ice

Mix lemon juice and honey. Shake well and chill. Add gin and cherry juice to mixture. Stir well. Add ginger ale and crushed ice to fill a 10 or 12 ounce glass.

May make ahead, adding ice and gingerale at serving time.

Julie Blalock

FRESH BLUEBERRY MUFFINS

Preparation: 15 minutes   Yield: 12 muffins
Cooking: 25 minutes

2 cups flour, unsifted (stir to aerate   1 large egg
   before measuring)   1 cup milk
3 teaspoons baking powder $1/3$ cup butter or margarine, melted
1 teaspoon salt $2/3$ cup to 1 cup blueberries
$1/2$ cup sugar

Combine flour, baking powder and salt. Stir in sugar. Set aside. Beat egg and milk until combined and stir in melted butter. Add dry ingredients, stirring only until moistened. (Batter will be lumpy.) Fold in blueberries. Bake in a preheated oven at 425 degrees for 25 minutes.

Beverly Gwinn

FRUIT PIZZA

Preparation: 45 minutes   Serves: 10 to 12
Cooking: 1 minute

1 box Duncan Hines Sugar Cookie   Glaze:
   Mix $1/2$ cup white sugar
1 (8-ounce) package cream cheese   1 tablespoon cornstarch
4 ounces prepared whipped   Dash of salt
   topping $1/2$ cup orange juice
Fresh, canned, or frozen fruit. Use $1/4$ cup water
   at least 4 to 5 different fruits   2 tablespoons lemon juice
   (bananas, blueberries,
   strawberries, pineapple, kiwi,
   oranges, cherries).

Prepare cookie mix according to package directions. Pat in a 12-inch pizza pan. Bake until light brown. Cool. Blend cream cheese and whipped topping and spread on cookie. Arrange fruit in a pretty pattern on cheese mixture. Put glaze ingredients in a saucepan and bring to a boil. Cook one minute, stirring constantly. Spoon glaze over whole pie. Refrigerate. Will keep several days.

Judy Stuart

COUNTRY FRENCH OUTING

Budget Boursin with Crackers
Chicken Dijon
Ratatouille
Potatoes Vinaigrette with Dill
French Silk Pie
Fresh French Bread
Chardonnay

BUDGET BOURSIN

Preparation: 20 minutes   Serves: 8 to 10

12 ounces cream cheese   6 tablespoons chopped parsley
2 medium cloves garlic   Salt, pepper, lemon juice

Peel garlic cloves. Cut into 6 pieces and insert into cream cheese. Leave out of refrigerator in covered bowl one to two hours. Remove garlic pieces and force through press into cheese. Add chopped parsley and mix well. Add a few drops lemon juice, salt and pepper. Mix well. Refrigerate until ½ hour before serving.

Joan Rowan

CHICKEN DIJON

Preparation: 20 minutes   Serves: 4
Cooking: 45 minutes

1 (3-pound) broiler, quartered   ¼ teaspoon pepper
2 tablespoons butter   2 egg yolks
2 cups dry white wine   2 tablespoons Dijon mustard
¼ teaspoon dried tarragon   2 tablespoons sour cream
Pinch thyme   Pinch cayenne pepper
1 small bay leaf
½ teaspoon salt

Brown chicken in butter. Add wine, tarragon, thyme, bay leaf, salt, and pepper. Bring to a boil. Cover and simmer 45 minutes or until tender. Remove meat to heated serving dish and keep warm. Discard bay leaf. Blend egg yolks, sour cream, mustard, and cayenne. Add to pan. Heat, stirring briskly and constantly. Do not allow to boil. Pour over chicken to serve.

Titsa Dermatas

RATATOUILLE

Preparation: 30 minutes   **Serves: 8**

3 cloves garlic, finely chopped
2 onions, finely sliced
3 to 4 tablespoons cooking oil
1 green pepper, cut in strips
1 or 2 medium eggplants, diced
1½ teaspoons salt
Pinch thyme
1 medium zucchini, sliced

1 medium summer squash, sliced
Several very ripe tomatoes, peeled
  and diced
1 teaspoon dry basil or ¼ cup
  fresh chopped basil
Sliced mushrooms (optional)
Grated Romano or Parmesan
  cheese (optional)

Sauté garlic and onions in oil until soft. Add pepper, eggplant and squash. Cook for 5 minutes over medium heat, tossing well and shaking pan. Add tomatoes and seasonings. Simmer, covered, about 10 minutes. If mushrooms are used, add at end of the 10 minutes. Remove cover, correct seasonings, and continue cooking until vegetables are cooked through (about 10 to 15 minutes). Stir while cooking. Serve sprinkled with grated cheese if used. Can be served hot or cold.

Jackie Kaldon

POTATOES VINAIGRETTE WITH DILL

Preparation: 30 minutes   **Serves: 6**

2 pounds potatoes, small and
  uniform
1 cup vinaigrette sauce (see recipe)
1 cup plain yogurt
1 tablespoon dried dill weed
2 tablespoons fresh parsley for
  garnish

Vinaigrette Sauce:
4 tablespoons vinegar
12 tablespoons salad oil
2 teaspoons salt
Black pepper to taste, freshly
  ground
2 cloves garlic, remove before
  serving

Vinaigrette Sauce: Beat all ingredients together. Makes 1 cup.
Potatoes: Boil potatoes and peel while hot. Coat each in vinaigrette sauce and allow to stand overnight if possible. Drain. Roll or coat with yogurt to which dill has been added. Sprinkle with parsley. (Yogurt travels better to a picnic than the traditional mayonnaise.)

Recipe shared by Anne Byrd, former Greensboro resident and past President of the International Association of Cooking Schools.

FRENCH SILK PIE
(see page 203)

PATIO FIESTA

Prairie Fire
Texas Barbecued Brisket
Corn Pudding
Calico Bean Salad
Texas Sheet Cake
Sangria or Blond Sangria

PRAIRIE FIRE
(see page 13)

TEXAS BARBECUED BRISKET

Preparation: 30 minutes   Serves: 8
Cooking Time: 3 hours + 1 hour

Beef Brisket, 4 to 5 pounds

Sauce:
1/2 cup sugar (can use Sweet and   1/2 cup Worcestershire sauce
  Low)   1 tablespoon salt
1 cup vinegar   1 tablespoon seasoned salt
1 cup catsup   1 tablespoon black pepper
1 cup water   3 tablespoons dehydrated onion

Mix all sauce ingredients and boil for 5 minutes. Place brisket in pan. Pour 2 cups of barbecue sauce over it. Cover tightly with foil and bake at 300 degrees for 3 hours. Allow to cool, place in refrigerator overnight. Next day remove all fat from brisket and sauce. Slice meat across grain of meat in thin slices. Place in baking dish, pour sauce over meat, adding additional sauce if needed. (can freeze at the point). When ready to serve, bake 300 degrees for one hour. Can be served as a main dish or in sandwiches.

Mamie Snider

CORN PUDDING

Preparation: 10 minutes   Serves: 8
Cooking: 40 minutes

2 (16-ounce) cans creamed corn   4 eggs
1/4 cup flour   1 1/2 cups milk (Half and Half)
1/3 cup sugar   1/4 teaspoon nutmeg (optional)

Combine all ingredients and beat. Pour into greased 2-quart 9 × 13 inch casserole and dot with butter. Bake at 400 degrees for 40 minutes. Let stand 5 minutes before serving.

Mary Elizabeth Irvin

CALICO BEAN SALAD

Preparation: 15 minutes   Serves: 6

2 (16-ounce) packages frozen   2 small onions, separted into rings
  French style green beans,   1 clove garlic, minced
  cooked slightly and drained
1 (9-ounce) package frozen   Dressing:
  artichoke hearts   1/3 cup red wine vinegar
1 (1-ounce) jar olives, sliced   3/4 cup olive oil or corn oil
1 (6-ounce) can mushrooms,   1 teaspoon salt
  drained   1/4 teaspoon pepper

Mix all salad ingredients and marinate in dressing for several hours. Drain to serve.

Elizabeth Ray

SANGRIA

Preparation: 10 minutes   Serves: 6

2 cans frozen pink lemonade   Lemon, thinly sliced
4 lemonade cans red burgundy   1/2 orange, thinly sliced
  (Spanish if available)   Club soda
Juice of 1/2 orange

Mix and refrigerate 2 hours. When ready to serve, add one lemonade can of club soda and serve.

Pat Carter

TEXAS SHEET CAKE

Preparation: 20 minutes   Serves: 24
Cooking: 20 to 30 minutes

Cake: Topping:
2 eggs   1 stick margarine
1 cup sour cream   1 tablespoon cocoa
2 cups sugar   6 tablespoons milk
2 cups flour   1 box confectioners sugar
½ teaspoon salt   1 teaspoon vanilla
1 teaspoon soda   1 cup pecans, coarsely chopped
2 sticks margarine
4 tablespoons cocoa
1 cup water

Cake: Mix eggs and sour cream together in large bowl or mixer. Sift together flour, sugar, salt and soda. Add to above. Bring to a full boil margarine, cocoa, and water. Then add to flour mixture and mix well. Grease and flour a 16 × 11 × 1 inch pan. Pour mixture into pan and bake at 350 degrees for 20 to 30 minutes.
Topping: About 5 minutes before cake is done, bring to a full boil the margarine, cocoa, and milk. Add confectioners sugar, vanilla, and pecans. Remove cake from oven when done and pour topping over warm cake. Cool and cut in squares.

Jeanne Rives

BLOND SANGRIA

Preparation: 10 minutes   Serves: 8

1 seedless orange, thinly sliced   ⅓ cup brandy
1 lime, thinly sliced   1 (25.4-ounce) bottle dry white
2 tablespoons sugar   wine
½ cup orange-flavored liqueur   2 cups club soda, chilled

In a bowl or pitcher, combine orange, lime, sugar, liqueur and brandy. Cover and let stand for several hours at room temperature. (The sangria can be made ahead to this point, covered and refrigerated up to 24 hours.) Just before serving, pour in wine and club soda. Stir well and serve over ice. Makes 1½ quarts.

Light, lovely and refreshing!

Darlene Young

The first performance of the Greensboro Symphony Orchestra was held in Aycock Auditorium in 1927. This historic building, an integral part of the University of North Carolina at Greensboro, continues to be the site of numerous cultural and musical events.

Index

INDEX BY CATEGORY

(see also Index by Recipe Title)

A

B

C

INDEX BY RECIPE TITLE

(see also Index by Category)

BRAVO

The Greensboro Symphony Guild
P.O. Box 29224
Greensboro, N.C. 27408

Please send me _____ copies of **BRAVO** @ $11.95 each $ _____
Postage and handling @ $ 1.50 each $ _____
Gift wrap @ $ .50 each $ _____
N.C. residents add 4½% tax @ $ .54 each $ _____
Total enclosed $ _____

Name _____
(please print)

Address _____

City _____ State _____ Zip _____

Please make checks payable to "BRAVO."

All proceeds from the sale of cookbooks benefit the educational projects of the Greensboro Symphony Guild.

BRAVO

The Greensboro Symphony Guild
P.O. Box 29224
Greensboro, N.C. 27408

Please send me _____ copies of **BRAVO** @ $11.95 each $ _____
Postage and handling @ $ 1.50 each $ _____
Gift wrap @ $ .50 each $ _____
N.C. residents add 4½% tax @ $ .54 each $ _____
Total enclosed $ _____

Name _____
(please print)

Address _____

City _____ State _____ Zip _____

Please make checks payable to "BRAVO."

All proceeds from the sale of cookbooks benefit the educational projects of the Greensboro Symphony Guild.

BRAVO

The Greensboro Symphony Guild
P.O. Box 29224
Greensboro, N.C. 27408

Please send me _____ copies of **BRAVO** @ $11.95 each $ _____
Postage and handling @ $ 1.50 each $ _____
Gift wrap @ $ .50 each $ _____
N.C. residents add 4½% tax @ $ .54 each $ _____
Total enclosed $ _____

Name _____
(please print)

Address _____

City _____ State _____ Zip _____

Please make checks payable to "BRAVO."

All proceeds from the sale of cookbooks benefit the educational projects of the Greensboro Symphony Guild.